Can We Stay Up and Watch the Bombs?

RECENT BOOKS BY THE AUTHOR:

Communication By Design

Hold Fast the Heritage

Winning Ways

I'll Be Over In The Morning

Can We Stay Up and

WATCH THE BOMBS?

James Pilditch

Introduced by
Charlie Chester

Verulam Publishing

First published in 1996 by
Verulam Publishing Limited.
152A Park Street Lane, Park Street,
St. Albans, Hertfordshire AL2 2AU

Printed in the United Kingdom by The Ipswich Book Company

ISBN 1-874504-11-3

A CIP catalogue record for this book is available from the British Library.

Preface

Biographies, often, are about the large deeds of famous people. This is not. Indeed, it is not meant to be about one person at all. Rather, through one pair of eyes, it tries to describe experiences many of us shared: being young in the 'forties and 'fifties.

This book has at its core two ideas. The first is that history is not only the grand sweep of events, but the details of what we did and how we felt. The second is a loving and cheerful idea picked from Robert Louis Stevenson. He wrote:

> *The world is so full of a number of things*
> *I'm sure we should all be as happy as kings.*

Ortega said we are what happens to us. The values echoing through this book were set when Britain was still the heart of a great empire. Although many seem today romantic, some will say awful, and certainly long gone, not all lacked merit. People who shared them will remember.

Charlie Chester **M.B.E., O.ST.J.**
London
August 1995

Imagination and memory... Two wonderful assets of entertainment....James Pilditch has both, and brings them vividly to the mind in his entertaining book. What a good read!

Can We Stay Up And Watch The Bombs is both amusing and nostalgic... In fact the very title took me back to 1917/18, when as a boy nearly four years old I climbed on to a sink in our kitchen at Eastbourne....to draw the curtain for my mother when the German Zeppelin went over and crashed on Beachy Head.

The author will certainly evoke many such memories for those who read this book.

Since reading it, I have discovered that James is an avid fan of mine and I can do no more than to say that I am certainly a fan of his.

Sincerely

Acknowledgements

The publishers would like to thank the following for permission to reprint material in this book.

Guys and Dolls
Words and Music by Frank Loesser
© Copyright 1950 Frank Music Corporation USA
© Copyright renewed 1978 Frank Music Corporation.
Published and administered by MPL Communications Limited.
Used by permission of Music Sales Limited
All Rights Reserved. International Copyright Secured.

Any Old Iron
Words and Music by Charles Collins, E A Shepherd and Fred Terry
© Copyright 1911, Reproduced by permission of Herman Darewski Music Publishing Company Limited, London WC2H 0EA

I Get A Kick Out of You
Words and Music by Cole Porter
© Copyright 1933 Harms Inc, USA.
Warner Chappell Music Limited, London WIY 3FA
Reproduced by permission of IMP Ltd

The following photographs used on the book cover:
Listening to the BBC
Richard Dimbleby reports bombing raid (BBC War Reporting Unit)
ITMA - Tommy Handley
Forces' sweetheart - Vera Lynn
© Copyright BBC

To Julie and Richard, Ray and Robin, Victor and Connie, Freddie and Jane, Patience and Ian, Charlotte and Kevin, and their children.

Sadly, James Pilditch CBE died of cancer in London on 23rd August 1995 just two days after finishing this book. He also changed the title from *When Cows Had Names* to *Can We Stay Up and Watch the Bombs?* which he thought was more fun!

Contents

One

Eagle and Two Veg

In the early days of the war metal drums were placed every hundred yards or so along the roads. They were filled with thick, black oil. At night the oil was lit. Filthy, choking smoke poured out. It was a smoke screen put up, we supposed, to hide the nearby Hawker aircraft factory. Walking through it, you couldn't see a yard. It was worse than any fog, and stank.

When the sirens first sounded at night, Freddie, my twin, and I were bundled under the stairs. Swaddled in blankets, we crouched there and tried to sleep. After a night or two the idea was abandoned. My father had had a brick shelter built in the garden (fifty years on it is still there). We slept there once. But it was dank and cold. Apart from keeping our bicycles in it, and smoking our first furtive cigarettes, we never used it again.

Although I always felt more akin to soldiering, and felt excitement when troops of the 51st Highland Division tramped down Syke Cluan and Canadians meandered around wearing the darker khaki uniform I was one day to wear, and although I pored over every picture I could find of soldiers, RAF pilots were our heroes, their top buttons undone, a polka-dot scarf slung artlessly around their throats. We gazed at the high, twisting vapour trails of the Battle of Britain, saw recovery trucks piled with wrecked wings driving to a dump on the Bath Road, devoured newspaper accounts, cut and collected photographs from magazines.

Our talk was splattered with RAF slang, "Wizard prang," "In the drink," Whack-o," "Bang on." Everything easy, or what heroes would have you think was easy, was "a piece of cake." Nor was this talk confined to children. A David Langdon cartoon of the time shows two civil servants at their desks. "Give me a buzz on the intercom," one says, "and we'll bale out for coffee."

Kept in bed with what they said was glandular fever, I began my first writing. In a lined exercise book I told how a Spitfire pilot was flying on patrol over the cliffs of Dover. The sea glistened below him. Suddenly he was surrounded by enemy aircraft, one with a yellow nose cone coming straight at him. He jerked the joystick, kicked the rudder bar and banked sharply. The Spit shuddered, its powerful Merlin engine gasping for air. Clouds were high on his right. Looking down, far below he saw streams of bombers, in formation, moving steadily on London. He was alone. Ginger and Sandy were nowhere to be seen. He dived, the bombers coming closer and closer at alarming speed. He picked one, a Ju 88. He flicked off his safety catch and roared towards his prey. As its black cross wing markings inched into his gunsights, he pressed his firing button. Tracer bullets from his eight machine guns curled towards the target. He pushed the nose down, screaming under the black belly of the Junkers, then swung back for another attack.

The pencilled story went on, page after feverish page. It ended, unfinished, with the pilot shaking straw off himself. He had no idea how long he had been asleep. He was in a French barn, having been shot down....

The sweet-purring Spitfire, with its elegant, curved wings and slim profile, was the most beautiful thing we had ever seen. In a film made about it, the designer, R.J. Mitchell, played by Leslie Howard, dreamed up its perfect name. Lying on a grassy bank, wearing a tweed jacket and sucking at an empty pipe, he explained: "It breathes fire and spits flame." Christopher Frayling, a design historian, says it wasn't quite like that. The prototype had a number. The specification of the first was F34/37. Frayling claimed the Air Ministry coined the famous word. "Just the sort of bloody silly name they would choose," Mitchell is reported to have said.

I had a beautiful flying model aircraft, a Hawker Fury. A bi-plane, the Fury was the main fighter in service in RAF squadrons when the war started. My model was about fifteen inches from nose to tail. The engine cowling was metal. The fuselage and wings, decorated with red, white and blue roundels, were made of silvered paper stretched over accurately copied wooden struts. The fixed undercarriage had metal 'oleo' legs with rubber wheels. The 'oleo' was a new device for cushioning impact on landing. One rod slid into another to take pressure. The wings unclipped and that was useful for when the 'plane landed roughly. They simply snapped off. The single propeller was connected to rubber bands inside the fuselage by the tail. You wound up the 'motor' by turning the propeller. The plane flew well, maybe eighty yards.

My father had taken us to fly it one afternoon. In the evening, in the sitting-room, I was repairing a tear. There was a raid on. Vroom-vroom-vroom-vroom; the uneven drone of German bombers was above us. Ack-ack guns were banging, bombs fell but not near. Then we heard the terrible whistle of one coming our way. We dived under the table. Ungallantly, I got there before my mother. With a bump she pushed on top of me — and the aeroplane I

was holding. The blast of the bomb smashed glass in the french windows and billowed the heavy curtains. But no other harm was done, except to my model. My mother had sat on the tail.

Grainy black and white newsreels of the time showed the Blitz. In one, a cockney woman crawled from the rubbled ruin of her house, through bricks and shattered glass and fallen timbers. "One day," she muttered to the camera, "that 'Itler, he'll go too far."

In that sitting-room in Iver, hushed, we heard Churchill's speeches. After one, in June 1940, when he warned that invasion was 'imminent', I went into the garden and stared into the black sky, afraid, waiting for Nazi parachutists to fall. They would be fierce, cruel, dark-eyed, wearing black leather jerkins and boots, with glinting daggers and snub-nosed machine guns.

We know now that that was more than the fanciful imagination of a boy. The German army had swept through Europe in six weeks, experienced, equipped, victorious. Against it Britain had the RAF, the Royal Navy and Churchill's eloquence. On the ground, after Dunkirk, what was there ? I looked up the figures. The most vulnerable part of the British coast was the area from Sheppey to Rye. One division defended it. It had no tanks, no armoured cars, no AFV's (armoured fighting vehicles), no medium machine guns, one-sixth its complement of anti-tank rifles and twenty-three field guns. Invasion, I am sure, was more than half expected, though no one I met seemed dismayed. I remember our mother and father wondering what they could do to protect us. They checked that the windows were shut, pulled the blackout curtains more firmly than usual and tried the lock on the back door.

On the wireless too, we heard ITMA. Short for *It's That Man Again,* the theme song that introduced the programme.

> *It's that man again, it's that man again,*
> *Tommy Handley is here.*

The song described him as 'Mother's pride and joy, Mrs Handley's boy'. Tommy Handley and the cast with him in the 'Ministry of Aggravation' were surely the joy of the nation. Hearing ITMA every Thursday at 8.30 pm was essential.

Anticipating the formula used by *'Allo, 'Allo* (I shall say theez only wairnce,) we waited each week for the same lines, exploding with laughter when, predictably, they came. There was Colonel Chinstrap, who turned every comment into an offer of a drink: "It's very risky," one would say. "Have a whisky ?" misheard the colonel — and here it came — "I don't mind if I do."(Laughter.) There was Mona Lot — "It's being so cheerful," she'd say in a dirgeful voice "as keeps me going." Week after week Mrs Mop, the char, would say: "Can I do you now, sir ?"

(Laughter.) There was Funf, the German spy. And the diver. After the glug, glug of bubbles you'd hear "Don't forget the diver, sir.""Boss, Boss, something terrible's happened," we'd say, and Alley-Oop's "I go - I come back." And two polite workmen. Going through a door, one would say "After you, Claude." To which, every week, the other replied "No, after you, Cecil" - all catchphrases we used constantly.

The Brains Trust was another programme we wouldn't miss. Professor Joad, a round man with a grey goatee beard and high-pitched voice, who was later prosecuted for consistently not paying his fare on the train, answered every question in a philosophic way. "It depends what you mean by..." he started. Perhaps he defended himself in court that way. By contrast, a former naval officer, Commander Campbell, blunt, rough-hewn, down-to-earth, answered questions from his experience of life. "I remember when I was in Patagonia..."

In a rich, round, deep voice, Dr Charles Hill, who later became chairman of the BBC, was the 'Radio Doctor'. Each week he spoke of health and food. To us, of course, as children, our food was normal, we knew nothing else. To mothers it must have been a daily worry. In the garden we kept rabbits, often unfed, and ate them (I haven't eaten rabbit since.) Perhaps from the hours we spent scouring the hedgerow opposite our house for weeds, I do remember Dr Hill talking about "my old friend the dandelion."

I looked up what food people could buy. Although amounts varied from time to time, the usual ration for everyone each week was this: tea, two ounces; butter, two ounces plus six ounces of fats, four of which had to be margarine; bacon, four ounces; eggs, thirty per year. You could also buy, every two months, a packet of dried egg powder. That gave about twelve eggs. Cheese, at first, was rationed to one ounce per week. You could buy three pints of milk a week (children received one-third of a pint free each day at school). Meat was controlled by price. Each person was entitled to what we would now call 6p worth of meat a week, children half that. Records say that bought about one pound of meat. Chicken and game were not rationed. In Scotland, Granada cinemas put on their restaurant menu 'eagle and two veg'.

Oddly, bread wasn't rationed until after the war (1946), although people were fined for wasting it. The Government produced a National Wholemeal loaf. Dark and coarse, it tasted awful. In the course of a Cabinet meeting at which he was saying he simply couldn't digest it, Ernest Bevin burped loudly. "There you are," he said, as conclusive evidence.

There was always something 'under the counter' and a flourishing black market (ration books cost about £5, a good week's wages), but housewives, I read recently, welcomed rationing. Nine out of ten approved of it in one of the many surveys. They thought it was fair — and saved lives of those in peril on the sea.

Though we knew about U-boats attacking convoys, I wonder whether anyone had any idea of the real damage being done. In 1940, in three months, U-boats sank 142 ships. Aircraft sank more. Each month some 300,000 tons of shipping, bringing us food and supplies, was sunk. In February 1941 that rose to 400,000 tons. In March, 500,000 tons. Nor was it all one way. Some 227 German U-boats, from a total fleet of 600 went for ever to the bottom of the sea.

Potatoes were never rationed. Bending over the sweet-smelling earth, eyeing girls in the Women's Land Army dressed in bottle green sweaters, corduroy breeches and khaki socks, we dug potatoes during school holidays on local farms. Sir William Beveridge, who later laid the groundwork for the National Health Service, encouraged people to eat more. He called the potato "that puckish vegetable".

Newspapers advised mothers to try turnip juice as a way to give babies necessary vitamin C. They were supplied with rose hip syrup, the hips picked by children. In 1943 the House of Commons offered on its menu 'Canapé Cheval'.

Dunkirk I remember and the Battle of Britain; high, white vapour trails swirling and criss-crossing in the cloudless blue sky, newspaper headlines blazing the 'score' each morning, as if it was more an exciting match than an earnest and deadly struggle. One rainy night a newspaper outside the Crown Hotel in Slough announced HOOD SUNK. It must have been May, 1941. I saw it across the busy, wet street. Although not understanding, I was sad to tears. Nearly 2000 sailors drowned. The ship, pride of the British fleet, had been hit by gunfire from the awesome, 45,000-ton *Bismarck* on her first voyage into the Atlantic. It was also her last. Stunned and alarmed, the Royal Navy sent forty-eight ships to find the *Bismarck*. Swordfish, slow bi-planes known as 'Stringbags', took off from the *Ark Royal* in search. They launched torpedoes, but HMS *Dorsetshire* probably put in the killing shots. The *Bismarck*, too, was sunk, and another 2000 men died.

We thrilled to Pathé newsreels of Alamein; tanks trundling through swirling sand, helmeted infantrymen crouched behind them, an officer running up a dune, his pistol held in readiness. "Not the end," in Churchill's words, "nor the beginning of the end, but the end of the beginning."

In 1944 we moved to Tudor Cottage. It looks as it sounds. Like other houses in Richings Park, it was mock, differing only in three ways. It was built to an original Tudor design. All the timbers came from a Tudor barn found in Devon. The house was built by the architect of the whole estate, for himself, so materials were excellent. It was a solid building.

My parents bought the house for £2000, a lordly sum, from Dorothy Varrick, sister of Alfred Drayton who, with Robertson Hare, starred in the hilarious Whitehall farces before the war.

The front door, recessed behind black timber beams, was heavy, hard to push open. The back door, to the side, led into the kitchen. Floors were parquet and, except in the drawing room, uncovered. Walls, where you could see them for all the furniture, were rough white plaster. We had a lot of furniture. It is a comment on the times that I had no idea what my father did for a living until I was sixteen or seventeen. What he did, as well as make wings for Mosquitoes (fast light bombers) as his war work, and it explains much, was to make fine reproductions for Harrods, Waring and Gillow, Maples and other furniture emporiums. He also bought furniture at auctions for those companies and supplied beds and other furniture to Tubby Clayton, who ran Talbot House, the hostel for men. (Toc H, as it was called, was perhaps better known then than it is now. The symbol on its vans was a lamp. 'Dim as a Toc H lamp' was an expression of the time). And my mother was acquisitive. The result was that whenever anything good came by it ended up in our house. Our house was stuffed.

I think of the hall inside the front door now, small, dark, those walls covered, as the stairs were, with stained mock oak panelling. A grandfather clock ticks loudly. My mother is standing there. She has received the telegram we dreaded, to say one of her sons, our brother, in the RAF, was missing. I see the doctor, too, come to see our father who lay dying upstairs. Why only sad images?

The drawing room, through a latched door, was long and wide. Dark-stained oak beams crossed the low ceiling. Here were Persian carpets, a rare curlybacked-sofa, stuffed chairs, a Queen Anne desk overflowing with papers, its drawers full of curling photographs, Coalport figurines, floor to ceiling bookcases, silver trays and a bust of Dante.

Below an American mirror, surmounted by an eagle, was the piano where my twin and I variously played Schubert's 'Marche Militaire' as an unco-ordinated duet, one always finishing before the other, and I scraped Handel's 'Largo' on the violin, and our mother sat and played any tune she heard. The piano stool was full of sheet music — Chopin, Schubert, Lizst, and *Rose Marie* and *HMS Pinafore* and *Patience* — but Mummy was happier extemporising. She could play anything. When the Russians became allies and the loud-speakers at Woolworth's in Slough blared 'The Volga Boatmen' and I, patriotically captivated, hummed it to her, she just played it, fully, generously, making up bits she didn't know.

There was a Jacobean cabinet, used for drinks. The inside lit when you opened the doors. There was a large walnut-veneered radiogram, replaced in time by an equally large television set. A great beam arched over the open hearth. Fastened to it were pairs of duelling pistols and miniatures and, when the war was over and my brother came back safely after all, a Japanese bayonet he brought from captivity. There was an oak refectory table, and a silver tray and a tapestry covered trestle stool. The curtains were heavy, plum-coloured velvet. At one end were french windows which led to the garden. The room was hot; my mother liked to be warm. It was an incestuous, stuffy, room where we had to behave properly .

When Lawrence Durrell, as a young man, announced that he wanted to live as a writer, his mother said, "Be as Bohemian as you like, but not in the house." Tudor Cottage was the same. One hot afternoon, years later, now in my forties, I flew into Heathrow after a very busy week in Germany. I drove over to see my mother. In the car I pulled my tie off, to be more comfortable. When I entered the drawing-room, her first words were, "What DO you look like ? Put your tie on at once."

It was also, sadly, a room to which few visitors came. Two who did were priests. One was Father Crawford, from the convent in Langley. Though young, broad-shouldered and handsome, with wide, cheek bones, he spoke as a saint might, in whispered, beautifully-enunciated Anglo-Irish. Everything about this gentle man was so tentative we thought he might blow away. How unlike the bluff canon who came in his Jaguar to scrounge money for his orphanage in Sheringham.

Canon Hunting filled our doorway and overflowed the

wing-backed chair he always sat in. Ruddy-faced with a booming voice, he conceded that he might just have one,then possibly two, then three, glasses of my father's better

brandy and, oh goodness, that cigar is hard to resist. As ash fell on his bursting waistcoat he smiled and joked and roared with laughter at the goodness of life. Careless for himself, he lived for his boys. "Why shouldn't they wear whites when they play cricket ?" he demanded. "That is what they should do and that," taking another puff, "is what they will do." With terrible irony, that good man had a car accident — and killed a boy.

Another visitor was a solemn policeman, come to ask about the thunderflash three of us put through someone's letterbox one foggy night. (It went off with a wonderful bang...the man whose house it was came charging up the road in his pyjamas, but didn't catch us.) If there had been a fire, my brain raced, that would be arson. And I was convinced that, like murder, arson was a charge punishable by hanging. But nothing came of it. And once that room was filled with Polish officers, come to spend Christmas. Why were they there ? It was the custom then to invite soldiers in nearby billets to share Christmas with you at home. It would have been thought selfish not to do so.

To one side of the drawing room was another latched door. This led to the breakfast room where we lived and ate, although there was scarcely space. The room was triangular. A glass cabinet, where we kept most of the china, including fine Czech gold-lined brown cups and saucers decorated with pastoral scenes, all too good to use, filled one wall. A Welsh dresser, decorated with Quimper plates bought in Normandy before the war, blocked another. At the small table we had our meals, did our homework, and cleaned the brass and silver every Saturday morning, the cause of endless wrangling. My father, home from work, would open his tobacco-smelling briefcase and take out papers and spread them across the table.

On Sundays, back from church, we ate 'Swiss dish', a wonderful egg and chopped bread omelette our father had fried, then listened to our mother rant on about how awful the Germans were. She was proud to be half French, and believed that conveyed a special knowledge and claim to hate. Hadn't her mother, a girl in Paris, seen rats hanging in butchers' windows during the Franco-Prussian war of 1870 ? Weren't 'they' the same as they always were?

I always thought rats hanging as food was an exaggeration until I read Cynthia Gladwyn's book about the British Embassy in Paris. In 1870, when Bismarck's troops were at the gates of Paris, the British Embassy was left in the hands of a wealthy banker, Edward Blount. He had two cows, one killed, salted and ready to eat, the other to provide milk and butter. He hoped to be allowed to keep just one horse (as quickly as they disappeared they arrived on the table) but he was not allowed to. The ambassador, who had fled Paris, sent Blount a message by pigeon, "a salubrious meal," Lady Gladwyn called it, "from out of the blue", but he resisted the temptation to eat that too. In the cold bathroom downstairs at Tudor Cottage was a yellow loo seat made of an early marbellized plastic. It belonged to Greer Garson, the film star who made us cry in *Mrs Miniver.* We were proud of that.

The bare wooden stairs by the bathroom creaked. When they didn't give us away as we came home in the small hours, the grandfather clock in the hall did: our lightest step was enough to set off the chimes. Upstairs were three bedrooms. The over-satined, over-stuffed one we seldom entered. That belonged to our parents, or more in tune with the spirit, mother. It was her room, her style. Our younger sister lived in a second, and my twin brother and I shared the cold one over the front door, looking up the road, lined with blossoming trees in spring, invisible in damp fog in autumn, which ran towards the station.

An arch and covered way separated the kitchen door from a garage filled not only with the car, but with several bicycles, rows of tools, a stirrup pump, my father's fireman's axe and belt, and boxes of forgotten bits. Behind were two stables where Sunshine, a chestnut, and Harlequin, Rosie and Mistral in turn stomped and neighed.

Sounds of Rosie clumping her hoofs on the stone floor of her stable, the sweet smell of wet coal stored behind the garage, the sight of fallen damp rhododendron petals on the drive; all stay in the mind, part of one's life.

As well as hacking nearby, my mother and sister, Patience, rode in Windsor Great Park. When she was five or six, Patience was sent ahead to find the time. She rode off, then returned. A minute or two later they overtook the couple who had told her the time. Patience waved. They were the King and Queen.

The garden was small by country measures, but overflowing with rhododendron, roses, lupins, weeping willow, silver birch and fruit trees. After Mr. Digweed left, five German prisoners-of-war came to garden. My mother cut ten rounds of sandwiches each evening. Always the same man collected them. It was some weeks before we found out that he told none of the others, but ate the lot. Another gardener had been in jail. My father wanted to help him re-establish himself. Soon we saw he couldn't garden at all, but was a good bricklayer. So paths were laid where paths had not been before.

Two

CAN WE STAY UP AND WATCH THE BOMBS?

Fifty years after she wrote the book, Daphne du Maurier watched an episode of *Rebecca* on television. She rang a friend to say, "It is so exciting. I wonder what happens next." A friend asked me to return a book he had lent me. I had no idea what he was talking about. But there it was on my shelves. The book was called *How to Develop a Power Memory*. Yet, still without that power or most others, I can say that fifty years ago our telephone number was Iver 419. It is strange how memory works.

Freddie, my twin brother, and I were four when we moved with our parents to a village called Iver, Buckinghamshire. The place and the people, as a boy saw them before and during the war, remain as close and clear as the cup on the kitchen table.

One day that memory came in useful. In the mid-1970s, going to see my mother who still lived in Iver, I was early. I went to the park where once red squirrels scurried in the chestnut trees and, as boys, we collected conkers and skated on a frozen pond, and later, in the evenings, walked girls to a stone bridge over a stream. Curious, I looked for and found the foundations of an old building, now covered in scrub. "Used to be a monastery, you know," called a man walking his dog. He waved across a field. "You can tell," he went on, " because there's a tunnel comes up over there, where the monks could escape." To his surprise, I asked him how long he had lived in Iver. Twenty-three years, he said. So monastery it was; that was the local knowledge. "Come with me," I replied. Somewhere there was a ha-ha, a ditch, brick-walled on one vertical side to keep cattle off lawns. I showed him. "Can you see where new bricks have been put in? That was where the bomb fell."

When we were boys the building was a fine white Georgian mansion, once belonging to Lord Bathurst. The RAF took it over when war started. It was made some sort of secret headquarters, all barbed wire and patrolling guards. Even we boys, who heard rumours before grown-ups ever did, had no idea what went on there. (In 1990 I asked the RAF's Historical Branch about it. They claimed to have no knowledge). But there is no doubt the RAF was there and the Luftwaffe knew. One night two landmines fell. One landed in the ha-ha and exploded with a deafening noise we all heard, damaging the house and shattering glass for miles around. The other didn't go off.

"Bigger than a pillar box," neighbours said it was. It hung from a tree on the verge of a row of big houses. All but one was evacuated. In that house lay an old, bed-ridden lady. My mother, then in the Red Cross, was asked to sit by her and comfort her until the bomb, a few yards away, could be made safe. Think of the unseen courage of ordinary people. I told this to the man who scarcely believed me. Only the new bricks in the ha-ha, which you would only see if you knew where to look, were evidence. As memory fades history changes. For that local man it had.

Iver lies seventeen miles west of London. Old as time, it was first mentioned in the Chronicles of Aethelweard in 893, although earlier Neolithic remains have been found there. Until a few years ago it was still and leafy and undisturbed. The church, squat, square-towered, built of flintstone, is Norman, from Anglo-Saxon beginnings. Beyond the lychgate is a 16th century pub, the Swan, and as the road winds to Uxbridge, Bridgefoot House, a tall-windowed, red-brick Georgian house owned, when I was a boy, by Martin Secker, the publisher and visited by D.H. Lawrence and Compton Mackenzie. From the house they would have looked over a glistening brook, the Colne.

Today, a deafening motorway, the M25, slices the churchyard from the stream and from cornfields beyond. The M4 now cuts in half woods we played in and where the landmine dropped.

Although Pinewood and Denham, then busy film studios, are near and the Duke and Duchess of Kent lived in Coppins, and cars took men to their work in town, the village was quiet. There were people in Iver who had never been to London.

Up the High Street, beyond dusty shops and a garage, is the bow-fronted, semi-detached house where, in the cold front room, I had stilted piano lessons from a pince-nez'd Mrs Tucker who wore brown crêpe de chine and had what I quite inexplicably called 'music-teacher's neck'. I think I meant her neck was crinkled and slack, like a chicken's, wobbling as she beat time, and, above a lace modesty vest across her V-necked dress her skin was redder, as though that part only had been coloured by the sun.

Lower down is the village school where my brother and I went the year the war started. Further down, though gone now, was the Cottage Hospital where our mother who, with loyal foresight, had trained before the war to become a Red Cross nurse, spent many days. There is a hall nearby, too, where our father passed his nights when not fighting blazes in London and Coventry, Portsmouth and Birmingham, as a member of the AFS, the Auxiliary Fire Service.

Every other night, for much of the war, after hard days trying to run his firm, twice bombed out, he would come home, have a meal, change into his black serge uniform, then go on duty. In the mornings, often stained with soot, his eyes red-rimmed with exhaustion, he had a bath (four inches of water was all you were allowed), changed, ate a hurried breakfast and then went to work in London. One morning I saw him slumped into a chair, too tired to eat. "I have been though hell," he said. Another morning, shaking his head in a daze, he told us, "We ran out of water last night... we ran out of water."

On such a night 2000 fire engines were rushed, rattling and clanging, to London from wherever they could be found. Douglas Reed, a foreign correspondent of *The Times*, was there. He wrote: "The amateur firemen who stood and fought the flames on swaying, unaccustomed ladders while bombs fell about them, these are the heroes." A punishing life shared by many, it took my father, we believe, to his death too soon, when he was no more than 52. He is buried in the once quiet churchyard, our mother sharing the same stone.

The church, its bells silent during the war, to be sounded only if parachutists landed, stands at the foot of the High Street. That turns past council houses where our gardener lived. His name was Mr Digweed. His wife, who cleaned in our house two or three mornings a week, had worked for Churchill before the war, a "two bottle a day man" she told me once when she was dusting the piano, although that legend has been refuted since. For years after the war you could spot Digweed's house, opposite the Fox and Pheasant. One night an incendiary bomb went through his roof. The replaced, lighter-coloured tiles were there to see.

Digweed left us to manage a horticultural farm, growing gladioli. Working on that farm one summer when a student, I met Nobby. After hours bending to cut flowers, then box them for Covent Garden as the chill early morning mist cleared to bring another hot, dusty day, we drank tea from white enamelled mugs. Nobby had been a soldier in England: Yorkshire, then the East coast. He remembered the girls he'd met. His style, he said, was to collect them by their uniforms, as others might collect stamps. All the obvious ones done, the WAAF, the WRNS, ATS, Land Army, his quest became increasingly esoteric; the New Zealand Auxiliary this and the French that. Whether peace came too soon for Nobby or was a blessed relief I can't say.

The road goes on. You cross the canal. Further, on the left, tucked in cornfields, is where the ack-ack site was. Across the road are fields where I watched a fighter aircraft, a Typhoon, crash. The pilot was a woman, a ferry pilot, an 'Attagirl', member of the Air Transport Auxiliary. She climbed out, took off her helmet, shook her blonde hair, lit a cigarette, and walked off.

Then you go over a narrow hump-backed bridge to cross the railway, the main line from Paddington to the west of England. Facing you is what was then an over-large modern post office where, on moist, misty mornings during Christmas vacations we young people collected sacks of mail to deliver. To the right is Iver station and, reaching behind it, Richings Park, an area a mile or so square of houses built in the 'twenties.

Conscious now of town-planning, and distressed by much that occurs, I see Richings Park as meeting almost every criterion of excellence. The pastiche architecture isn't what it might be, but it has the merit of being what people wanted. To a boy brought up there, it was a complete world.

The northern boundary was the railway line. To the east, south and west stretched fields, farmland and the great park after which the estate is named. Many of the houses, each in its own leafy garden, were mock Tudor, with black boards nailed on rough, painted stucco.

The railway station and post office were the nodal points of the estate. Roads fanned out asymmetrically. There was Thorney Lane to the east, where we once lived and, one remembered night, stood as small boys in front of our high hedge to look at the red glow of London burning. "Mummy," my twin brother and I asked, "can we stay up and watch the bombs?" I see now searchlights probing and sweeping the sky and even an aircraft twisting to evade the beams of crisscrossing lights. Ack-ack guns banged, shrapnel from their bursting shells whistling to earth near enough to drive us indoors.

The Tower Arms at the bottom of that road was the pub we used as we grew up. Behind it is a hall where we had dances, sticky hands pressing the backs of satin dresses. We were always the same group, boys and girls who saw

each other daily and indeed had all learnt the same steps from the wife of our maths master and cricket umpire. She was short with dark hair and red lips and a rather pointed face. She stood square, straight, shoulders back, making the most of her excellent bosom which, like her strong calves, we boys dreamt about. In her bare-floored front room, to 'You're dancing on my heart' and other strict tempo records of Victor Sylvester, she taught us to dance waltzes and foxtrots, quicksteps, the veleta and military two-step and the 'Dashing White Sergeant' and, best of all because you bent girls over backwards till their hair nearly touched the floor, the tango, all practised puffingly and alone at home. Dances in Iver then were with a five or six-piece band; saxophone, clarinet, double bass, drums and piano, as well as a compere and girl singer.

That hall was used for everything. In rough green tweed uniforms, the women of the WVS (Women's Voluntary Services or Widows, Virgins and Spinsters as they were called) held whist drives. The St John Ambulance Brigade gave First Aid lectures. There were plays, flower shows, cookery and sewing classes, parties and dances, even, for a while, a church. One June, my mother organised a concert there to raise money for prisoners of war in the Far East. The programme included Haydn, Bach, Delibes and Ravel, but had an English touch. There was 'Love is meant to make us glad' from *Merrie England,* 'Greensleeves', 'In England, Merrie England', something from *Tom Jones* and, as a 'first-half closer', 'Let our torches light up the gloom' from *Les Cloches de Corneville.* The evening ended with sea shanties. The programme from another concert, held at the Tower Arms in July 1943, records that I played two violin solos — the first movement from a concerto by Rieding and Handel's 'Where'er you walk'. I am unable to scratch a note today. It is hard to believe.

The Home Guard drilled in the same hall. It was started at the beginning of the war as the Local Defence Volunteers, meant to encompass a million men too old or too young to serve. Jokers nicknamed the LDV 'Look, duck and vanish'. J.B. Priestley called it "half absurd, half glorious". Churchill, perhaps unknowingly coining a term from the American Civil War, re-named it the Home Guard.

Robb Wilton, a shy, stuttering North Country comedian, told us what they did. "The first day I got my Home Guard uniform — I'm getting the trousers next year," he told audiences, "I went home and slipped upstairs and put it on. I came down into the kitchen and my missus said, 'What are you supposed to be ?' 'Supposed to be? I'm one of the Home Guard'... She looked at me and said, 'Well, what do you do in the Home Guard ?' 'I've to stop Hitler's army landing,' I explained. 'What, you ?' asked my missus. 'No,' I replied, 'there's Harry Bates and Charlie Evans — seven or eight of us altogether. "

Our Home Guard patrolled the unlit, black lane that ran down to St. Leonard's Church. I went with them, as a boy relishing the damp cold on my face, the rough collar of my greatcoat pulled about my ears, the crunch of boots on gravel. "Halt," a voice from the ditch called one night. "Who goes there ? Friend or foe ?" "Foe," replied the corporal with me. After a pause the unseen sentry said, "Don't be a bloody fool, George."

In the Tower Arms on drill nights charts of the Lewis gun and other weapons were pinned up; a blackboard was pulled into place for instruction. Although all the men were older, most wearing First War ribbons on their battledress, they kindly let me, by then a young army cadet of fourteen, take part. There was a song at the time: 'They're either too young or too old/ Either too grey or too grassy green.' That is how I felt. I especially wanted to do well, not least the first night I went. It was arms drill. Good, I could do that. Weapons were handed out. Drill started — slope arms, order arms, slope arms, present arms. It all went wrong. I was late and clumsy, then I saw why: the rifles we had were P14's, American rifles used in the Great War. I was unused to their weight and balance. At school we had the latest Lee Enfields. And while I don't remember firing them then, at school we stripped and carried Bren guns, then in service. Military policy, plainly, was to give boys current weapons.

The Tower Arms stands at the south-east corner of Richings Park. From there, a road cuts across. One way the Danes, then on to West Drayton. The other forms the southern boundary of the estate. It is called Richings Way. That, too, is noisy now.

Across fields once peaceful, traffic roars along the M4 and you see aircraft after aircraft dipping into Heathrow. Along Richings Way, then a leafy rural road, in a house set back, were two brothers, Maurice and Barrie Budden. They had come from Sussex. By their back door was a shed for the boys only. It housed a Hornby train track. You opened the wooden door, then bobbed down under the track to come up in the middle of it. Around the walls a landscape was painted. The track filled the shed. Trains ran in both directions, through miniature fields, under bridges, past stations. There were shunting yards and goods wagons you could arrange and re-arrange.

In their long garden backing onto the 'Rec', the recreation ground, the Buddens had a cricket net where we spent days, warned only not to break any windows. Both boys were good at cricket. An uncle, Maurice Tate, had played for Sussex and England. His nephew, named after him, was best of all of us. When he was nine, in 1939, he played in a 'grown- ups' match. He scored a century and took several wickets. Then, terribly, he contracted a rare illness. By the time he was thirteen or fourteen he could hardly see. At twenty Maurice was blind.

In the same road was another boy, John Travis. Like the rest of us, he was out each morning collecting bits of war material. Some bush telegraph told us early what had happened the night before. We'd go where the incendiaries had fallen, and pick up remnants, or sometimes to see a fallen bomber. On the edge of the woods a Wellington had crashed. Its tail jutted to the sky, the rear gunner still sprawled over his guns. On the way to West Drayton, on the cricket pitch we sometimes used, a Whitley had exploded. The stench of burnt rubber lingered as we approached tentatively, then, emboldened, stepped closer to gaze helplessly at the torn fuselage, smashed wings and propellers. We were never brave enough to climb inside. "You must keep away," our mother warned, "they might blow up." I think we saw six crashes, all English and all brought down, we believed, by the cables of barrage balloons that flew to protect the nearby Hawker factory (now the Ford factory at Langley you see from the M4 beyond Heathrow).

While we cluttered our bedroom with scraps of sharp-edged shrapnel, incendiary bombs and torn fragments of fuselage, John Travis did better. He had an exhibition in a hut by his house, to which he charged an entrance fee. Amazed we may have been, but we went anyway, and paid. John joined the Navy, then settled in Australia where, we may be sure, he prospered.

'Dusty' Miller lived in the same road. His son was a scout with us. We knew Dusty because at night, during the Blitz, after his day's work, he drove an ambulance. My mother was the nurse with him. She made our supper, then cycled off, her weak, hooded bicycle light waving and flickering in front of her. She went into the black night, through the dark, through fog and rain, even snow in 1940, the coldest winter for forty-five years, to West Drayton, two miles away, to the ambulance station.

Along Richings Way there is what we called 'the island', a rising hump of tree scrub that divides the road. As boys, we played in the scrub, hid, ambushed, fought battles with wooden swords, often as Robin Hood searching for the wicked King John. If one of the girls was with us she had to be Maid Marian, a dull part. Older, we sat shivering on damp nights in the church porch with those same girls, icy hands exploring goose-pimpled skin.

Winding west, towards the Hawker factory where Hurricanes, Typhoons and Tempests were built, is North Park. Oda Slobodskaya, said by musicians to have been one of the great sopranos of the twentieth century, lived here. She was, as she said, 'Rrrrooshan', born in 1888 in a poor family in Tsarist Russia, in Vilno, on the Polish border. Her story was remarkable. Working in a shop, she was encouraged to travel 300 miles to St Petersburg to compete for a scholarship to the Conservatoire. Although she couldn't read music and, when asked, didn't know what key she sang in, she won a scholarship. Prokofiev was a fellow student. Rimsky-Korsakov lectured to them. Even before her nine years tuition finished, she took the lead at the nearby Maryinsky theatre. She lived through the Revolution, escaping from the Bolsheviks in 1922 hidden in straw in a cattle train. In Berlin a critic wrote that she had 'the loveliest voice ever to come from Russia'.

Diaghileff, in Paris, invited her to star in a new opera by Stravinsky. Invited to New York, she received rave reviews for a solo evening at Carnegie Hall. Even so, after a year touring the United States in a Russian troupe, she couldn't find work. Undaunted, she changed her name (to Odali Careno) and sang all over America in variety and music halls for seven years, earning £500 a week (maybe £5000 or more today ?). She was invited to come to London to sing at the London Palladium and indeed at a Royal Command

Performance, still under her false name. She appeared at the Lyceum and elsewhere and the BBC gave her lots of work. Sir Compton Mackenzie wrote that 'such a glorious voice would make a poem of an income tax form'.

Bravely, she shed her music hall name to resume her operatic career.

Her husband, a British army officer named Pelly, was an admirer who came to her dressing-room. They married in Bangor, in Wales, where she chipped five years off her age on the marriage certificate, then went to live in Iver. That was in 1932. "Our house," she wrote of those days, "had a lovely garden with an oak tree in the centre and a bed of roses at the bottom. How I loved that cosy home of mine. We were happy there and it was ideal, as I realised every moment we spent there."

When we saw her during the war, she marched to the station, always in the middle of the road, her gas mask, tied with a ribbon, slung over her shoulder. It was said she still couldn't read music. My music teacher, Mrs Fenton, used to play the piano for her and help her. One day she arrived at Mrs Fenton's house and announced with characteristic dramatic intensity, "My deeeerr, my husband he is DEAD."

In 1942 we heard her sing in a BBC Promenade Concert (its forty-eighth season) at the Royal Albert Hall. A Russian concert, its first part was conducted by Sir Henry Wood, the founder of the Proms, himself. Sir Adrian Boult conducted the second part. Eileen Joyce was the solo pianist. The programme noted, 'In the event of an Air Raid Warning (the programme's capitals) the audience will be informed immediately, so that those who wish to take shelter, either in the building or in public shelters outside, may do so. The concert will then continue.' While the bombing went on, that meant. The Albert Hall had an infamous echo then. Asked about it, Sir Thomas Beecham said he liked it. "It is, after all, the only chance most British composers have to hear their music twice."

On the western side of Richings Park are two roads, Syke Ings and Syke Cluan. The Klemperers were among several friends who lived in one of them. Two boys, Hugh and Derek (re-named when they came to England on the edge of war, from Uwe and Dieter), were nephews of the great conductor. We were at school together. Hugh, always studious, won a scholarship, then read medicine. Unlike his simpler, cheerful, brother who told me one night while we were talking after lights-out in a rain-sodden tent on a Scout camp, that women had fur inside them to keep babies warm, Hugh was serious and solemn. Then, doing a postal round one Christmas, I met him in the street. "Hallo," he beamed, "how are you ?" He chatted away so freely and openly that I was rude enough to ask him why had he changed so. "Oh," he replied, "do you like it ? I realised that to be a doctor you need a bedside manner, so I am trying to cultivate one."

At the top of Syke Ings lived a beautiful, tall, pale Baptist girl. Her Sundays were spent indoors, behind curtained windows, reading the Bible. We were all conscious of that. Whatever the poor girl might have felt or wanted, and robust hockey player though she was, we boys treated her like a fragile saint.

Quite unlike her was another girl in the same road. We didn't know how to treat her at all. Older, she reduced us to helplessness because, undoubtedly, she Had Had Experience....in London. Hidden behind the bushes of someone's garden one night, she recited a poem about a car. "There's marks upon the cushion / Where someone has been pushin' /And there's footprints on the dashboard upside down..."

Her suntanned brother, whom we glimpsed occasionally on the touchline of the hockey pitch, was at sea, an officer in the Merchant Navy. He gave me a banana which I thought at the time came from Australia. During the war we never saw, perhaps never had seen, a banana. There was a joke about that. Two boys were in a train. A soldier, back from the Far East, hands them a banana. One peels it and starts to eat. As he does, the train roars into a tunnel. All is black. "Here, Alf, don't eat that banana, it makes yer go blind."

Three

You mustn't sigh, you mustn't cry

If we wonder now who will be the world's conscience and guardian and policeman to tame the next Saddam Hussein or Bosnian warlord, there was no doubt about the policeman in 1899, the year our mother was born. Only six months before, at the height of British imperial power, Kitchener had routed tens of thousands of Dervishes at the battle of Omdurman, while in South Africa, where war had broken out, the public mood was illustrated by a cartoon at the turn of the century: 'The Boers will cop it now. Farfer's gone to South Africa an' tooken 'is strap.'

Outside her bedroom window in London, when my mother was a baby, jubilant crowds celebrated the relief of Ladysmith, Mafeking and Kimberley, railway towns in South Africa which had been surrounded and starved by the Boers. She was two years old when Queen Victoria died.

Yet although, more than ninety years later, traces of those imperial days still swell old hearts, the early influence on my mother's life was neither British nor Victorian, but French. Her mother came from Alsace. She had been sent by a brother, Emile Kern (a civil engineer said to have designed one of the bridges of Paris) to study English at Taunton. Mathilde's husband was English as roast beef. His name was George Priest. Too big to be a jockey, as he wanted, he owned livery stables in Portobello Road, no distance from the site of the old Hippodrome race-course in Holland Park.

Then, for years, he looked after the Duke of Norfolk's horses. He lived with his family in Arundel Castle and behind Norfolk House in St. James's Square where, in the Second World War, General Eisenhower had his invasion headquarters.The Duke took my grandfather to France, to race meetings at Neuilly and Longchamp where, as children we were constantly told, "He struck a fine figure, gambling and giving away his money." "When his money disappeared," repeated my mother as a solemn warning of man's infidelity, "so did his friends."

Are there ghosts ? My mother's father told her he had seen a headless coachman driving a coach and horses up the long drive to Arundel Castle. Years later a secretary of mine interviewed the current duke for television. She asked him whether the castle had ghosts. "Oh yes," replied the Duke, "there's a headless coachman, but don't say so...it will keep the tourists away."

There were two children of my grandparents' marriage, my mother and an older brother, George, who was wounded in that Boer War. In Canada in the 1950s I met a man with the same name, George Priest. "How odd," I said, "I had an uncle with your name. He was in the East Surreys." "So was I," replied the man. Writing of those days in *Something of*

Myself, Rudyard Kipling recalled that "French as an accomplishment was not well seen... knowledge of it connoted leanings towards immorality." Even so, my mother, christened Marie-Therese, went to a French convent behind Leicester Square, where she was in the same class as John Barbirolli, a London boy who became a fine soloist and, without a lesson, a brilliant conductor. Caught in the United States when war started, where he was conducting the New York Symphony Orchestra, he returned to war-torn and poverty-ravaged Manchester in 1943 to re-build the Hallé Orchestra.

That convent school could have lessons for us now. In the mornings, one week, all the lessons were in French. In the afternoon they were in English. Next week they would change about. My mother became totally bilingual, being chosen by the school to greet the French ambassador when he visited and, later in life, to meet President de Gaulle.

Like her children a generation later, as a girl she grew up in the noise and confusion, shortage and fear, excitement and patriotism and posters of war. When she was sixteen she married, in Henrietta Street, Covent Garden, a young medical orderly in the Middlesex Regiment. Surprisingly, in view both of the hate-filled times and of her French roots, her husband was a German, born in Berlin. His name was Ernst Herrmann. For his military service he was granted British citizenship. His younger brother, too, served in the British army, in the Rifle Brigade. Two weeks after he reached the trenches, in 1917, he was shot dead.

By the time she was nineteen, my mother had three children, Julie, Raymond and Victor. Perhaps many mothers are the same. When ours was old and fat and comfortable and lonely, sitting in a winged armchair by the fire, stroking her cat and sipping whisky, she told the same stories over and over and over. She told how, newly-married, they moved to Yorkshire. Then her husband walked out. Mother made her way back to London and took a basement flat in Ogle Street, near where the Post Office Tower now stands. With three small children and almost no money, before the age of social security, her life was dire. By day she worked in Pinet's, the French shoe shop in Bond Street and at the Savoy Theatre, translating a French play for C.B. Cochran. At night she cleaned and laundered and ironed and fed the children, having to ration slices of bread.

A nun, a Sister of Mercy, visited and comforted her. "You should get out," she said, "and meet people." She persuaded my mother to go to a rehearsal for a Gilbert & Sullivan opera. At the rehearsal my mother met my father. They were doing *Patience*, the name now of my younger sister. They married and moved to Ealing. My twin brother and I were born there, in 1929.

On my bookcase is a fading photograph of my mother taken soon after that. Smiling, she is dressed in white, with a white bandeau across her short, dark hair. Crouched on the steps of a pavilion, she holds a tennis racquet between her knees. Her skin was pale, her eyes light blue. She was slim, not tall. Later, as we remember her, she became heavier, moving slowly. The darkness of her hair faded. The smile in the photograph was replaced by the stern downlines of disapproval. She became a dominant disciplinarian, with a voice that could shout and hand that could slap. It would be hard to say we liked her or were not afraid of her or that with her we were happily relaxed for long . She was house-proud and as she cleaned she made our home an uncomfortable museum, with rooms not to enter, chairs not to sit in. But, seared by her early years, she was brave, a fighter. In her strict way, she looked after us well, cooked generously, mended and cleaned our clothes, took us to church, put us into schools, made us do our homework and music practice and, every Saturday, polish the inordinate amount of brass in the house. It was she who taught us to clean our teeth, brush our hair, clean our shoes, put our caps on straight, stand up when a lady enters the room and, in the street, to walk on the outside, to shield them from mud-spraying traffic.

Dust came with age. When she was widowed and as she grew older, cleaning mattered less. She preferred to sit as a grande-dame in the green sofas of Harrods' banking hall, which was then on the ground floor, and meet friends in her club in Belgrave Square. And, later still, to drink whisky and eat shop cake in front of a television set and tell us repetitive stories of her youth each time we went to see her. "You've just told us that, Mummy," said my sister when, having finished a tale we had heard a hundred times, she began it again, with the same words, pauses and emphases. "Don't interrupt," replied my mother sharply, and on she went.

Although she bossed our father equally, she may well have loved him; never more than when he died. "You will never be half the man your father was," she told my twin and me repeatedly.

If Daddy's presence was lighter, less felt, we loved him more. He was a good man. Called Freddie, as my twin is, he was broad-shouldered, well-built, a pipe smoker, solid, safe. He had brown eyes and a gentle manner. No doubt he surrendered too much. In a turbulent household, he strove for peace. "Even when the darkest clouds are in the sky," he sang as he mended something in the house, "You mustn't sigh, you mustn't cry/Just spread a little happiness as you go by." That was him; kind, loving, generous. Another song was, "I've got a motto/ Ever so merry and bright/ Look around and you will find/ Every cloud is silver-lined." And a third: "I'm shy, Mary Ellen, I'm shy," as, indeed, he was.

Then, once in a while, perhaps remembering his father's stories, (not unlike recent Hovis advertisements), of going to the West End, having something to eat and a pint of beer and seeing a Music Hall and still having change from a shilling, he sang at high speed faster and louder, louder and faster, Harry Champion's song:

> *Any old iron, any old iron, any any any old iron ,*
> *You look neat, talk about a treat,*
> *You look a dapper from your napper to your feet.*
> *Dressed in style, brand new tile,*
> *Father's old grey tie on.*
> *Oh, I wouldn't give you tuppence for your old watch chain,*
> *Old iron, old iron.*

He went faster and faster, as we egged him on, helpless with laughter. He took on our mother's three children as his own, never making the slightest distinction, loving us equally. Good with his hands, he made an aeroplane for me, told us to take off our hats when we passed the Cenotaph, taught us how to hold a straight bat, keep our elbow out and stand with our feet together, side on to the bowler... and not to answer our mother back.

Although his family came originally from the West Country — the chief engineer of the Torbay/Saltash bridge, Brunel's famous railway bridge, had the same name — my father, born in 1901, was brought up with his sister, Emmie, in Hounslow. Their mother was a loving, gentle creature. Their father, with a grey 'Old Bill' drooping moustache, owned a second-hand furniture shop, then a workshop with two or three craftsmen in All Saints' Road in Westbourne Park, London, the firm my father took over. Every Monday morning, on the way to work, he drove to see his parents, sometimes taking us. Every Monday my mother grumbled about it.

Although I remember Grandpa bent over, wheezing and with palpitations, doctors said there was nothing wrong with him and never had been. Legend had it, perhaps wrongly, that after the First World War he went to bed and there he stayed.

Our parents moved with all their children to the green fields of Iver, in Buckinghamshire, one Saturday afternoon in 1933, to a house called Brooklyn. Within an hour of their arrival, J.S. Anthony, the local milkman, left on their step a pint of milk, half-a-pound of butter and six eggs— with his compliments. Later we moved to a house with nothing before it but a small, tarred and gravelled road, wide verges and far-reaching fields of waving corn. My mother named it St Christopher's, after the patron saint of travel. We lived there for seven or eight years, through the beginning of the war and worst of the air raids.

St Christopher's is a square, upright house, covered today in dun-coloured shingle. The façade has a central section, the width of the drawing-room, jutting out. The roof is pitched and tiled. Windows, a single frame, then four together, then another single one, identical on both floors, are painted timber, with leaded lights. To one side is a garage.

There is a short garden in front with a drive dividing it diagonally. At the back is a lawn, then vegetable garden. Beyond, trees screen the garden and backs of houses.

Both the front and back doors of the house are on the left. Downstairs there was a cold drawing room, used mostly for entertaining and at Christmas, when it was hung with looping paper chains we had pasted for hours. After a roast turkey lunch which took several days to prepare and ended with us poking for — and finding — silver threepenny bits in the Christmas pudding that had steamed for a day, then cracking nuts and listening to the King, Daddy would throw open the door and step in, disguised in red cloak and fur-trimmed red hat. He handed out presents stacked around a Christmas tree that reached to the ceiling.

Behind was the sitting-room where we listened to *Children's Hour*, with Uncle Mac and S.G. Hulme Beaman's *Toytown*, with Ernest the policeman, Larry the lamb, Mr Growser the grocer and the Mayor "wearing his chain of office". In that house before the war my twin brother and I became Ovaltinies ("We are the "Ovaltinies," we sang, "happy girls and boys," an early advertising jingle).

When darkness fell we lit the fire and pulled the curtains across french windows and sat raptly listening to *In Town To-Night*, a magazine programme of interviews, and *Monday Night at Seven O'Clock.* (It changed to *Monday Night at Eight O'Clock.*) "It's Monday Night at Seven O'Clock," a girl sang, "Oh can't you hear the chimes, they're telling you to take an easy chair..."

The singer was Judy Shirley, who was the first to sing 'A Nightingale sang in Berkeley Square'. Her son, who later became a good friend, told me that after the war, with her actor husband Roy Finlay, she left England for Cyprus. They bought the Harbour Club in Kyrenia, and created the best restaurant on the island. All during the troubles in Cyprus, even though half the British High Command ate there, never a pane of glass was broken by what were then called the terrorists. The reason given was that during the war Roy Finlay, a gunner twice decorated with the MC, had saved the life of George Grivas (leader of the terrorists). Remembering, Grivas had given orders that Roy and Judy weren't to be touched.

Unlike Sir Compton Mackenzie who wrote a book about his life up to the age of two, and who remembered feeling his pram bump on the kerb as he was taken to Kensington Gardens when he was one, I have no picture of my early days. Or have I ? I see pools of water on a wet beach and my father rushing towards us, then feel him grabbing us from waves. That was when we were very small.

A recurring dream is of being a small child at the back of a crowd watching an air display. A gyroplane, forerunner of the helicopter, is flying. I hear its engine buzzing like a wasp. Suddenly, the aircraft lifts its nose. It stalls and falls, disappearing beyond the big backs of the crowd. A pall of smoke billows up. Daddy, my twin and I turn to leave, everyone trailing slowly behind us. I think that happened, I even imagine seeing a picture in the paper next day of the exact moment the frail craft tilted its nose too high. But maybe it is just a dream. Newspaper files would tell.

I can feel, as if now, the wire cutting into my knees as we climbed a fence to watch a special train roar by. Shining green engine barrelling forward, purposeful, important, urgent, smoke billowing behind, glistening cream and brown coaches, shadows of faces at windows; in a trice it was gone. It was the end of January, 1936. The train was taking the body of King George V to Windsor.

Freddie and I cycled to school every day, with Mother, through Thorney to the village green in West Drayton, pushing our little legs hard to climb a humped-back bridge, then swooping, legs akimbo, down the other side. We paused as a slow, shining green steam-roller with a tall chimney and great brass Invicta badge on the front, laboured slowly down the road. At the water-mill where in winter mistletoe blossomed on the top of trees, we turned left. We came to the village green where, behind St. Catherine's Church, was a primary school. There we got our first school reports and made our first, and my last, appearance in a play. Even then, at five years old, I wanted to be a soldier, a Crusader. Mummy made me a white tunic and pinned on it a big red cross. She fashioned a helmet from silver cardboard. Daddy made me a wooden sword. All I had to do, stiff and frightened, was to stand on the side of the stage, holding the sword upright.

'Any time you're Lambeth Way / Any evening, any day / You'll find us all doing the Lambeth Walk. Oi.' In a darkened hotel bedroom in Ostend, Freddie and I lay in bed listening to roistering English tourists dancing and singing down the road. It was August 1939, a week or two before the war started. We were in Belgium on holiday. Strange, spicy smells, cobbles, clattering trams, engraved glass doors with curved brass handles. At the back of a crowd we glimpsed a passion play being enacted before the spired town hall in Bruges. In Brussels we giggled with embarrassment at the Mannequin Pis and, following our father, bowed our heads before the eternal flame of the Unknown Warrior. Again summoning the seriousness expected of us, we gazed respectfully at four wooden stumps of wood set in stone. They were remnants of the seat in which Nurse Edith Cavell was executed by the Germans on 12 October 1915 accused of being a spy. To us it meant nothing, although of course we have learnt since that together with sinking the *Lusitania* and the alleged shooting of nuns at Louvain, her execution was an atrocity which fanned First World War fury.

In the Bois de la Cambre, we watched Belgian cavalry trot and canter, drilling on horseback. They wore khaki, with tassels falling from their forage caps. This was eight months before the Panzer tanks swept them and a world away.

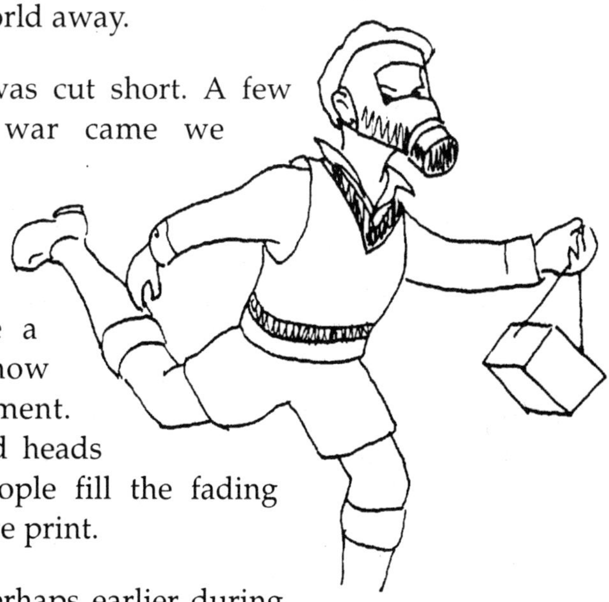

The holiday was cut short. A few days before war came we crowded to the quay at Ostend to catch a ferry home. I have a photograph now of that moment. Ferryboats and heads of waiting people fill the fading black and white print.

Back home, perhaps earlier during the Munich crisis, Freddie and I were sent one day to an empty shop at the end of the line of shops in Bathurst Walk. There we were fitted with gas masks, black rubber things with straps you put over your head. In front was a metal cannister. You looked through a plastic visor.

Although there was a quick frisson of fear, wearing them soon became great fun. If you blew hard the visor misted over, but you made marvellous rude noises. We walked home wearing them and snorting through them, proudly. To our surprise, when we showed them off to our mother she burst into tears.

We were in the garden of St Christopher's with a friend when Chamberlain, the Prime Minister, made his grave announcement that Sunday morning, 3rd September 1939. Daddy called us in, through the french windows to stare at the wireless. "...No undertaking having been received, we are now in a state of war with Germany," we heard. My father switched off the wireless. There was silence. We sat, not moving. Clearly, it was a large moment. Something important had happened. But what did it mean? Neither parent said much. Mummy sent the friend home. In a moment or two the sirens we had heard rehearsing for months wailed. We ran to the garden and looked up to the high, white, clouds drifting across a blue sky, expecting to see black bombers. But there were none. The 'All Clear' sounded.

Our older sister, Julie, was to have celebrated her 21st birthday party in London the next evening, but the party was cancelled. She had been sharing a flat in London with an Italian girl-friend. Doubtless fearful of the expected bombing, they came to live at home. An exotic, fulsome woman who clouded the bathroom with sweet-smelling talcum, and wore scarlet lipstick and smelt exciting, the Italian girl went with Julie one day to a local dance, a 'hop' we called it. The quintessence of continental sophistication, she was asked to dance by a farm worker. 'One, two, three, one two, three,' he puffed as he pushed her around.

The year the war began, when we were ten, my mother thought we should be near. She sent us to the village school, Iver Board School, a low, sandy-coloured 1897 building, with high windows edged in red brick. Above the steeply-pitched tiled roof is a white bellhouse for the school bell. All the children sat in one room on benches, behind long, low desks. Mornings began with prayers and 'Jerusalem'.

And did those feet in ancient time
Walk upon England's mountains green ?
And was the holy Lamb of God
On England's pleasant pastures seen ?
And did the Countenance Divine
Shine forth upon these clouded hills ?
And was Jerusalem builded here
Among these dark Satanic mills ?

Bring me my bow of burning gold !
Bring me my arrows of desire !
Bring me my spear ! O clouds, unfold !
Bring me my chariot of fire !
I will not cease from mental fight,
Nor shall my sword sleep in my hand,
Till we have built Jerusalem
In England's green and pleasant land.

Scoffed at as this hymn may be when patriotic ladies from

the shires sing it in the Albert Hall at the annual conference of Women's Institutes, I have no doubt its stirring words shaped me. My feeling for England stems, in part, from that small schoolroom.

Behind the school allotments had been dug. Even then, we 'dug for victory'. Two or three pupils each shared an allotment. In the summer, everyone's potatoes suffered a blight, ruining the entire crop. The cause was pinned down to my allotment.

Four

Movies were movies

A white picket fence and bank of grass kept you from the gravelled platforms. You had to pass the ticket office, a small, cream and dark brown painted box, then climb stairs to cross a bridge. There were four pairs of sparkling lines, fast and slow up to London, fast and slow down to Reading and the West Country. This was Iver station on Brunel's Great Western Railway. It was different then. Railwaymen planted flower beds, edged with whitewashed stones. On platform 4 there were metal billboards. One, blue and white, advertised pens. "The Owl, the Pickwick and Waverley pen" it read, "They come as a boon and a blessing to men, the Pickwick, the Owl and the Waverley pen." Later, when the war moved into gear, it was replaced by a warning about security and spies: "Be like dad, keep mum."

Every morning streams of men converged there to take the 8.27 or, for a few, the 9.04 train, past the timber yards in West Drayton, the gasometer at Hayes, the asylum at Hanwell, the dirty and damaged flats of London, past Royal Oak and Westbourne Park, to the glass arches and the steaming, smoky, hissing bustle of Paddington. In the evening, back they streamed, fanning out their different ways.

One who did was Mr Crowther. He was a Yorkshireman. To

us boys, he could have come from the moon, except that we knew they played cricket in Yorkshire and we never thought of the moon. Mr Crowther was portly. You don't see portly men like him anymore; stout, leaning back as they walk, a gold watch-chain stretched across their waistcoat. Mr Crowther smoked a pipe and wore his hat jauntily, on the back and side of his balding head, as Clark Gable might have worn his regulation US Air Force cap: dashingly. It was said Mr Crowther was a reporter on Fleet Street, a wonderland away of words and ink and print and rolling machines. Each morning, his first after-breakfast pipe billowing smoke, he would step slowly to the station. Often as not, we boys would be waiting for him.

"Hey, Mr Crowther," one of us would call, "have you heard the terrible news ?" "Nay, lad," he'd say, time after time, "what's that ?" "Hootton's out," we'd cry, holding in our giggles. Then, after a pause, "For a dook." Morning after morning.

Before he was cast from our fickle minds by the 'terrible twins', Compton and Edrich, Hutton was our hero. Had he not scored 364 runs at the Oval in that timeless Test match of 1938 ? And Hutton, 'Len o' Pudsey' to us, was from Yorkshire. That we did know.

It is small wonder we were impressed. In 1939, the last

year of proper county cricket until it resumed after the war, the first seven names in the English county batting averages played for Yorkshire, Hutton leading. The two top bowlers in the bowling averages that year were also from Yorkshire; Bowes and Verity.

When Sir Len Hutton died in 1990, Sussex Cricket Club reminded members of the last match played in England before the war started. It was Yorkshire playing Sussex at Hove in what must have been an epic match. In Sussex's first innings George Cox scored 198 not out. In their second innings, Hedley Verity took seven of their wickets for nine runs. Then they all went their ways to war. Verity was killed in action in Sicily in 1943.

By Iver station was the Plaza, the cinema where we saw old films on Saturday mornings for threepence and on Sundays, in red cassock and loose white cotton surplice, I served as an acolyte at mass. In a cinema? That was make do, because there wasn't a Catholic church within miles. As well as shuffling solemnly across the cinema stage behind the priest (who came from the girls' convent in Langley and had a petrol ration to visit his outlying flock), and trying to remember where to kneel and when to shake the tinkling bell, this included cleaning the brass candlesticks. "What you need," some devotee chided me one morning, "is a bit of elbow grease." "Where will I find it ?" I asked. "Try the cupboard," he answered. I pulled aside brooms and lamps and chairs and even a disused projector, but there was no elbow grease to be found.

Cleanliness was part of politeness as well as godliness. My elder brother rebuked me one Sunday morning for my dirty shoes. "You'd clean your shoes if you were going to see the King, wouldn't you," he said. "Well, this morning you are going to see the King of Kings." How a chance remark of fifty years ago set values that stay.

In 1940 the Plaza closed as a cinema. It became a furniture warehouse. In 1962, the Plaza was pulled down to make way for a block of flats. When the cinema closed we went to mass in the village hall in Iver village. Invariably, there had been a play or dance there the night before. The hall smelt of dust and stale beer. The altar went on the stage, in front of a lurid backdrop of painted scenery.

Maybe because the mass was droned in Latin and I didn't like or understand a word of it, and such singing as there was was Gregorian plain chant, austere, without flourish or joy, I wasn't engaged in the slightest. From boredom and because I had some artistic interest, however unformed, I spent hours studying those backdrops. They varied. The usual one was of an Italianate garden, with urns and poplars and an oblong lake narrowing with perspective. The sky was a violent blue and everything tinged with a hideous orange which failed to give the impression it was meant to convey of a scorching Mediterranean sun.

While we knelt on the hard, boarded floor, then sat with relief in the canvas-backed brown metal seats, then knelt again, one lady wearing a fur-collared coat and flat pork-pie hat tilted to one side, stood throughout. She was Baroness de Stoeckl, a refugee staying with the Duchess of Kent, who often accompanied her.

One devout Catholic who attended mass while it was held at the Plaza was Miss Bamber. Short, wide, dressed in long black clothes with, invariably, a high, boned lace collar around her throat, she was elderly. From her neck hung a glass-fronted gold pendant, the shape of a fan.

In it, to see, was gold dust her father had panned in the second Californian Gold Rush in the 1860s. As a girl Elizabeth Bamber had lived in the *Gone With The Wind* world of parkland and horses, columned houses, crinolines and balls. Although many years in England, she retained a delightful Southern drawl.

When, after the war, she heard I was going to America, she advised me of something she claimed most Englishmen don't learn. "Never forget," she said, "that the world is yer erster." Then, doubtless recalling moustachioed villains of another age, she warned me, "Look out for those smart fellers you'll meet in the bar of your hotel. They'll be feeding you drinks and be nice as pie. All the while," she shrugged, "their confederates will be upstairs rifling your luggage in your room."

I met her one day, leaning on her silver-topped malacca cane, hobbling to the railway station. "Where you going, Miss Bamber ?" I asked. "To Baath," she replied. "I've just been reading about a church there, and thought I'd like to see it." "You're wonderful," I said. "Well, you gotta do sumpin'," she said, "otherwise you jest set and rot like an old cabbage." She was then 86.

Because the smell and thrill of those Saturday mornings at the Plaza floods back when I hear one song from *Mack and Mabel*, a show about Mack Sennett, an early producer, and Mabel Normand, an actress on the silent screen, I realise the films we saw were pretty old.

"Movies were movies when you paid a dime to escape/ Cheering the hero and hissing the man in the cape./ Romance and action and thrills/ Pardner thar's gold in them hills/ Movies were movies when during the

titles you'd know/ You'd get a happy ending.

"Dozens of blundering cops in a thundering chase/Getting a bang out of lemon meringue in the face/Bandits attacking a train, one little tramp with a cane/Movies were movies when I ran the show.

"Movies were movies when Pauline was tied to the track/After she'd trudged through the ice with a babe on her back..."

As well as Keaton and Chaplin and Roy Rogers on his white horse, we saw strings of English films: Will Hay as a station master, Will Hay as governor of a prison, George Formby with his ukelele, Gracie Fields, the 'lass of Rochdale' who, in one film, had a skirt made from an old parachute and someone pulled the rip-cord, Jack Buchanan in Mayfair.

Fred Astaire and Ginger Rogers must have been among them. In one film Ginger Rogers, working for a dancing academy, tries to teach Astaire to dance. Although we know already that he is a professional dancer, she doesn't. He pretends to be hopeless, slipping and falling. "I can't teach you. You'll never be able to dance," she cries in exasperation. Her boss hears her and fires her. To save her job, Astaire shows what he has learnt. Of course, they dance divinely, with a lightness of step beyond clumpy mortals.

How finely social strata were defined then. We were told never to speak to 'boys from the village'. For a while a gang of them came to the Plaza on Saturdays, an alien invasion looking for fun. While we thrilled to dusty cowboys or adored Vivien Leigh, then so slim and young, they crawled under the cinema seats, along the unswept carpet, and tied our feet to the metal struts. We responded by letting down the tyres of their bikes. We were poor sport. The village boys soon gave us up.

The Plaza had plays too. There was a theatrical company called the Richings Players. My sister, older than we were, blonde, blue-eyed, attractive, acted with them and won good reviews in the local newspaper. We hoped she'd go on the stage, but she never did. She married an RAF officer and had a family. It took a generation for the nascent talent to flower. Her daughter has an Equity card and is now an actress.

Facing the Plaza was a row of shops. On the corner was the estate agent, called King. The son, older than us, went off to the war. A door or two along was the sweetshop. Once a week we ran there to buy our sweet ration, three ounces, always hoping to find gob-stoppers in the large glass jars on the shelf behind the shop-keeper's head, or, in packets, those slim white sticks with a red tip to look like cigarettes. There was no chocolate that I recall. (A friend told me recently how in Stanmore at that time he bought the nearest thing, Choclax, from the chemist. Results were unexpected. It was a laxative.) I was always at a disadvantage in wartime. My twin has a good memory. I remember little. Each week, or so it seems, my brother would say I owed him a coupon, or tuppence. Did I ? I couldn't recall. So I gave it to him. He shared generously, so it amounted to little except a few arguments and pleading.

The road from the station, between the shops and cinema, cuts down into the heart of Richings Park. To the left runs a row of shops; the grocer where our ration books were registered (he was allocated just enough food to match the number of customers registered with him) and Wilkinson's hardware shop where we took our bikes to be mended and, late at night in the damp Thames mist, I left his daughter to creep in the back way without being heard. Paddy had high, almost Slavic, cheekbones, full, finely-carved lips, arching eyebrows and firm breasts. In summer she wore flowered cotton dresses, with more buttons undone than her father would have liked.

On the corner, opposite Keats the papershop, was a dairy. When the premises became vacant Mr Wilkinson took them, to start a small garage, where he tinkered with our father's Wolseley.

After a few yards the road from the station forks. One divide, swinging to the left, is Somerset Way. Richard Haddon lived in that road, as did his cousins, Gerald Eilouart and his sister. Richard, with dark hair brushed back, full lips and a nervous manner, an Harrovian, always wanted to get into films. After early forays, he moved into advertising, where they were then hiring what they would have called the 'right kind' of young man. As deputy advertising manager for British American Tobacco, he travelled without pause to all the extremities of the globe, to Omsk and Tomsk, everywhere. Everywhere, that is, except New York, Nassau and Paris. When one of those more comfortable, even luxurious, trips was due, his boss always said, "Mmmm, I think I'll take, this one, Richard."

In the 'sixties, before gambling was legalised, Richard was invited to a poker party in London. He took a few pounds to lose. On the first turn of the cards one side of Sloane Square changed hands.

Mr Eilouart, Gerald's father, started an enthusiasm for me that continues to this day. He first took me to the pavilion at Lord's. We watched the Eton and Harrow match. Before the war this was a two-day game, attracting crowds of twenty thousand and more. Started as long ago as 1821, the Eton and Harrow match has dwindled now to a sparsely-watched one-day game. Sadly, it is less of an occasion.

When we went horse-drawn coaches lined corners of the ground. Most people wore morning coats. As was the custom, at lunch and perhaps again at tea-time, we perambulated the pitch. Years later, the chairman of Moss Bros, told a story about that. His father, he said, was strolling with everyone else around the ground when someone called his name. "Hallo, Moses," said the voice,

"what are you doing? Stock-taking?"

One score card I have now describes the match of 1949. Robin Marlar, who now writes for the *Sunday Times,* not only made the highest score, 45, but took five wickets for Harrow in the first innings, including Ingleby-Mackenzie who later captained Hampshire and Alastair Aird who, in turn, bowled him out. Alastair Aird (now Sir Alastair) became the Queen Mother's equerry. Robin Marlar became the captain of Sussex. One long-standing player there, George Cox, spoke of those days. "Some captains," he said, "we followed with enthusiasm. Others from loyalty, still others out of curiosity...and speaking of Robin Marlar..."

Lord Home played for Eton at Lord's. Later to be president of the MCC, his passion for cricket never dimmed. When he was Commonwealth Secretary and Sir Robert Menzies (Pig-Iron Bob), who called Lord's "the cathedral of cricket", was Prime Minister of Australia, the two of them 'managed' in the words of a letter he wrote me 'a regular coincidence between the Prime Ministers' meeting and the Lord's test matches.' Such is the way affairs of state may be arranged by civilised leaders.

That passion can take surprising turns. When he was Foreign Secretary, Lord Home, then Sir Alec Douglas-Home, was invited to a cathedral city, Ely or Worcester. The bishop took him around the cathedral. Lord Home admired the soaring arches, reaching columns, magnificent stained-glass windows. "Do you know, Foreign Secretary," the Bishop interrupted, "I never walk up this aisle without wondering if it will take spin."

While at Lord's, Mr Eilouart took me to a room where they

repair bats. I was shown Denis Compton's. The blade was clean white. Only in the plumb of the bat, the sweetest and perfect place, was there a mark; a black depression. Compton, judging by that, hit only with the middle of the bat. Although I have been to Lord's a thousand times since, I have never found that room again.

Ernest Stevens, tall, upright, was another of those who walked to the train each morning. He had a button factory in Soho. Like him, his wife was sandy-haired, perhaps auburn. She had a way of tilting her head as she spoke, always smilingly. Her house was like a new pin. The garden, too. Roses bloomed there as nowhere else, the lawn was perfect as a bowling green. Brian, their son, also tall and sandy-haired, was leader of our scout troop. He wore three white stripes on the left breast pocket of his uniform and the green and yellow lanyard of a First Class scout. His sister, Brenda, vividly auburn-haired, was a year or two older than we were, an unbridgeable gulf.

The Elliotts lived nearby, in Wellesley Avenue. The father, Fred, ran a coal business in London. He had the firm, quick movements of a sportsman, pushing back with his elbows and leaning forwards as he walked, short, greying hair and a clipped military moustache. His wife had died. He brought up his family strictly and alone. Two sons had gone to war. One, Kenneth, was killed in a tank battle in the North African desert. His name appears, below that of HRH The Duke of Kent, KG KT, on a plaque in Iver church.

Fred, or Mr Elliott as he always was to us, had two daughters. Barbara, who preferred to be called Kay, maybe nineteen or twenty, was beyond us. Angela, our age, was my girl friend. We didn't have the term 'going steady' or 'petting', but we were one and did the other.

How innocently, though. Fear of our parents, the respectability of our time or middle-class dread of 'getting a girl into trouble' and, if you were a Catholic, the sureness of swift and terrible retribution, were inhibitions enough. In Canada, years later, a lady came bounding up to me at a cocktail party. "Hallo," she said, "my name is Marjorie. I am 63 and I have never missed an opportunity." Never, more sadly, have I been able to make such a sensible boast. Perhaps our idea of 'sowing wild oats' wasn't quite, as I read recently, 'to keep library books overdue', but that is the timid extreme to which we erred.

Here it is worth dismissing the idea of homosexuality. You can't pick up a paper today without being aware of it. Then, it didn't exist for us. We called boys 'queer' and perhaps 'pooffy' and 'cissy', but to us that meant they were feeble.

Further down Wellesley Avenue was where Russell lived, a newcomer. One day he asked me indoors and, to my surprise, took me upstairs to a bedroom. There, strewn on the floor, was a muddy battledress, a belt and boots, one on its side as it had been dropped. In bed, dead to the world, was Russell's brother. A paratrooper, he had just come back from Arnhem.

Later, he told me his company commander had announced they were to be evacuated from the battle to England, to "a place called Iver. Ever heard of it ?" he asked. As soon as they found their billets the brother came home. While he slept I took his gun, a Sten. We went behind the cricket pavilion. Playfully, I aimed at the wooden wall and squeezed the trigger. There was much too loud a bang. In the wall of the pavilion were two holes. Anxiously, we looked across the cricket pitch, to gardens and houses beyond, fearing I had killed someone. But apparently not. When he heard, the brother was horrified. "That gun was jammed," he said. A free round had blasted out the jammed one. All highly dangerous.

In Wellesley Avenue, too, was The Grove House, the broad double-fronted white home of the Fentons. Two 'vaccies' (evacuees) were billeted on them. Donny and Stanley Perkins, both from Stepney, slept in a cupboard under the stairs, with their feet sticking out. Later, two airmen, manning the local barrage balloons, were billeted there. They worked shifts. One insisted his food was kept warm in the oven. The other, no less emphatically, demanded that his meal be kept warm over a saucepan of boiling water. Mrs Fenton, perhaps the most enthusiastic and uncomplicatedly good woman I ever met, complied.

I can't see a picture of Joyce Grenfell without thinking of Mrs Fenton. They shared the same look; pronounced jaw, lively eyes, hair pulled back in a bun, wispy traces uncontrollable, the same urgency and vivacity. She came from a distinguished and benevolent Edinburgh family. Her brother was General Sir Philip Christison who served under Slim in South East Asia. Mrs Fenton had been a leader of the Queen's Hall Light Orchestra. Her husband, serving in the London Scottish in Flanders during the First World War, had been gassed and given up for dead. But he recovered, to became a 'stage-door Johnny'. On leave, high in the gallery, he saw her, fell in love and waited for her after each concert. When they married they had two daughters, Dids and Robin (Deirdre and Rosamond). The family formed its own quartet. Mrs Fenton, Dorothea, played the violin, her husband the 'cello. Dids played the piano. Robin, not in the least interested, was stuck with the double bass. My older brother fell for Robin. To ingratiate himself, he borrowed her double bass, and took lessons. His campaign triumphant, they decided to marry. When they did both ended, forever, their musical careers. They sold their instrument and, with the money, bought a tandem bicycle. They had their honeymoon in Bournemouth, where the beach was mined and, on their wedding night, they locked themselves out of their room.

Mrs Fenton didn't have time for her house. For her, food was a nuisance. She was always on the go, her cloak flowing behind her as she cycled up the road, perhaps to shop, more likely to give another lesson, or, to accompany Oda Slobodskaya. One day, from her bicycle, she told me she was teaching herself Russian. "It's wonderful," she cried as she sped off.

She taught me, with a success which would not have troubled Menuhin, to play the violin. Lessons, for a few shillings, drifted long after the hour was up, past tea, past time for an hour in the nets. Swaying in ecstasy at her flowing interpretations of our scratched out music, she taught enough children to form her own orchestra. We won prizes in local music festivals, and toured with a choir singing *The Messiah,* once in the freezing church in Iver. Mrs Fenton used, too, to have terrifying concerts in her drawing room, where each of us had to perform before anxious parents. One poor child, unable to scratch a note on a violin or peck a tune on the piano, recited a poem. Twice he started, twice he faltered. Blushing, he turned to Mrs Fenton and said, loudly enough for all doting parents to hear,"Oh shit, I've forgotten it."

Even now when I hear, say, Haydn's No 1 in B, or Brahms or Mendelssohn (Mrs Fenton always wanted us to have 'a jolly tune') my elbow pumps along with the music, making up the bowing forgotten so long ago.

As children, then teenagers, we grew up together; all in the same happy, busy, sheltered community. Older ones went away. David, once my patrol leader in the Scouts, died in a bomber. Rex, son of a photographer, became a glider pilot and was missing. Norman was crushed under a tank.

Five

To Defend Old Ladies

The centre of our world was the 'Rec', a large playing field edged on all sides by the gardens of houses. "Play in the Rec," my mother commanded, "or in the garden, but not in between." Left to overgrow when war started and with a barrage balloon site in one corner, it hardly recovered its earlier, greensward beauty, although we boys cut and rolled the cricket pitch. We heaved and struggled to pull what was once a horse-drawn roller big enough for three of us to hide in when it rained, rust flaking on us. There was one central cricket pitch with sight-screens at each end, and later two pitches, as there had been before the war. There were two, then three, hockey pitches. There was a hedged-in bowling green we weren't allowed near, and an aloof, high-fenced tennis club.

The tennis club-house was a small timber building which had once been a butcher's shop where the Plaza stood. On rainy or wintry nights I used to climb in through a high window, then open the door to let a girl in,'just to save her,' as the song says, 'from the foggy, foggy dew.' Apart from that, we never went there. The cricket pavilion was our home. Today an imposing brick building with dormer windows cut into its tiled roof, and bars and a snooker table and plastic-topped tables, it was then a small, dark-stained, shuttered wooden structure, raised above the ground a foot or two, with steps leading up to a planked verandah. Inside was one square room, with changing rooms on one side and a small kitchen and lavatories on the other.

The floors were boarded, knotted and indented from the spikes of a thousand cricket boots. The room smelt of dust and embrocation, linseed oil and men. In summer boys and men played cricket. I was a wicket keeper and once, most unusually, took six wickets, four catches and two stumpings.

In winter we played fierce hockey. Often the goal mouth was churned into mud, our maroon and pink-squared shirts and dark blue shorts stained and wet as we charged and ran and blocked and hit. Mr Elliott, as umpire, ran up and down the sideline. Mike Brining kept goal, or sometimes Padley-Smith, a fat, bustling major with heavy-rimmed glasses and curling moustache. Padded, in goal, crouched to fend off an attack, he'd encourage us. "C'mon," he'd cry "you're playing like Trojans." Had he known, our desperate, puffing, effort would have pleased one headmaster of Wellington, a Mr Malim, who dismissed tennis and golf as "not sufficiently painful".

On Boxing Days, while parents slowly braced themselves to face common day after the hot, rich indulgence of Christmas, and laid cold left-over turkey on the lunch table, we played on hard, frosted ground, the sky blue and fresh, the air cold. Clouds of breath pushed from us as we ran. We played both days of most weekends, and I kept it up later, at the university, in the army and, with Indians and Pakistanis, on sun-scorched pitches in Canada.

In the pavilion, too, the Scouts met. In summer we lined up in front of the pavilion, before a flagpole. As the Union Jack was raised we would salute, three fingers of our right hand outstretched, the index finger touching the broad brim of our hats. In the same trinity, we would affirm allegiance to God, the King and who was the third ? Our parents, or the troop ? Those hats were as the Canadian Mounties wear, the brim starched flat, the crown shaped into a pyramid. Our shirts were khaki. Around our necks we wore square scarves of light and dark blue. They were gathered at the throat by a woggle and a blancoed white lanyard with a whistle on the end which looped into our left breast pocket.

Scarves were useful for a number of things. Making a sling for a broken arm was one purpose we learnt. Our shorts were khaki corduroy. We wore long socks, folded over and held up by green tasselled cotton garters. Finally, we carried staves, straight sticks about five feet long. They were cut with notches every inch or so. Using those marks you could work out, based on some trigonometric theory, the height of trees, hills and buildings. Of course, staves had other uses; to protect yourself, for example, or vault over rivers or defend old ladies from savage animals.

Neville Howlett, with a beaky face, dark eyes, and wiry body, was our enthusiastic Scoutmaster. Scarcely ten years older than we were, he led us and disciplined us, his large Adam's apple jerking up and down with the tension he felt when he had to be firm. Neville was a friend and father to us. He took us camping, when we stowed tents and billy-cans and bedding onto 'the truck' and pushed it, in turn, for miles.

What he taught us about putting up a tent came back from nowhere, a few years ago, when my wife and I were on safari in the north-west of Kenya. One evening we camped by Lake Turkana, formerly Lake Rudolph (named originally after the Austrian prince who, with his mistress, committed suicide in the hunting lodge called Mayerling). Every night, we were warned, a strong wind blows across the lake. Without reflection, not knowing I knew, I went at once in search of large stones. I laid them on the guy ropes of our tent. After supper we went to bed and slept soundly. By next morning several tents had blown down. The stones had spared ours.

Neville taught us to tie knots. When I became a patrol leader, of the 'Lions', I both painted a lion on the wall of the corner of the cricket pavilion where we grouped, and made a board with examples of all the main knots. There was a reef knot for joining ropes of equal thickness, and sheet bend for joining ropes of unequal thickness. There was the round turn and two half hitches, like the clove hitch, ideal for lashing a boat to a mooring. There was the bowline you used to make a loop, good when you wanted to lift a person who, perhaps, had fallen down a cliff. I remember, too, the sheepshank, for shortening a rope, and the fireman's bend. That was a good one. One end fastened a rope securely. You tugged the other and the whole rope was released. You would use that, for example, if you were upstairs in a burning building. You would look around for sheets, then tie them together (reef knot). Then you would lash one end of the newly-made rope of sheets around a bed or something firm. You'd throw both ends of the rope out of the window. Grasping the secure end, you would shin down to safety. Tug the other end, and the whole rope of sheets would be freed, to fall down after you. That knot would be good, too, if you wanted to make an escape without leaving a tell-tale rope hanging from an empty window.

We spent long summer evenings in the woods. Neville taught us how to make a hide from nearby undergrowth, and how to make rickety rope bridges. We looked for footprints and broken twigs, signs of people having passed there. By putting twigs in a certain pattern or by twisting grass, we could tell friends looking for us where we were. We learnt to camp, light fires, leave without trace. We worked for badges. Incredibly, I got one for cooking, though only by pairing with a stocky, strong South African boy (who became a life-saver off the coast of Durban after the war. He gave up when his companion had his arm bitten off at the shoulder by a shark.) We made an oven from a biscuit tin turned on its side, then roasted a chicken. We learnt to send messages by semaphore, waving flags, and, di-di-da-dit, Morse. I went to a RAF corporal in Langley for special lessons. We became very quick. I got another badge for first-aid, a fourth for aircraft recognition and others I forget.

Hour after hour we practised aircraft recognition until, with the briefest glimpse at a silhouette, we could identify anything. One Sunday we were playing cricket. The sky was overcast and on the edge of rain. We saw an aircraft poke its nose out of a cloud, then vanish. As boys,

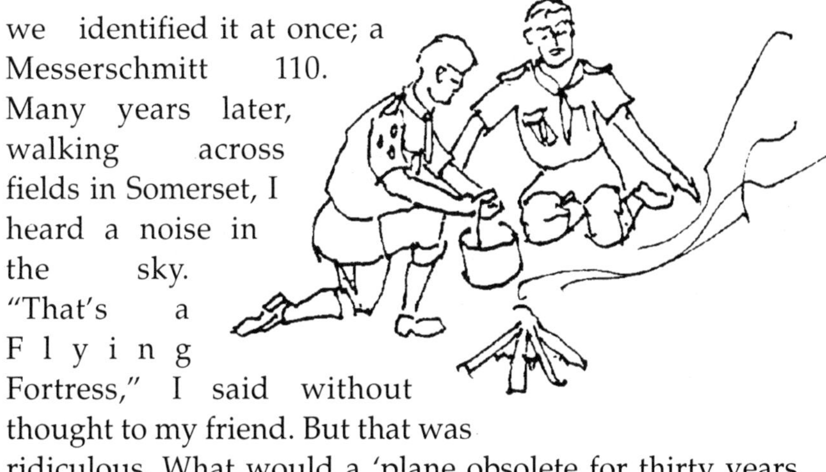

we identified it at once; a Messerschmitt 110. Many years later, walking across fields in Somerset, I heard a noise in the sky. "That's a Flying Fortress," I said without thought to my friend. But that was ridiculous. What would a 'plane obsolete for thirty years be doing there ? Two days later there was an air show at Yeovilton, the Fleet Air Arm base. There was the Flying Fortress.

I recapture, too, the fresh, shivering new days of scouting, when you woke up, crawled from your blanket, untied flaps on the tent and gazed at trees grey and glistening with dew. You rolled the flap of your tent, securing it with tapes, then stepped into grass, always wet. Slowly, others stirred. If it was your chore to light the fire you would have smuggled dry twigs into your tent the night before, to keep them dry. For some reason that was thought insanitary and was not officially allowed. You found water and balanced a soot-blacked billycan on the crackling fire.

To become a First Class Scout you had to have six badges, pass other tests, then go on a trek for a weekend. You travelled on foot, following clues you'd been given, finding your way by map and compass. Two of us set off. Our destination, we found when we were there, was a field in Eton, by the Thames. As we'd been taught, we first went for a reconnaissance, to see what was around. 'Time spent in reconnaissance,' they say in the army and I have repeated a thousand times since, 'is seldom wasted.' Nor was it then. I found part of the river marked off as as a pool, where Eton schoolboys swam. I plunged in the chilly, murky water and felt fresher, if not much cleaner.

In early evening we put up a tent, carefully pinning a ground-sheet to the sides so that no insects could enter. (That lesson, too, where there really were snakes and scorpions, was handy in Kenya.) We searched for twigs and logs and lit a fire. After a few minutes, an inspector appeared. He was a house master at Eton. He said he had broken his arm. Would I fix it ? From sticks I made a splint, then tore off my neckerchief to provide a sling. He made no comment, but asked us questions for a while. Apparently satisfied, he asked what we were cooking, then sat and ate our stew with us.

Although the furthest we trekked was to Chalfont St Peter and Gerrards Cross, we were aware of a wider world of scouting. We had seen a grainy newsreel of the King, George VI, beaming with happiness, surrounded by boys, at a jamboree.

> *"Underneath the spreading chestnut tree, "*

he sang with them.

> *"There she said she'd marry me.*
> *'Oh, how happy we will be*
> *'Neath the spreading chestnut tree."*

In time with the song, along with the scouts around him, the King touched his hips, shoulders, head, then stretched out his arms. Often around the camp fire we did the same.

Another song we sang came from Ralph Reader's *Gang Show*, held at London's Victoria Palace for a number of years.

We're riding along on the crest of the wave
And the sun is in the sky.
All our eyes on the distant horizon
Look out for passers-by.

We'll do the hailing
When other ships are round us sailing.
We're riding along on the crest of the wave
And the world is ours.

Those early experiences of learning both to be self-reliant and to be dependable for others, the craft and fun, seem to me good. It is sad that in the 1980s, ILEA (Inner London Education Authority), red as a cardinal's hat, as well as letting school cricket grounds run to seed, declined a request for a grant from some Scouts because Scouting, as they put it, is a 'fascist' movement.

Six

DINNER JACKETS IN THE JUNGLE

"Greece fell, Rome fell, Hindhead's turn will come," George Bernard Shaw is "reputed to have said, in Heaven knows what context. Apart from leaving leafy Buckinghamshire to become part of Berkshire and electing a Labour member of Parliament, Slough's hasn't yet. 'Come, friendly bombs, and fall on Slough,' Betjeman wrote unkindly, 'It isn't fit for humans now.' Slough, Slough, quick, quick, Slough. While Freddie went to school in Windsor, I went to the grammar school in Slough. Wycombe, say, or Buckingham would have been better; both sound softer, more sympathetic to the ear.

But there it was, five miles cycle ride from Iver. On many mornings I rode to school along the empty gravelled roads through the woods, now dripping and dank, now touched with early morning sun, around the guarded, camouflaged Hawker factory. Then I swung right, into the traffic on the Bath Road, past the wrecked aircraft dump beyond the Golden Arrow garage, then piled high with crumpled tails and bent wings and oil-streaked cowlings of Messerschmitts and Dorniers and Junkers, Hurricanes and Spitfires. Near my school, hidden behind tall trees on the right, stood St Bernard's Convent where girl-friends, my sister and Jean Shrimpton who, known as 'the Shrimp', became a famous model in the 'sixties, went to school. I swung left, into Lascelles Road. The school, red brick with Georgian flourishes, built in 1935, was set in wide, manicured playing fields. Beyond was farming land and, grey in the distance, the familiar shape of Windsor Castle.

Friends who talk often today about their school days never ask about mine. Even today, when there are second thoughts and a friend could ascribe the fall of Welsh rugby to the demise of the grammar schools, 'those great fly-half factories' as he called them, it remains a gap between us. 'Grammar grub' is the term they might use in unguarded moments.

If unfair, they are right. English public schools give a boy or girl more than social grace although, often, a charming amount of that. Anthony Powell, the author, says he was told at Eton, "If you don't learn some sort of civilised behaviour England will become uninhabitable," perhaps half joke, half not. But when (and if) such snobbery is shrugged off, assured, insouciant yet reliable lifelong qualities remain. Boys and girls who go to public schools are lucky. I see the crumbling medieval, Hamstone buildings around the quadrangle at Sherborne and hear the deep and mighty swell of five hundred boys singing on Sundays in the ancient abbey; all is splendid.

Not that public schools hand out *laissez-passers* to life. A large, bumbling, careless, very clever friend of mine was competing for a job as a marketing consultant. After the interview he heard he had won. "It is not because you were at Winchester," his new client told him. "But how did you know I was there?" asked my friend. "I didn't say and I wasn't wearing a tie." "Oh yes you were," smiled the client. "It was holding up your trousers."

There are many theories. One is that the public schools flowered in Victorian times to supply the Empire with leaders. But since boys would be sent to places their masters had never seen, it was hard to teach them what they should know. Instead, they planted in boys a gyroscope, the theory runs. You could spin them around and drop them, confidently, in a jungle. The fools might wear dinner jackets after six, but they would cope.

When Sir Peter Tennant, a dear friend, was in Sweden during the war he used to meet the Russian ambassador, Alexandra Kollontay. The Soviet Union, she said, was very interested in education. She also remarked that while the Soviet army was good, and its officers well trained, they could lack the flair and initiative of British officers. Deducing that it was something to do with their boyhood, she asked Peter which were the best English schools. Taking his advice, the Soviets developed a huge report. It recommended to the Comintern, in sum, that schools in Russia should copy Eton. The first plan was to build sixty. Indeed, after the war headmasters of four English public schools were invited to Russia, though nothing came of their visit.

Nor does the formal education explain the public school difference. Although the classics are enviably better taught, the general academic knowledge covered may not be so superior. It's not that. I have another Wykehamist friend who learnt nothing but Greek and hates his wasted years. Alan Ross, the cricket writer and poet, says that at Haileybury he didn't have one lesson, ever, about any kind of science. While both extremes would be unheard-of today, the gift of these great schools lies somewhere else.

A story of Ludovic Kennedy's, in *On my Way to the Club,* gives a revealing insight to excellence. At Eton in 1938, with three other boys he wondered whether it was possible to leave school after morning roll call, have lunch in France, then return in time for the evening roll call, without anyone noticing. They achieved it, taking a taxi after the morning call to White Waltham, then flying to Le Touquet, having a lunch of ham sandwiches and champagne, then flying home. Puffing, they ran in to school just in time to answer their names. Nothing was said; they'd got away with it.

Weeks or months later, Ludo Kennedy was in the Lake District. In the same hotel was his headmaster, Sir Claude Elliott, a distinguished mountaineer. Spotting him, the head said, "Ah, Kennedy, care for a little climbing tomorrow?" For hours they climbed. When they reached a plateau and unpacked sandwiches, the head said, "Now, tell me, Kennedy, how DID you do that trip to France?" In other words, the school had known all the time. Not many schools would have taken the same attitude to an initiative that broke the rules.

Sir Claude's son, Nicholas, indeed, created a prize at Eton for initiative. Of Claude Elliott, his son told me,

"He liked mountaineering," (as president of the Alpine Club he helped arrange Hillary and Tensing's ascent of Mount Everest in 1953) "so he went to Cambridge." Cambridge is flat. Sir Claude took a teaching post there because it gave him long breaks for his climbing.

Nicholas told an endearing story about his father. At Eton he was promoted from being headmaster, or head man, to Provost. That meant he had to sit in another part of the chapel, closer to the choir. Although tone deaf and unmusical, he noticed that choristers on one side of the aisle were singing a different melody from choristers on the other. Unaware of descant, Elliott went to the young choirmaster at the end of Service and said, "I wouldn't dream of interfering, but, you know, it costs a great deal to send boys here, and I really do think they ought all to sing the same tune at the same time."

Nicholas, who was the senior MI6 officer sent to Beirut to interview Kim Philby and who claimed that his great-uncle Edgar, on holiday on the Continent, once fired both barrels of his gun and shot a woodcock with one and a Bulgar with the other, published a book recently with the title, perfect for his walk in life, *Never Judge a Man by his Umbrella*. I asked him where the phrase came from. It was Eton again. A housemaster had pinned up a notice. The second line was 'the one he carries may not be his.' Boys exposed to wit like that or, as one master wrote on a report, 'the only thing he could pass is water,' can only benefit. I once asked Nicholas whether, in the war, he was ever wounded. "Only by Maltese claret," he replied. The drawback, of course, is that such privilege may be earned and may not. In Kenya Masai warriors move naturally to become elders, rulers of their villages.

But, to become a warrior, these young men must have killed a lion with a spear. English schoolboys face no such test; yet often they move, just as inevitably, to the upper reaches of national life.

By contrast when, in 1991 a group of visiting Americans published a report on British schooling, they regretted that in most state schools neither teachers nor children have any expectation of success. That is an unkind start.

England was very divided when I was a boy; sadly, it still is. A few children went to public schools, some went to grammar schools, pale imitations, most went to council schools or technical schools from which not much was expected. Now even the grammar schools have gone, destroyed by Shirley Williams, like Margaret Thatcher a child of the system herself, in what the *Sunday Times* described as the worst official pillage since Henry VIII dissolved the monasteries.

There have been grave consequences. In the 1950s an American taking a thesis at a Scottish university took as his subject differences between executives in Europe. To his astonishment, he found that, hierarchical and class-ridden though it was thought to be, Britain had by far the most 'socially-mobile' industry in Europe. It was easier, in other words, to move from the factory floor to the board in Britain than anywhere else. The reason was as chilling as it was informative: the top is not blocked. In Britain the 'elite', as he put it, doesn't go into industry in the first place.

A friend of mine was the European vice-president of ITT. In the 1970s his son was at Oxford. Asked by his tutor what he wanted to do, the son replied, "International marketing, like my father." "Ah, what a pity," continued the don, "we look on men who go into business as our failures." Nor has such snobbery changed much. At dinner recently I asked whether anyone present knew a single young man or woman who worked for a manufacturing company. Not one did.

Of Slough Grammar School I have few memories and never think of it. That is part of the difference. But because education is so discussed today, it is interesting to see what happened fifty years ago.

In front of me now is a school magazine, *The Swan,* from July 1945 when I was in the Upper Fifth. I see there were 500 boys. Fourteen old boys were listed as killed in action the previous year and eight had been decorated, mostly in the RAF. 'For coolness and good judgement,' reads one citation. 'For skill and bravery, bringing in a burning aircraft and saving the crew,' reads another. 'Outstanding devotion to duty,' 'utmost courage, fortitude and devotion to duty,' 'skill and fortitude,' 'conspicuous gallantry,' the magazine records. While those great events were going on above our heads and across the sea, I passed the army cadets' 'Certificate A', was in the cricket team and became intermediate champion at athletics. By then, I read, I was house captain of Hampden. While the Allied armies, tired and strained, were smashing towards Berlin, my activities were pale, slight things in comparison.

There were four houses in the school, each named after a distinguished Buckinghamshire man: Milton, the poet, Herschel, astronomer, Gray, whose 'Elegy in a Country Churchyard' was written in nearby Stoke Poges, and Hampden, Cromwellian soldier.

Some masters I remember: Mr Leftwich who had the blushing task of teaching us about sex, the maths master who gave me two marks out of a hundred in one test because I had spelt my name correctly on the paper. (When, under another teacher, I scraped a credit for mathematics in School Certificate, still with no idea what a sine or a cosine is, the earlier master took trouble to congratulate me, a generous gesture.) Being wartime, there were occasional drastic measures. They employed a woman teacher, a Miss P. Joyce Smith. She was slight and slim. Her dark hair was pulled back and tied, haphazardly, in a bun. Her movements were quick, her voice charged with enthusiasm. Away from the classroom we imagined she would be full of fun. After months of gamely absorbing our mockery, she became a favourite. We had old, pen-knife carved, individual desks, each with an inkwell. One day, before Miss Smith was to come to our form room, we made hydrogen sulphide in the inkwells. The smell was unendurable. Holding our breaths, we just did endure. Miss Smith came in, paused, and asked one of the boys to open the window. Without another word she started the lesson. Her *savoir faire* won us over.

Music was one of her subjects. It may be through her teaching that I first began to appreciate Mozart and Bach, Haydn's 'Surprise' and 'Clock' symphonies, and Sibelius, Dvorak and Rachmaninoff (composers listed in the magazine as taught that year). So there is much to thank her for, although her report in that school magazine added wryly: 'Progress has been considerably hampered by the frequent indisposition of the radiogram.'

My musical taste was less informed than that. During dull lessons I filled an exercise book with words of songs.'I'll be with you in apple-blossom time' was one. 'It's a lovely day tomorrow' was another. Of course, Vera Lynn's 'There'll be bluebirds over/ The white cliffs of Dover' and 'When the lights go on again/ All over the world' were as evocative then as now.

We played records too, on a gramophone we wound up. Strewn across the grey carpet at home were 78s in thin, printed, wartime brown-paper sleeves. Artie Shaw's 'Frenesi' was one. There were Tommy Dorsey, Harry James and the Andrews Sisters, Glenn Miller's 'In the Mood' and 'String of Pearls' and 'I'm Going to Buy a Paper Doll to Call my Own' sung in close harmony by the Ink Spots. Other records we played were the 'Warsaw Concerto' written by Richard Addinsell for an emotional film about Poland called *Moonlight Sonata* and, bought in a wave of emotion when Russia joined the war, Tchaikowsky's first piano concerto.

The lyrics I recorded so carefully were sentimental. Dinah Shore, Anne Shelton, Rita Hayworth, more for her husky sexiness than voice, were stars in my eyes. Perhaps you had to have heard Vera Lynn then, the 'Forces Sweetheart', to know the emotional effect she had. That power stayed. In Worcester, Massachusetts, years later I worked with an American who had been a liaison officer with the Commonwealth Brigade in Korea. "The most moving moment in my life," he volunteered, "was listening to Vera Lynn sing to the troops."

Perhaps it was Anne Shelton who sang 'I haven't said thanks for that lovely week-end/Those two days of Heaven you helped me to spend'. Verse after verse I knew, even if the full meaning escaped me. Then, as American influence in the war grew and Glenn Miller's US Air Force band became the dominant sound, I wrote:

A B C D E F G H I've got a gal
In Kalamazoo

and

Pardon me, boss, is this the Chatanooga choo
choo ? Track 29,
Boy, you can give me a shine.

While those words are silly and most are trivial, popular songs can be brilliant examples of the English language.

I think of Cole Porter's:

Flying so high with some guy in the sky
Is my i/dea
Of nothing to do.

See how the 'i's sound as the 'plane soars, optimistically, upwards, i,i,i,i,i,i. Then hear the 'o's, as the 'plane swoops down.

Or think of 'Cold Cape Cod clams 'gainst their wish/ do it.' And 'good authors, too, who once knew better words/ now only use four letter words/ writing prose.'

In *Kiss Me Kate* Cole Porter, mimicking the clipped way American ears hear English English, rhymes 'the British ambessader' with 'Troilus and Cressida.'

Songwriters can be masters of words; witty too. Remember Noel Coward's 'Englishmen detest a/siesta,' or 'the simple natives hope he /will impale his solar topee / on a tree.' Alan Jay Lerner, in *My Fair Lady,* sums up Professor Higgins's ideal home: 'an atmosphere as restful as an undiscovered tomb' and Eliza's familiarity with St James's

Palace — 'I go there so often I call it St Jim.'

Benny Green tells of two song-writers walking along Broadway. One asks the other how quickly he can write lyrics. "Give me a tune," said the other. They picked 'Jealousy'. With hardly a pause, the man sang:

> *Cyd Charisse*
> *Up there on my mantelpiece,*
> *She's quite a shock there,*
> *We need a clock there.*

If my sophisticated friends smirk at such simple tastes, I might say that some popular songs are part of everyone's life. Who can't hum 'Tea for Two' ? Vincent Newman wrote that in 1924 and it is still going strong. Glenn Miller's 'Moonlight Serenade' was first played in 1939. Desmond Carrington, on the BBC, said that every year, including 1991, it is in the top fifteen records he is asked to play. There are lots of other songs we all know. But maybe writing lyrics really is something they don't do as well any more.

To this day I relish every line in *The Music Man* and *42nd Street* and *Guys and Dolls*. If enthusiasm for popular music is scoffed at, I would agree that practically everything after the Beatles (thought by William Mann, when musical critic of *The Times*, the most creative musicians since Beethoven) leaves me cold as well as deaf. The greasy hair and dirty vests, not to speak of white Rollers, that go with the strobe lights and unremitting din, appal me. My ignorance, of which I am ashamed, embraces 'good' as well as bad modern music. Every morning I wake to Radio 3, Haydn, Brahms, Mozart, Bach, all heavenly. In a serene mood I step into the bath. Then, out of reach, the radio announces a concerto for two chain saws, first performed in 1989 in Cracow University.

Apart from the enchanting Pavilion Opera which performs in the drawing rooms of country houses, and a jolly *La Bohéme*, I am unlucky with opera too.

My last three operas at Covent Garden have been dedicated to death, one consisting entirely of moaning ghosts rising from their tombs.

Nobby Clarke, the headmaster of Slough Grammer School, a lumbering pink-faced man who, though quiet, had won the MC in the First War, had the unpleasant though rare job of beating us. He whacked us on the bottom with a cane. The thing to do afterwards was to sit on a hot radiator as soon as you could. Someone said tracing paper in your drawers lessened the pain, but I think it actually made it worse. Some masters carried short canes, to rap your fingers. Vincent Evans, the art master, a hairy Welshman who wore a no less hairy tweed coat, who had studied at the Royal College of Art and who rhapsodied, by turn, about New Zealand where he had lived and Michelangelo, Titian and Degas, used his hand to cuff us. That, as he knew, 'wasn't done' at all.

Another Welshman, Mr Llewellyn, who stood square-shouldered and erect as short men may do, taught physics. Although once or twice we crocodiled to the shelters, more in practice than earnest, the only time I remember a bomb coming down while we were at school was during a physics lesson. Hearing the scream, we dived under the lab benches. A window burst into a thousand slivers. When it was over and we sheepishly sat again, we saw Mr

Llewellyn standing where he was, by the blackboard in front of us. He hadn't budged. A small trickle of blood ran down the side of his nose.

The French master, Mr Taylor, who wore large, round, black-framed glasses on the end of his beaked nose, looked through the criss-crossed strips of brown sticky tape that covered every window, supposedly against the effects of blast, as bored by the irregular verbs as we were. Did he think they were any match for our dreams, of being in a bomber droning across Europe, expecting flak, tail-end Charlie lonely in his turret, cold, rubbing his gloved hands, scanning the dark sky hour after apprehensive hour ? Or was he dreaming too, of tall elms on the banks of the Loire ?

There was no fooling with Mr Hampshire, the strict Latin master. His gown wrapped tightly around him, he strode into the room, sat, opened a book and, unsmilingly, began the lesson. Geography we enjoyed because the master drove an open red MG. 'Wheat, maize, millet, rice,' he taught us in simple words how crops alter as you go south. The wall atlas really was pink then with the British Empire a quarter of the world. It was assumed that some of us, at least, would go to live in strange parts; in the East, perhaps, where people wore broad, sampan hats, in Africa or in the snows of Canada. When, every year, officers from the Indian Army came to recruit no one was surprised.

I suppose one should feel mortified by, or not admit to, the difference and advantage one felt, just being British. Perhaps it was as unforgivable then as it seems absurd today. I record it in the way of an historian. In defence, I'd say I remember no bombast, no wish to exploit. Quite the reverse; the assumption was that we were born to serve, guide, protect people across the broad brotherhood of nations, the Empire. Our model might have been the boast of civil servants in the East India Company. They claimed to be 'minutely just, inflexibly upright'. That's not a bad examplar for a boy.

Lord Annan, in *Our Age*, summed up where we stood. 'The word "empire" was frequently coupled with the word "heritage", he wrote. 'It was a sacred trust that children must learn to cherish. These English-speaking countries were nearer our hearts and interests than the jabbering European states. The dominions were shining examples of the imperial spirit. Had they not given their sons to die on Flanders fields, on Vimy Ridge and Gallipoli ?'

That view of the world given to English boys took years to unlearn, if it ever quite has been unlearned. I still love it.

That school imposed a healthy regime. Sergeant Major Luck gave us PT most days and two afternoons a week we had games. I preferred cricket and athletics, running the 100 yards, 220, half mile, jumping the high jump (once for the Buckinghamshire army cadets at the White City, where we won the Lady Margaret Shield and I came second to a man jumping with his broken arm in plaster). 'Elliman's Embrocation' was the name of the pungent grease we massaged into our muscles, quite as vigorously and more often than we rubbed linseed oil onto our cricket bats which already smelt with excess of it.

Both, we believed, would help us do better. Each year,

everyone in the school had to run a cross country chase of several miles. As house captain one year, never able to find my way, I took a short cut. We ran home first, through a funnel of cheering spectators. Then my mistake was found. The whole team was disqualified.

"The English," someone observed, "not being a spiritual people, invented cricket to give themselves some idea of eternity." At school the cricket was good. We had a beautiful wicket and travelled often to play against other schools. Eton Upper Sixpenny was one of only two sides that beat us that year. While we were playing at home one day a droning noise made us look up. A Lysander, the high-winged aircraft used to drop agents into France, landed on the outfield. It was an old boy 'dropping in'.

Freddie and I, sometimes with our father, sometimes with friends, went to Lord's when we could. The great players were in the forces, but were given time off to play. There was even an Australian side in England, the Royal Australian Air Force, whose most dashing player, perhaps, was Keith Miller, a tall, broad-shouldered, grinning swashbuckler. I saw Washbrook, known as a wonderful cover fielder, and all the players whose names I could look up. Above all were Edrich and Compton. Edrich was a squadron leader in the RAF, who had won an immediate DFC for a daring raid on Cologne. He flew Beaufighters. If you can imagine any man more likely to be an English boy's hero than Squadron Leader W.J. Edrich DFC, who played cricket for England, I don't know who he'd be.

Bill Edrich wielded a cricket bat like a bludgeon, hitting any loose ball with power and gusto. Compton, then in the Army School of PT, no less strong, was delicate. He flicked the ball, caressed it, almost. But it went like a bullet. I see him now. At the pavilion end, he moved on to his back foot to play a dull, defensive shot. Next I knew, the ball had hit the far sight screen and bounced back thirty yards onto the pitch.

Neville Cardus said Compton was "touched by the grace of genius in his cradle." E.W. Swanton thought the same. 'As he strolled out to play a ball from Goddard,' he once recorded, 'the stud of his right boot somehow caught in the laces of his left and he toppled headlong forward. As he did so, he remembered the ball and, in the act of falling, flicked it sweetly away for four. Have you ever tried walking on water, they asked him.'

The score cards at Lord's divided 'gentlemen' from 'players'. A print works beneath the Grand Stand kept the score up-to-date. At the fall of each wicket they published a new score card. On it, you would read Compton D.C.S. and W.J. Edrich. Having initials after his name placed Compton as a 'professional'. His initials before his surname meant Edrich was a 'gentleman'. Indeed, while 'gentlemen' came to bat through the Long Room in the middle of the pavilion, 'professionals' used a side entrance. A popular three-day match each year was Gentlemen v Players. It certainly continued until 1950, a match at Lord's I saw. Freddie Brown, then aged forty and captain of the Gentlemen, celebrated his century with a six into the pavilion.

If that division was snobbish nonsense, it may have had valuable roots. Arthur Bryant, the magisterial and romantic writer of English history, claimed that cricket prevented an English version of the French Revolution. His theory was this: the sons of landowners went away to school. There, they learnt to play cricket. When they returned to their estates they needed twenty-one other players, as well as two umpires and a scorer, to make a game. A farm-worker was hardly likely, Bryant asserted, to chop his lordship's head off if he played cricket with him every week.

Grown up, years later, I met both Edrich and Compton. Sitting next to him at dinner I asked Edrich if he had seen a match we went to when a doodlebug fell nearby, in Hamilton Terrace. High in the old Mound Stand, Freddie and I heard the unmistakable buzz. Then the engine cut, meaning the bomb would fall. We crouched as best we could. The players lay down, where they were, on the pitch. The bomb exploded. As we went back to our seats, the bowler bowled. His second ball the batsman hit for six. That was Robertson, who had been a captain in the army at Dunkirk and, before, had opened for Middlesex. The crowd cheered his marvellous defiance. Yes, Edrich had been there. The match was the Army playing the RAF. He was captain of the RAF.

Seven

CHILD OF EMPIRE

Fidgeting at our desks, gazing at prints on the walls, one a portrait by Roualt, another a landscape by Cézanne, thinking about the game in the afternoon, we followed Ulysses' travels and half-heard how Socrates died. We read some classics, but not much. Snatches only stay in the mind. Plato and Aristotle and Pericles. Paris and Menelaus fighting before the walls of Troy, watched by Helen. There was that comedy by Aristophanes in which the women of Athens refuse to make love until the men stop fighting; pictures, snapshots.

Until I went there a year or two ago I didn't even realise Troy and Ephesus were not on the Greek mainland. I envy people who had a more thorough grounding, though perhaps not as excessive as that of Tim Renton, once Minister for the Arts. When he was seven he was beaten for not construing a Greek adjective. To win the Newcastle scholarship at his school, he remembered, you had to recite an epistle in Greek. We were nowhere, nowhere near that. Not at all. I read Tacitus and we learnt some Roman history, though of that, too, I remember little.

Our history seemed to revert annually to the Anglo-Saxons and the Norman Conquest, strip-farming and medieval housing, only later moving to the Civil War.

Perhaps for fear those days were too pulsating, we seemed, in memory at any rate, to jump to and dwell on the dull Corn Laws, fencing acts and the Reform Bill of 1832.

We had a good deal of United States' history; the Pilgrim Fathers, War of Independence, the trek West and the terrible Civil War, all alive with romantic names and sturdy adventure.

Of European history we learnt little, except as it affected Britain; the wonderful triumvirate of Pitt, Wellington, Nelson keeping Napoleon at bay, and strange treaties at Amiens, Tilsit and .... where were they ?

Only recently have I read a footnote to the conference at Tilsit, held after the battle of Friedland, at which Russia's Tsar, Alexander, was forced to come to terms with the victorious Napoleon. So that they could speak in private, away from British spies thought to be everywhere, the meeting was held on a barge moored in the River Niemen. The suspicion was right, but the solution failed. The British secret service was indeed there. It bribed a Russian nobleman to perch beneath the barge as best he could. His feet dangling in the water, he heard every word.

There was also the Schleswig-Holstein question, that squabble over land between Denmark and Germany. The argument was so arcane, it was said, that only three people understood it; Palmerston who'd forgotten, a professor who went mad, and Bismarck who was dead.

But it was the glorious, mainly military, exploits of empire that stirred us. 'Into the valley of death rode the six hundred.' Think of Tel-El-Kebir, in 1882, where Sir Garnet Wolseley beat Arabi Pasha. Or Rorke's Drift, where fewer than 100 men, mainly from South Wales, held 4000 Zulus and eleven VC's were won in one afternoon. Or the Black Hole of Calcutta... or the scramble for Africa, Khartoum and 'Chinese' Gordon, of whose complex character we knew nothing... Think of the brave subalterns who disguised themselves as Muslim holy men and horse traders to map the northern reaches of Afghanistan during the days of 'the great game'. These were the stories that brought history alive and no doubt formed us.

Apart from Lucknow and the Indian Mutiny, the names we relished were mostly in the far north of India and over its borders: Kandahar, Kabul, where in 1841 an army of 16,000 soldiers and families was tricked and massacred by Afghans and, it was at first thought, only one man, an assistant surgeon called Dr William Bryden, survived. Lady Butler's moving painting 'Remnants of an Army' shows him riding into Jellalabad, exhausted, on a broken, foaming, horse. There was Sind (*'Peccavi,'* signalled General Napier when he conquered it — I have sinned), Lahore, the Punjab and, of course, the dusty mountains of the Khyber Pass.

Even if a contemporary observed, "Dr Livingstone is a hard man to ignore, although you might think it worth the effort," we heard about him and Stanley and Burton and Cecil Rhodes. Rivers like the Limpopo ('the great, grey, green, greasy Limpopo' as Kipling called it) and Lualaba and Zambezi and Congo were closer by miles to us than the Seine or Meuse or Rhine.

As boys we sweated under the burning equatorial sun,

plodding forward in unknown land. We plunged to our necks in malarial swamp and hacked elephant thorn to clear a path, always forward. Hiding our fear, we watched Livingstone offer beads and bibles, with chilling pacific courage, to fierce tribesmen. (Not always. *The Dictionary of National Biography* describes one encounter: "Livingstone got off his riding-ox and, in spite of his weak health, presented a six-barrelled revolver at the chief's stomach. This prompt action converted him into a friend.")

History, for us, stopped with the death of Queen Victoria. As far as I remember, we learnt nothing of this century, even of the Great War, a mere twenty-two or three years before. Our mother spoke of Vimy Ridge, which she had visited, and we heard the words Ypres, Mons, the Somme and Passchendaele. The Battle of Jutland, yes, and blocking the harbour at Zeebrugge, but little more.

We may have had engrained pictures in our mind of mud and machine guns and 'going over the top' and black-shrouded widows in rainswept and cobbled Northern towns, though none of the tragedy, anguish or futility crossed our minds. My throat chokes and heart pounds when poppies flutter from the high ceiling of the Albert Hall on the eve of Remembrance Day, one for each life lost. No hamlet in England is without its memorial. A tear touches my eye when I see them, or hear 'Roses of Picardy' or 'Keep the home fires burning', but such emotion flows from knowledge gained later.

Physics, biology, zoology, chemistry slowly came into focus and, indeed, although I was inept at most of them, these were my sixth form subjects. But, for me, English was the wonderland.

'The clatter of rain on galvanised roofs,' the English master rolled around his tongue, swaying with the beauty of it all, to explain onomatopoeia. And, clutching his gown about him tightly, taking tiny steps between the lines of desks, his lips pinched small, 'mincing in time with a girl' to show how words can mimic movement.

The Canterbury Tales, Milton, lots of Shakespeare, Wordsworth, Keats, the well-turned papers of Addison and Steele, Dickens, Tennyson, the Brontës, Kipling, Wilde, Shaw, Lawrence... so many writers, so varied.

Then, as now, I read every free moment. From *The Wind in the Willows* and *Just William* to the gentle delights of Arthur Ransome's *Swallows and Amazons* and *We Didn't Mean to Go to Sea.*

(A year or two after this, another keen reader of Ransome and contemporary of mine spent his summer in Brantwood, John Ruskin's house on Coniston Water. He and another boy rowed in Ruskin's boat across the lake to an island. It belonged, they found, to Arthur Ransome and was, indeed, his famous 'Pirate Island'. Bravely my friend, then about fourteen years old, went to pay his respects to the great author. A wizened old man pulled open the heavy door. "Are you Mr Ransome, sir ?" asked my friend. "Yes, I am," growled the creator of those charming children's books, "and you," he continued " are the horrid boy that has been playing on my island. If you are not off my land in one minute I'll set the dogs on you." What being an unrepentant Bolshevik, as I now know Ransome was, had to with this disillusioning tale, I don't know. But I am glad I hadn't heard it then.)

We rushed towards every new Biggles book and read the school yarns of Talbot Baines Reed. We recited the poems of Henry Newbolt. Here, again, the adventure of empire is central:

The sand of the desert is sodden red,
Red with the wreck of the square that broke.
The Gatling's jammed and the colonel dead,
And the regiment blind with dust and smoke.

In the verse before that Newbolt links schooldays to those of Empire. In both cases, boys are urged to "play up, play up and play the game."

There's a breathless hush in the close to-night
Ten to make and the match to win,
A bumping pitch and a blinding light,
An hour to play and the last man in.
And it's not for the sake of a ribboned coat
Or the selfish hope of a season's fame,
But his captain's hand on his shoulder smote,
Play up! Play up ! And play the game!

If that makes us smile or scoff today, or feel a hint of regret, remember the poem Newbolt wrote for his old school, Clifton:

To set the cause above renown,
To love the game beyond the prize,
To honour, while you strike him down,
The foe that comes with fearless eyes;
To count the life of battle good,
And dear the land that gave you birth,
And dearer yet the brotherhood
That binds the brave of all the earth.

Reading that now is a shock; the values are as remote as they are romantic. Yet there is no doubt they inspired boys at school for generations, including mine.

Think how a boy would be touched by the example of Captain Oates, leaving his tent in an Antarctic blizzard, stumbling to sure death to spare the dwindling supply of food for his friends. And the scratched notes of Captain Scott, found in that tent, 'Had I lived I should have had a tale to tell of the hardihood, endurance and courage of my companions which would have stirred the hearts of every Englishman.'

Nelson's signal before the battle of Trafalgar, known to everyone, was no less inspiring. 'England expects that every man this day will do his duty.' The irresistible appeal lies in the word 'expects'. Nelson didn't 'command' or 'require' his thousands of sailors and marines to do right. His original word, too long to relay in flags, was 'confide'. He was confident; his faith more compelling than any threat. Which boy, in the midst of war, would not be moved by such trust, or fail to want to live up to the example set then ?

Muscular christianity and the ideals of Victorian empire intertwined. When Peter Ustinov went to his prep school he was surprised to see, in the entrance hall, a painting of God. With one hand he clasped the hand of a Boy Scout. God's other hand pointed to a map of the British empire.

Of course, I came to G.A. Henty.

With a sheet over my head and a torch, in bed late at night, I trudged through the barren hills of the North-West Frontier. Horses, pulling the creaking and rumbling guns, occasionally neighed. Sweat-stained troopers cussed. As the dusty column wound its way up the pass my eyes ranged over the crests and ridges on either side, searching for a tell-tale glint of metal caught in the sun, sure sign that Pathan tribesmen were up there, watching us, perhaps setting a trap.

When I went to India years later the image was undimmed. As I have never felt elsewhere abroad, I was at once at home, another victim or proud suitor of Britain's long love-affair with India. The great red sun rising at dawn, geese flapping in the early light, a funeral procession, white and yellow turbaned Sikhs, bungalows, the Club, gates now rusting, paint peeling, once manicured lawns wild.

While I have no doubt that the British days in India were glorious and their influence benign, not every lasting lesson of the legacy is wholesome. An interior designer was invited to India recently by a Maharanee to design the entrance hall of her palace. "What do you want it to be like ?" the designer asked her. "I want it to make my visitors bloody nervous," she replied. The Raj might recognise that.

Yet G.A. Henty let me down. A year or two ago a friend said she was selling old books. I had a brainwave. "What about G.A. Henty ?" I asked. "I loved him as a boy. I haven't seen one of his books since then." After a week or two my friend 'phoned. She had tracked down three of his books. "Buy them," I said. When they came, first editions, I pounced on the first. It was unreadable. The Victorian sentences I had once devoured were long-winded, meandering, too slow for today. It was a terrible disappointment.

I read Siegfried Sassoon's *Memoirs of an Infantry Officer* in which, disgusted by war, he threw his Military Cross into the Mersey, and his *Memoirs of a Fox-Hunting Man*, smelling the damp, foggy mornings of Ireland. That mood was recaptured a few years ago for me in a book by Violet Pakenham, Lord Longford's sister. Sitting next to her at lunch in Somerset, her husband Anthony Powell across the table, I said how I had admired the description in her book of her girlhood in a great Irish house. "Which book was that?" she asked. Since I had no idea what it was called, she ended that topic abruptly.

At weekends my father drove us through the blackout to the Theatre Royal in Windsor. With covers over his headlamps allowing only three slits of dim light, no street lamps and often a fog, it was a probing, slow journey. The Theatre Royal, in the shadow of the castle wall in Thames Street, housed a repertory company run by John Counsell. Each week, actors read one play, rehearsed a second and acted a third. Of many we saw, comedy, restoration, drawing room, high drama, one by Terence Rattigan stays in the mind.

Flare Path was about a bomber squadron. A Czech pilot is missing. Everyone is cast down. Later, to their relief, they hear he has landed at another airfield, miles away. The squadron leader sees the Czech pilot's wife to give her the good news. He offers to provide an aircraft to fly her to her husband. The wife says 'thank you', then adds timidly, 'I'd rather go by bus.' Until then the play had been tense and emotional. The wife's small request triggered relief, laughter, even tears, in the audience.

As soon as I was fourteen I joined the school cadet corps. It became a unit in the Army Cadet Force. We were the 1st

Battalion, Oxford and Buckinghamshire Light Infantry. Boys playing as men, we did company attacks in Windsor Great Park, drilled, fired weapons, practised platoon tactics and learnt camouflage. We were in a field one day looking at a far line of trees. That was all. Then a whistle blew. Where we had been looking were soldiers, but we only saw them when they moved. The lesson was to show how inconspicuous a man is if he stands still. When that demonstration was over our instructor blew a whistle. To our astonishment, soldiers stood up a few yards from us. They had been lying doggo, in only a few inches of grass, and none of us had seen them.

Twenty or more years after that day a Dutch general told me how foolish he found Trooping the Colour. He was wrong. That drill, where men learn not only to respond instantly and move smartly, but also to stand wholly still for hours, helps them when it matters. There was an incident in the jungle of Borneo I read about. A four-man patrol of the SAS came across a 'bandit' camp. It seemed deserted. Experienced and cautious, the team decided to wait and see. They lay still as stones for over four hours. In the camp nothing moved. Then, believing all was safe, the leader moved. He knelt. He was shot dead.

I lack taste to quote the warning given by the commanding officer to boys in the cadet corps at Eton: "If you don't learn to stand still you will never get anywhere." There, too, on exercises, a boy in the school corps was challenged by an officer. "The enemy is in front. You are being enfiladed from the side. Your retreat is cut off. What would you do?" he asked. Blankly, the boy looked at him and replied, "What indeed ?"

'Cover from view is not cover from fire' was another lesson

learnt then, one most Hollywood producers don't know. You see the detective hero, or good cowboy, chasing a villain into a dark and deserted warehouse. Someone moves. Shots ring out. The good guy hides safely behind a pile of empty boxes, boxes a bullet would blast through.

On route marches and as we trudged home after exercises we sang songs with words beyond our years or understanding.

'Who's that knocking at my door ?
Who's that knocking at my door ? '
cried the fair young maiden.
'It's only me from over the sea,'
cried Barnacle Bill, the sailor.
'I'll come down and let you in,
I'll come down and let you in,'
said the fair young maiden.

There was 'Tipperary' and' Roll Me Over in the Clover', of course, and, as our boots crunched in unison.

I don't want to join the army,
I don't want to go war,
I'd rather hang around
Piccadilly Underground,
Living off the earnings
Of a high-born lady.

To the tune of Colonel Bogey we sang, as we marched:

Hitler has only got one ball
Goebbels' are rather small
Himmler is somewhat sim'lar
And Goering has no balls at all.

We were fourteen or fifteen at the time.

The war wound on. Late on summer evenings, by dusk, we watched stream upon stream of bombers drone overhead, more, then more, then more. They were ours, on their long, dangerous way to Germany. I don't know that we felt malice towards the enemy, but certainly the crews were in our minds. We imagined them settling down, then, after they crossed the coast we saw in our minds tracer shells arching towards them, their aircraft lurching; tea in Thermos flasks, freezing hands gripping guns, eyes peering into the darkness.

D-Day came. I counted myself then, as I do now, among the 'gentlemen in England, now a-bed' who ' shall think themselves accurs'd they were not here and hold their manhoods cheap...'

Chastened as we are now by the horror of war, it seems childish to say that although I was only a boy, I ached to join the party. Words I learnt parrot fashion (from the Prologue to *The Canterbury Tales*) filled my soul and still lurk as ideals:

> *A knight there was, and that a worthy man*
> *Who, since the time that he first began,*
> *To riden out, he loved,*
> *Truth and honour, freedom and courtesy.*

Not that the concept of chivalry was confined to English schoolboys. Long after the war there was a reunion of German fighter pilots. British aces were invited, one of them my friend Jim Goodson, an American who fought with both the RAF in the Battle of Britain (one of seven Americans to do so) and in the US Air Force. They were met by Adolf Galland, the most distinguished German pilot, who became a general. To the audience that evening he said, "We were the last knights."

There was the battle for Caen, through the 'bocage' of Normandy. And Arnhem. To the tune of 'Lillibulero' (now used by the BBC World Service), reports came on the wireless every evening 'live' from the battle. I hear now the Canadian reporter, Stanley Baxter, his voice choked with emotion, the sound of gunfire behind him, describing the epic courage of the Parachute Regiment. Equipped only with light arms, meant to seize a bridge for a day, they held off the tanks of a Panzer division for eight days and sixteen hours. "They'll go on fighting while there is breath in their body," said Baxter. He signed off his report with these words: "It is Monday, September 25th, at tea-time, only there isn't any tea." Imagine the impact of that on an impressionable boy. It is common today, with the light of history, to diminish that battle for the disaster it was. But then their gallantry moved us to tears. Even in the 1960s such emotion could be aroused.

Sir Peter Berger, then naval and military attaché in The Hague, organised a tournament in Amsterdam. He kindly invited me. The programme wore on. One display and band followed another. Then yet another band marched into the arena. Now something remarkable occurred. The entire audience stood. People had recognised the red berets of the Parachute Regiment. In the Netherlands Arnhem is not forgotten.

The war in Europe ended. I went to London on VE-day to be in the joyous, swaying masses, more people than I have ever seen, outside the Palace and in Piccadilly Circus. I went again to the glorious Victory Parade, hanging precariously to railings on the Mall above the crowds as pipes, drums, bands, rank upon rank upon rank upon rank of troops crunched by. In Iver we celebrated with a dance in the dusty hall of the Tower Arms. 'Oh give me land, lots of land under prairie skies above/ Don't fence me in' we sang, and 'I'm going to get lit up when the lights go on in London,' as the saxophone crooned.

In summer we went to cadet camp. One year it was Southwold. The next year we went to a transit camp in Newhaven, high on the Downs, overlooking the sea. We slept in metal Nissen huts put up to house men going to France. Those huts, like our beds, boots, rifles, mess-tins, mugs, everything, were coated with chalk from the Downs. Perhaps the men going to France were too; a novel insight into our invading army. Cleaning was constant and useless. What we did I don't know, except one day I had leave to watch Middlesex play Sussex at Hove and one night some of us went to an ENSA concert. ENSA (strangely meaning Entertainments National Service Association), had been started in 1939 by Dame Anna Neagle's husband, to provide entertainment for the troops. Later, the father of Jenny Agutter, the actress, ran ENSA. She told me the initials stood for 'every night something awful'.

In 1946, by now sixteen and a sergeant, I went to the Army School of Physical Training at Aldershot. There were cadets from all over the country, although they made less impression than the heaped plates of food at every meal. At breakfast, three fried eggs perched on a pile of crispy bacon and fried potatoes and fried bread. Cholesterolly catastrophic, perhaps, but it was astounding after the weekly dried egg one was used to. And maybe we needed it all. At any rate, we 'sprang at it', as Wodehouse said of black pudding when he was prisoner in a German camp, 'like wolves at a Russian peasant.'

From early morning PT, shivering in vest and shorts, we ran, jumped, pulled, heaved, stretched all day to the squeaky commands of the white-vested PTI's. "Wonn and tew, wonn and tew and push and push and wonn and tew," hour after hour. Under the words *Mens sana in corpore sano,* lettered high across one wall of the main gymnasium, we did log exercises for the first time. For two or three days we couldn't lift them. Eight of us were pinned under one great tree trunk, helplessly. After a while, though, we swung them over our heads, from side to side, without effort. We climbed ropes, at first straining and unable to reach the top, then going up and down half-a-dozen times with a few swift pulls. We threw ourselves over vaulting horses, touching the far end, then leaping upwards, arms outstretched, body straight, or diving into a forward roll. We learnt to swing on a rope across a river, scramble over high walls, throw ourselves and hope for the best. We also learnt a lesson so little remembered or practised since: the best way to get over things is to attack them.

One obstacle consisted of two planks nailed on top of telegraph poles and separated by a three or four-foot gap. You had to climb a rope to reach the plank, then cross it. Then you came to the gap. Pausing to look at it was hopeless. Although only a few feet, the gap seemed a mile wide. Below was barbed wire. The way was to run across the bouncing plank and, without hesitating, leap the gap. Then you shinned down another rope at the far end.

The evening before our final tests, we went to a theatre to hear a talk by a doctor major. He had been in India a long time, he said, and seen how badly long absence from home affected some soldiers. He came to work on their minds, often, he claimed, with success. His theme was the power of the mind over the body. He brought some volunteers on to the stage from the audience and gave each of them a matchbox. "In a few moments," he said, "you will lift the matchbox over your head, then open your hand and let the matchbox fall." You could see the soldiers didn't believe him and were intent to resist him. Yet their arms did rise, they did open their hands and, while sweat of fear poured off them, they let the matchboxes fall. No doubt he had hypnotised them. "Tomorrow morning," he said, "some of you are doing your final tests. Before you go to sleep, say to yourself over and over that you will jump higher and run faster than you ever have before." I did. And next day I surely exceeded anything I had been able to do before.

We qualified as PT instructors (only as cadets, far from the real thing) and that entitled us to wear crossed swords on our sleeves. Driven to London in a three-ton truck, we rolled up the side flaps and stuck our elbows out of the window. The cadets on the right of the truck faced forward, so that their crossed swords could be seen. Those on the left faced backwards, again so that their right arms, with those precious swords, were visible. We went to Wembley stadium, where the Army School of Physical Training was to put on a demonstration during the interval of a football match. Waiting, we kicked a ball around the pitch. So I have, sort of, played soccer at Wembley.

That August, on the 6th, the *Enola Gay* dropped Fat Boy, the atom bomb, on Hiroshima. The war in the Far East ended abruptly. Later that year our brother Vic came home. He had joined the RAF when he was seventeen-and-a-half and been sent to the Far East. Before he was nineteen he was captured in Java, a prisoner of the Japanese. Much of his time he spent in Japan, at first on the north island, then in the south, no distance from Nagasaki. He suffered terrible years. "If you saw someone stop cleaning his teeth," he told me later, "you knew he'd be dead in three weeks." Starving and thin, he was liberated by Americans. The first food they gave him was ice-cream. One rich and extravagant meal followed another across America and Canada when they travelled, as heroes, across the continent. When the ship which had brought these prisoners of war home docked at Liverpool, Customs officers came on board to search their kit, looking for duty to pay. At last in England, these former prisoners of war were taken to an RAF camp. Their first meal, either intelligently or as insensitively as the Customs men, was rice pudding.

We met Vic in the dim lights of Iver station one warm, though damp and misty, autumn night. More yellow and less tanned than expected, and though suffering, as we later learnt, from tuberculosis, he was round as a barrel. All that Yankee ice-cream. He had three kitbags full of American army clothing, including five pairs of boots, and a Japanese bayonet, his spoils of war. He had his chopsticks and a small canvas bag, about six inches square, which held all his other possessions.

Eight

THAT MAN'S LOOKING AT ME

Freddie, my twin, joined the RAF, then studied furniture design at the Central School. He was there at the time of Sir Terence Conran, already making money sewing florid waistcoats, David Carter, who has recently designed the cross-channel train, and Alan Fletcher, a graphic designer of international stature. All went on to tower over the design profession in Britain, the world I was to join. But in those days, ready to leave school, what was I to do ?

The Merchant Navy officer whose sister had 'Had Experience... In London', invited me to visit his ship, then in the great, busy, grey maze of London docks. Dozens, hundreds, of cranes ground and wheezed and rattled cargo from the holds of ships jammed stem to stern along the quays. Seagulls wheeled and screeched, lorries bumped over ropes and cables, men were everywhere. His ship was new, smelling of paint and oil. He showed me the crew quarters and the bridge and navigation room. His idea was that I should join the ship, leaving in a few days for the Far East. I would work my way up to take a Master's ticket.

Conrad, a brave ship yawing and climbing and smacking through towering seas, rivulets draining across the decks, unknown sights and smells in hot, strange ports... it was an awesome, exciting prospect.

One sunny afternoon my mother and I stood outside the kitchen door. She had prospectuses from two universities. She thought I should explore that future first. Cleverly, she had found places where I could study fine art, my favourite subject. One was Ruskin College, Oxford, the other was the University of Reading. Oxford sounded marvellous, but wasn't Ruskin College something to do with the Fabian Society or Labour Party, both anathema ? Anyway, if I went to Oxford I would have to be in residence, and that would cost my father more. My career before the mast forgotten, I enrolled in the fine arts department of Reading University. Today Reading has thousands of students on a huge, ugly tower-blocked campus in Whiteknights Park. In 1946, the year I went up, there were a little over 600 students and the new site hadn't been bought. The university was a cluster of Victorian and red brick buildings sited around lawns, the Great Hall in the centre, behind an unassuming porticoed entrance on the London Road. Halls of residence, some Georgian houses, others built just before the war, spread alongside and up the hill behind the university.

Opposite the 'Virgin's Retreat', a ladies' hall of residence, was my own hall, St David's, a Georgian house on the south side of London Road. I reported there on an October day in 1946. All the other male 'freshers', with few exceptions, were ex-service people, back from the war. There was even one senior student who had lost an eye in the Spanish Civil War. Rumpled, overweight, with flowing black hair and his head tilted enough to see through his good eye, he claimed as his right a soft sofa in the common room by the hissing gas fire on which he toasted crumpets. Just seventeen, I felt terribly young. Nervously, I went into a tobacconists, bought a pipe and tin of tobacco, not to smoke but to look older.

To find the 'Art Department', as it was called, you went down a cloister, through the arch under the clock tower, then turned left to a group of low buildings, the oldest in the university. I spent much of the next three years in them. Although the art department was irritatingly insular and isolated from the world, more, in my view, than education should be, and I was far from a model student, it gave me many perspectives I enjoy now.

The course was more academic and less practical than most are today. At its heart was life drawing. We spent thousands of hours standing at easels grouped around a lifeless woman. Indeed, 'life' drawing seemed quite the wrong name. The large studio was lit from above. Its walls were bare. There was no noise, apart from the hiss of radiators, and occasional 'click, click' muttered by the professor. A pompous, strutting, short, plump man, his thinning hair was smoothed back neatly, his grey goatee beard and moustache trimmed short. While students wore anything, and lecturers invariably wore tweed coats, thick flannel shirts and wool ties, often yellow, Professor Betts always wore a chalk-striped, dark blue double-breasted suit and polka-dot bow tie. In the mornings you'd see him hurrying along, a black pork-pie hat angled on his head,

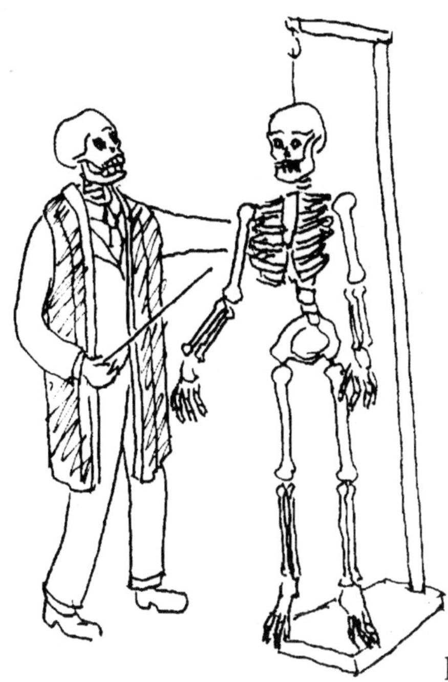

for all the world as though he was off to meet Sartre at Les Deux Magots.

His passion in life was Sickert, English disciple of Degas. His way of drawing was to to look at the line of the model's arm or thigh, then go from imagined point to imagined point, reproducing it on the student's paper before him. "Click" he said at the first point, then "click" at the second. One student was a handsome naval commander, who later married a fellow student, H.M. Bateman's daughter Diana. He was drawing one day, in that same silent, hissing room, when the model said, "That man's looking at me," nodding towards the commander. "Of course I am," he bellowed back. "How am I supposed to draw you, you fool ?" "No, sir," she said to the professor "he's looking at me in THAT way."

Although squeezing tubes of oil paint on to a palette and pouring measured amounts of sweet-smelling linseed oil and turpentine into little pots clipped to its edge anticipated excitement, Sickert dominated our painting classes too. His muddy colours were thought by Betts to be the exemplar we should follow. I think he wanted what might be called a moody accuracy, nothing abstract or too imaginative, something neither as precise as Ingres nor as honest as Max Ernst's father. It is said of him that once when he painted a picture of his garden he left out a tree, to improve the composition. This left him so full of guilt he went out and chopped down the tree.

One student who found this restraint unnatural was Ben Wheeler. Ben, with a deep, loud voice and flowing, unkempt hair, had been in the RAF in Italy. Every picture he painted was in the style of Chirico. Violent blues, yellows and reds zoomed in exaggerated perspective to distant white, colonnaded buildings. In the foreground, always, sprawled dead bodies.

We drew bodies a lot. This included learning anatomy. Another professor, Carter, taught that. A skeleton hanging by his side, he lectured to us dully. We had to be able to draw and name every main bone and muscle in the body. Then we were told to draw, say, an archer shooting an arrow. We first drew the skeleton poised as an archer would be, then laid on it the muscles, flexed as correctly as they were named. The skin came last. Tedious at the time, the value came to me later. It makes you think what's underneath, what causes the shapes you see. While we may have thought so deeply about the human body, the lesson didn't go further.

One day an inspector from the Ministry of Education, first intrusion by the new Labour government into university life, came to judge us. He hung up his grey raincoat, looked at us balefully, then, with a flat North country voice, said, "Draw a bus". A bus ? We were fine art students, far above anything as pedestrian as a bus. But we tried. The man went around looking at our work. With despair in his voice, he asked, "How many wheels are there on a bus ?" And "How do you get on it ?" None of us had any idea. His lesson was that we don't look.

Then he said "I want you to imagine a road going downhill,

with houses either side. Draw that." That was better; perspective came into it. When we finished his disappointment was clear. "What happens," he asked, "when it rains?" We had no idea what he meant. Then he pointed out that not one of us had drawn a window-sill or gutter. His uncomfortable point was that we don't think how things work.

For these two reasons, I believe learning to draw is good for life and surely right for anyone wanting to design. But there was more on that course of lasting value. We studied the history of art and architecture and every day that is a blessing. Nor do you have to go to Rome or Florence to enjoy it. If you look above the strident Perspex fascias of shops, every city street reveals its history.

Banister Fletcher's *History of Architecture*, known to every architectural student, was our bible. I read Burckhardt's *Civilisation of the Renaissance in Italy* and Benvenuto Cellini's autobiography and many other books of art history. Vasari's *Lives of the Artists*, a contemporary account of painters and sculptors of the Renaissance was, at that time, a labour to read. My friend, George Bull, has since produced a joyful translation. Omitting some artists who haven't stood the test of time, he wrote a loving work of limpid, plain prose. In 1952, when he was a student at Oxford, he was struggling through an old translation of *The Courtier* by Castiglione. Innocently, he wrote to E.V. Rieu, editor of the Penguin Classics, to ask whether a newer translation was available. Rieu replied that there was not a newer translation, nor did he want one. But, he continued, he would like an up-to-date translation of Cellini. George's translation, done when he was 22, was published for five shillings, in 1956. In 1991 it was reprinted for the fourteenth time. That is how, while still a still a student, George began an enthusiasm that has enriched the world with more than two million copies of books from the Renaissance now available in contemporary, elegant, plain English.

The Florence of Cosimo de' Medici became then, as it remains, a well of endless joy. Cosimo not only built his family bank into the largest commercial enterprise in the world with branches as widespread as London and Constantinople, Paris and Rome, and, despite the sophisticated democracy of Florence, effectively led the city state for forty years, he also showered his wealth on the artists of his time. Michelozzo, the rakish Fra Filippo Lippi who slipped out of the Medici palace in search of women , the pure Fra Angelico, Luca della Robbia, his favourite Donatello, Uccello (so-called because he loved birds) and Pollaiuolo, named so because his father was a poulterer; all these enjoyed Cosimo's informed patronage.

His grandson left as great a legacy. Consider the artists Lorenzo the Magnificent employed and befriended: Fra Filippino Lippi (Filippo's son), Verrocchio, Ghirlandaio, Botticelli and Michelangelo who lived with him, in his house, as a son. What a debt we owe.

It makes you wonder at the central power of patrons. Would we cherish such artists today without the Medicis? Affluence, they showed, is not the enemy of art to be scorned by artists, but its lifeline.

A gossiper of those days, Aretino, wrote to Michelangelo and nailed a copy of his letter to a tree, so that everyone might share it. 'The world is full of kings,' he had written, but there is only one Michelangelo.' There is more to that than flattery.

Nicholas Pevsner, Herbert Read and R.H. Wilenski were newer authors. Wilenski shattered our conventional view that all that was Greek was good. The statues we admired he dismissed as 'reconcocted ninepins'. The Venus de Milo, he pointed out, had been damaged, then buried, then dug up and repaired — and perhaps buried again, I forget. Like other adulated works, it was a patched up job, in his view. Still more shocking, it was painted. Far from the white purity we were meant to worship, Greek statues originally had painted hair, eyebrows, tinted cheeks, all shockingly realistic. I came to prefer, and still do, the ruder, though often exquisite, shapes of ancient Egypt.

We did 'sculpture', standing at high, turning tables, pushing and thumbing and modelling shapes in clay, then making moulds for them to be cast in plaster. We printed lithographs, drawing on heavy stones we had spent hours smoothing flat, swinging a heavy metal disc across the surface, back and forth, back and forth. I first smelt the pungent, exciting and, to me, still evocative smell of printer's ink at Reading. There, in the printing department, at first so slowly, we picked lead letters from a tray then set them in a forme. We learned to measure in ems and, half their width, ens. We printed our own elegantly-spaced poems and booklets, experience which helped me get a job later.

Robert Gibbings, a gentle man with flowing hair and pointed white beard, who wrote and illustrated *Sweet Thames Run Softly*, taught us engraving, and Mr Pearce, a former student there who was now its longest-serving lecturer, showed us the essential speed and discipline of watercolour painting.

Although some students specialised in fashion and

perhaps other subjects, the design element of my course was slight. It consisted of book jackets, occasional posters and illustration. One lecturer, Frank Ormerod, had designed some lovely posters for London Transport. One day he showed them to us. He was reprimanded for being more commercial than Betts thought proper. In three years, indeed, that was the only mention made of the real world we would all have to find jobs in.

When Sir John Wolfenden (who made his name with the Wolfenden Report, one of the first on homosexuality) became vice chancellor I asked him about this. Wouldn't it be better, I wondered, if people learnt useful rather than useless things ? "No," he replied, "our job is to train your minds. What you do with them is up to you." When, in recent years, I have had something to do with design education nationally I have made sure students understand very well what is often dismissed as 'the world of work'. Arguing the point one day, I was delighted to be supported by the head of a department at one university. "If there is another world," he said, "I'd be delighted to know where it is. I'll go there."

This more relevant view of education may have gained currency. In 1985 at a Design Council dinner, held in the Oxford & Cambridge Club in Pall Mall, John Butcher MP, then an Under-Secretary of State at the Department of Trade and Industry, gave a speech. To my embarrassment he read out a letter I had had published in *The Times* a few days before. It said that when I left the university I knew about Piero della Francesca and Fra Filippo Lippi, who ran away with a nun (whose name was Lucrezia) and had a son, also a good painter, and I wept at Masaccio's 'Expulsion from the Garden of Eden', but I couldn't DO a thing. Such education, the burden of the letter, seemed to me unfair to young people, all of whom have to earn a living.

In language that now seems both tortuous and trite, I kept a diary of my first year at Reading, 1946-47. Reminiscence recalls the smell of leaves burning in damp autumn, spring flowers, cricket on a beautiful wicket, a hot sun. The diary says something else.

It was a harsh winter. Heavy snow, sparkling under a bright blue sky, made the university beautiful. But it also immobilised trains. Movement became difficult. Coal was frozen at the pits, coal barges were frozen in ports There was a shortage of fuel, and £100 fines for wasting it. The Thames froze. Big Ben, its mechanics frozen, was silent. For three weeks in February the Observatory at Kew recorded no sunshine at all. Snow turned to flood. In Reading people had to boil water because the purifiers were flooded and in Maidenhead DUKW's, amphibious army vehicles, criss-crossed the streets, rescuing marooned people.

Wrestling with these worries and others, of shortage and poverty, was an ambitious but untried government under Attlee: 'the long streak of misery' Stafford Cripps, the dreadful Hugh Dalton, Strachey, Greenwood, Nye Bevan, who called the Tories 'vermin' and the blunt, square, towering Foreign Secretary, best of the lot and loved by those who knew him, Ernest Bevin.

Attlee was known for his economy with words as Bevin was for his forthrightness. Once, when he sacked a member of his Cabinet the minister said, "Are you making way for a younger man?" Attlee put him straight: "Not younger, abler." Of another minister he said, "That man's his own worst enemy." Bevin replied, "Not while I'm alive he ain't."

Shivering, we listened to the crackling cricket commentary on the wireless. The English team was enduring 'unbearably hot' weather. In the Adelaide Test Bradman was bowled for 0. Lindwall took three wickets in four balls and both Compton and Morris scored 100 in each innings.

1946 was the year, too, of the Britain Can Make it exhibition at the Victoria and Albert Museum. It was organised by the fledgling Council of Industrial Design. An attempt not only to convince the world that, after years of production for war, Britain could provide contemporary goods for a hungry world (Spitfires to saucepans - it displayed transparent shoes made from the plastic of gun turrets), it also introduced the importance of design. Sir Stafford Cripps, President of the Board of Trade at the time, made this clear. For a while, he said, we'll be able to sell anything we can make. But the time will come when other nations revive their manufacturing. How, then, are shoppers to choose between all the competitors ? Good design was his answer. With this as a belief, he had started the Council of Industrial Design a few months before.

The exhibition ran from September to November. It occupied 90,000 square feet, was a third-of-a-mile walk and showed some 5,000 products. James Gardner, prince of exhibition designers, designed the show together with Basil (later Sir Basil) Spence, who went on to create the new Coventry cathedral and, a few yards from the V&A but more questionably, Knightsbridge Barracks.

Misha Black OBE, (later Sir Misha), whom I came to know well and perhaps never saw without a yellow cigarette dangling, French peasant style, from his lips, had the daunting task of explaining to the public 'the meaning of industrial design, its fundamentals and the processes whereby a designer does his job'. No one was more able. With Milner Gray he started perhaps the first industrial design partnership in London, in 1936.

Only a year or two before this V&A task, Misha had worked in the basement of the National Gallery in Trafalgar Square as a designer for the Central Office of Information. Years later I asked him what he did there. One job he had was to design a bottle. It contained broad beans. The bottle was to be dropped into France, in quantity. What was the purpose of that ? Hidden in each jar was a rubber stamp. On it, no doubt well lettered by Misha, was one word: *merde*. Loyal Frenchmen, the idea was, would carry the stamp with them. When they saw a German 'Achtung, Achtung' poster, they were to stamp their word on it.

The British seemed to employ many such japes. One friend of mine had itching powder flown to Sweden. He gave it to friendly workers in the laundry of Stockholm's Grand Hotel. They rubbed it in the clothing of important German visitors.

When she was a girl, the sister-in-law of journalist Katherine Whitehorn was at an art school. Her first job was to work in the Ministry of Information for Edward Hulton, founder of *Picture Post*. Within a day or two of her arrival Hulton took her to a meeting of senior officers. An admiral at the far end of a long, polished table was holding a postcard. He looked at her. "You're a bit of an artist, aren't you ?" he asked. "Well then, draw on this the largest penis you've ever seen." Reflecting on her youth he added, "if you've never seen one, imagine it." He skidded the postcard down the table. It was a photograph of Hitler, standing, his hands clasped in front of him. Underneath was a caption: 'What we have we hold.' Her drawing done, the card was dropped by the million over Germany.

Another job Misha did for the Maquisards, the resistance force in France, was to design horse-droppings. The task was to design an explosive device which could be laid on roads quickly, without being noticed. At that time there was a great deal of horse-drawn traffic. Horse droppings were the answer. No one would spot them. When a truck passed, up it would go. Designing them, Misha Black and his colleagues faced the same judgements as Pinin Farina would when he designed a car, or Zandra Rhodes when she designs a dress. What is its purpose ? How big, how many ? How much should it cost ? What materials to use ?

Good design can take many forms.

My diary for that year describes events at the university: a procession, led by a band, on a crisp, dark Guy Fawkes night. While most of us tried to keep warm in wool hats and duffel coats, Dai Williams, who had been a Bevin Boy, drafted into the coal mines, wore 'a top hat, tails, red shirt, spotted bow tie, white trousers, football socks and suede shoes'.

It tells of the 55th Jantaculum, first after the war, held on December 7th, 1946. It was a feast 'to conform,' the programme said, 'as far as is possible, consistent with food restrictions, to the traditional style.' Meat rationing, remember, continued in Britain for nine years after the war.

We sang carols, then as a plum pudding (ersatz, notes the programme) was brought in 'raised on a brave trencher', we all chorused;

Oh we all love a figgy pudding,
We all love a figgy pudding,
We all love a figgy pudding,
So bring some in here.

Good tidings we bring
To you and your kin,
We wish you a merry Christmas
And a happy New Year.

The feast gave way to a play, or entertainment, then dancing.

The next year, the Jantaculum consisted of a masque and anti-masque, the music for which, I see from the programme, was written by a Mr Benjamin Britten.

Although, as the diary notes, I struggled to raise money to live in digs, it also says 'I must be prepared to travel 50 miles a day for the rest of my stay at Reading. In any case, dad is paying quite enough for me'. So most days of term I took the train from Iver, rattling through Langley, Slough, Burnham, Taplow, Maidenhead and Twyford to the approaches of Reading; river winding on the right, the jail which held Oscar Wilde on the left. I ran around the back of that jail hundreds of times, puffing up to the university. Then back, late at night. Of those many journeys I remember only the running, heavy naval duffel coat flapping, and, oddly, in the swaying train reading a red, cloth-bound edition of *War and Peace* and the autobiography of J.S. Mill in a green, tooled Victorian volume bought for sixpence.

At Reading I played hockey at least two afternoons a week in winter and spring, occasional rugby as a wing three-quarter, and enjoyed countless summer days of cricket. One match was against a ladies' side. They won. Whether Molly Hyde was captain that day I don't recall. She was at Reading and, in the season of 1948/49, captained the English ladies against Australia. She made over 1000 runs and scored five centuries. Her English ladies team won 28 matches in Australia and lost one.

Captain of both our hockey and cricket teams was Bill Birch, a strongly-built, dark-haired man with a deep voice and solemn way. Having travelled the world as a naval officer, it was natural that he should choose to read geography. He went on to get an excellent degree. We were playing cricket the afternoon he heard. He scored a century. Bill did well at whatever he tried. Concentration was his secret. If, practising, you tossed a ball at him, he watched it as if it was a poisoned arrow. That wasn't all. Of all the lovely girls in the university, he wooed and won perhaps the most beautiful; tall, blonde, blue-eyed Mary Stammers. But then, he did have a 1947 Ariel 350cc OHV teledraulic motor-cycle and maybe that helped.

Since I cannot play a note now, it is poignant to record that I played the violin, too, in the orchestra. At one concert we played Rossini, Mozart and Brahms. At another, Colin Davis (now Sir Colin) conducted *The Magic Flute*.

I became, as near as I ever was and then not for long, a socialist or worse. My poor father, trying to run a business; how I argued with him, such passionate nonsense. Years later a naval friend of mine told me of lectures given by another Hyde, Douglas Hyde, who had written a book called *I Believed*. Hyde, a senior communist who converted to Catholicism, advised the armed services on Soviet dialectic. My friend said it was impossible to break through his arguments, although, happily, one does. But even that brief experience was not a waste. Dealing with bitter left-wing students in education I have been better informed than they thought. One day all the students crowded into the Great Hall to decide a question. Should we become members of the National Union of Students? "No," someone said, "they're led by communists." That was the mood of the meeting. Then, just as we were to vote overwhelmingly against the idea, a voice in front said, "If we are in the union we can have a say. If we stay out we will have none." That swayed us and we voted to join a movement that then, as now, fought far more for revolutionary politics than students.

In the Great Hall we heard stirring talks. Haldane debated with a Professor Hodges, who taught philosophy, whether there was a God. First one spoke and seemed unanswerable. Then the other was no less convincing. Another day Hodges spoke about the German romantic philosophers, Hegel, Kant and Fichte. He described their impact on poets, then explained an inner sense of Wordsworth's 'Ode on the intimations of immortality'. He showed meanings that were revelations, a new vision. Feverishly, I scribbled six pages of notes, overjoyed to have seized his fleeting words. Back home, my sister, then small, tore my prized notes and threw them into the fire. All Hodges' insights went with them.

Ernst Gombrich, who had started to clean the pictures in the National Gallery, came to speak, shocking us with the vivid colours he exposed. We always thought the old masters painted in tones of brown. Indeed, Victorian painters laid a sepia wash over their pictures to help them resemble the great artists. But here were Titian and Tintoretto using bright blues and reds and Rubens fleshy and pink as could be. Betts lectured on Picasso. A Major Dent described Rowlandson as 'one hellova fellah'; the director of the Sorbonne, Professor Pauphilet, spoke in French on Paul Valéry.

Gilbert Spencer came to talk about his brother, Stanley, a local hero from nearby Cookham. Showing pictures on an epidiascope, he walked back and forth across what was, it seemed, a hollow platform. On one foot he wore a heavy, studded, country shoe. On the other, a tennis shoe. As he strode we heard 'bump' (pause), 'bump' (pause) 'bump' (pause). To point to details on his pictures, he held a long bamboo cane. It was frayed at one end. Every once in a while he paused to lean on the cane. When he did, it bent so that his nose was scarcely above the desk in front of him. Tears of silent laughter streaked down our faces.

The Great Hall was used for balls too. There were a good many, both there and in each Hall. Pasted in my diary are cards we used. Heavy board, folded two inches by four inches, on the cover was the university or college crest, the occasion, hosts and band. We danced, I see, to the music of Howard Lucroft and his Orchestra (Steve Race playing the piano, Ann Weaver the 'vocalist'), to the Embassy Players and George Watkins and his band. Dances started at seven o'clock, with a waltz, perhaps, then quicksteps, an 'old-fashioned medley', snowball waltz, rumba, slow foxtrots, through to a sentimental 'good-night' waltz until, at 11.20 pm, the band played 'The King'.

By each dance on the programme were dotted lines,

where you pencilled in the name of your partner. There were so many lovely girls. But soon my cards were filled by one, Brenda Langford. She wore, according to the diary, a long dress made from an old eiderdown cover. It might have been true; Brenda was studying fashion and cloth and clothing was not easy to buy. You needed coupons for everything. The ration, I think, was sixty-six coupons a year. One coat took twenty-two. Brenda and I became inseparable, not only at the university but at her home, too, a refuge of peace and humour. Doubtless making comparisons, I see I described its 'complete atmosphere of freedom' and 'lack of tension', all wonderful to me. Brenda's mother was a dear friend. 'Pleasant, calm and true' I wrote of her.

Films were popular then. Twenty million people went to the cinema each week. In 1947 we saw, according to the diary, *La Bête Humaine, Odd Man Out,* with James Mason, Robert Newton and Kathleen Ryan, *The Cabinet of Dr Caligari* (a surrealist German film, I noted, made in 1919). When we saw *Les Enfants du Paradis* at the Rialto, which had 500 seats, already 100,000 people had seen it there. We saw *The Edge* with Tyrone Power and Gene Tierney, *Notorious, My Favourite Brunette, Hungry Hill, Brief Encounter* and *Black Narcissus.*

B and I went to London to art shows, films and plays. One day in my diary records seeing the Spanish Exhibition at the National Gallery, first event of the Arts Council, founded the year before. We had lunch in a Lyons Corner House, then saw *Fantasia* and *Ils Etaient Neuf Celibataires.* Tea, then on to the Lyric Theatre, to see Emlyn Williams in *The Winslow Boy.*

Perhaps it was at that National Gallery show that I first saw, and was overwhelmed by, Picasso's 'Guernica', his outraged portrayal of the bombing of a Spanish village. Apparently disordered, with every image thrown at random onto the canvas, it was disliked at the time, although I believe I grasped the point of his innovation. It became a device imitated by film makers.

The start of *The Thomas Crown Affair*, a film made twenty years later, showed six or eight films on the same screen, each of men in separate parts of the city at the same moment, all preparing their part in a robbery.

'The mat the cat sat on' was the name of an article I wrote later about this . My point, tracing back to 'Guernica' and now television, was that perhaps since print began the writer or artist dictated the order in which we receive information. He decided priorities; the cat came before the mat. Painters were the same. Traditionally, they artfully led your eye; they decided what was most important. Picasso shattered that imposition. Now we, as viewers, decide whether the cat is more interesting than the mat. Or maybe the photograph of the Queen on the fireplace behind the cat takes our eye. My theory wound on, its aim to understand the effect of television on perception. Of whatever value, it is amusing to trace the roots to that afternoon, with Brenda, so long ago.

We were full of joy, though, as I noted at the time, 'The effects of the fuel cuts are obvious. I have never before travelled in a tube in such silence and state of brooding boredom, passive anger and exhaustion.' So soon after the war, the country was grey, long-suffering, poor. That was the year of the 'dollar crisis'. Britain, quite simply, was running out of money to buy food or anything else. Contingency plans were made, I have read since, to cut the food ration to half wartime levels. Hugh Dalton, a minister, noted in his diary that he was 'haunted by the thought of people starving, unemployed and in revolt.'

Of course, even though during the war the Cotton Board had the imagination to commission Paul Nash and Graham Sutherland to design cotton prints, clothing was drab and spare. At that time, the norm in Britain for a skirt, for example, imposed on manufacturers by the Government, was three to four yards. Imagine the shock, even anger in official circles, when, from France, there came a luxurious, spendthrift, extravagant wave of fashion. It was called the 'New Look'. Christian Dior, then thirty and holding his first fashion show, launched a line of soft-shouldered jackets and billowing skirts that took fifteen, twenty-five, even eighty yards of cloth.

Because it cast to the winds his imposed austerity, Sir Stafford Cripps was furious. "There should be a law against it (the New Look)," he declared. He urged a young Harold Wilson, then President of the Board of Trade, to ask fashion writers not to publicise this French flamboyance. It was in vain, of course. Women had suffered long enough. Princess Elizabeth and Princess Margaret set the tone: they were seen in little else but the New Look.

France was in our minds for other reasons, too. Over coffee in the smoke-filled Buttery at Reading we argued about existentialism. Sartre, whose theory it was, believed as far as I recall, that life is pre-determined. All we can do is decide between a series of choices. The way we do determines our character, he thought. There was a film at the time, *Les Jeux Sont Faits* with Jean Gabin, along those lines.

French songs were popular just after the war, *'Boom'* and

'J'attendrai' and *'Vous, qui passez sans me voirê/ sans meme me dire bonsoir...'*. Jean Sablon and Charles Trenet, whose song *'La Mer'* was on the wireless often, were singers we knew, as we did Edith Piaf, then filling the great theatres of Paris with the haunting *'La Vie en Rose'*.

During the Christmas vac Dai Williams and I hitch-hiked to France. The white cliffs faded away in mist. Then, a low dark line on the horizon grew larger, clearer. We churned towards Dieppe, still damaged after the Canadian raid. As our ship bumped alongside the quay, we saw dockers in blue blouses and gendarmes in cloaks and their round Képi caps. We smelt our first pungent Gaulois and read our first tin signs nailed to walls.

In the heart of Paris we slept in a tented camp on a bomb site. We went on to Rennes, capital of Brittany, where we stayed with a Dr Pelle, friend of my parents, in his house overlooking the river Vilaine. As far as we could see, all the bridges had been destroyed. One Sunday Dai and I visited La Cercle Celtique, where Bretons spun and wheeled in traditional costume to the notes of *cornemuses*, bagpipes, (then, as now, my most esoteric French word). Dai, as a Welshman, found he could speak sufficient Celtic both to understand and be understood.

At the University of Rennes we became friendly with students, some of whom had been in the Maquis. One gave me a FFI lapel badge, not the army's Free From Infection, but Force Française de l'Interieur. It was a generous gift of a prized possession.

A formal dinner was held for us. Dai and I sat opposite each other, at the centre of a long, white-linen-covered table. Champagne was served continuously. If you took a sip your glass was refilled. As time passed I looked across at Dai. He wasn't there. He had slid under the table, silently, where he slept.

At Easter Freddie, my twin, and I went again to Paris. Having heard of the Marché Noir, we filled our rucksacks with coffee and soap, both said to be scarce. By now seventeen, we hung around bars near the Gare St. Lazare until we found a buyer for our goods. We acquired enough cash to pay for the holiday. Not that we spent much. One hotel, on the left bank, cost 5p a night. After some days we went to Rennes to the Pelles, then to their cousins in Corneville, in Normandy. Staying on a farm, we went to a hopping, accordion-accompanied, dance in a dusty village hall. I was invited to a local girl's home. Squatting uncomfortably on her bed, sipping coffee, not knowing what to do nor what was expected, I was startled when a lean, thin-lipped, scowling woman burst in. Her greying hair was pulled back in a bun. She was wearing a flowered apron. And pointing a shotgun at me. She was, I assumed, thegirl's mother. She wanted me, I took it, to leave. Then. Which I did.

Nine

Asleep on a butcher's table

In darkness and driving rain, high on the top of a lorry, clinging desperately to ropes holding a tarpaulin-covered load, I hitch-hiked north that summer, headed for Norway. A second lorry driver, met at a transport café on the A1, let me hide under an upturned rowing boat on the back of his truck. Rain still lashing down, the truck rumbled into Newcastle at first, grey light. From there I planned to go to Acomb where, according to the map, there was a youth hostel. On a bus I asked the fare. The conductor didn't understand. I tried again, then a third time. "Ah," said the conductor at last, "tha means Yecoom." "How much?" I asked. Heaven knows what he said. I held out a hand full of coins. He took what he wanted. This was my first experience of the north of England.

Next evening I rolled out my sleeping bag in the hold of the SS *Jupiter*, moored on Tyne Commission Quay. The anchor chain rattled and clattered deafeningly against the bow plates, inches from my ear. Then, engines throbbing, waves slapping by my head, the ship heaved and dipped its way across the North Sea.

Hunched over a table in the saloon was an elderly American. His hair was cropped short, grey. He had grey stubble on his rumpled, worn face. "Main-t'nance," he announced as I bought him a beer, "that's the key to civilisation." I wondered what he meant. "You go south, you see. In northern countries people look after things. They repair them, they MAINTAIN them," he drawled. "You go down to Italy it starts falling apart. By the time you're in North Africa it's hopeless. A light-bulb breaks, it stays broken. I tell you, if you don' have maint'nance you don't have civilisation."

We called at Stavanger and Haugesund, then docked in Bergen. My idea was to stay in youth hostels. Delightfully, the one in Bergen was at the top of a high funicular railway, with majestic, long views. I went there, to find it was closing next day, as were all in Norway, except the one in Oslo. Late in August it was the end of their season. So much for that plan.

Two men from Birmingham University, mountaineers, were going north. Together, we found a small steamer that arched out to sea, then hugged the coast to the wide entrance of Norway's biggest fjord, the Hardangerfjord. Grey mountains rose sheer on either side. The water was still, black, deep. The little boat criss-crossed the fjord, stopping at communities nestled by each shore, black smoke from its funnel staining a sky of the palest blue.

To save money, we decided not to take a cabin, but to sleep on deck. Soot from the funnel whispered down on us constantly. To protect ourselves, we stretched out my tent, lashing one side to the rails, the other to a pile of logs, so that it formed a roof we could creep under. When the ship stopped to unload supplies and mail, we emerged to buy bread and cheese. At Utne, a trim, white-painted village at the water's edge, we disembarked. As we crossed the gangplank the captain called after us. We had been sleeping on the first-class deck, it appeared. He insisted we pay first-class fares.

Near Eidfjord the Birmingham men left. An Englishman from the Foreign Office and I camped in a glade of a silver-birch wood, by a stream. While I put up tents and lit a fire, he baited a makeshift hook and cast a line in the river. And he caught fish. We cooked them, then headed to a nearby inn for a 'digestif'. By now just eighteen, it was all very sophisticated and strong for me.

Next morning, rucksack pushing into my back, I set off to trudge up the dusty road that snakes through mountains, winding and turning, winding and turning, up and up to Fossli at 6000 feet. Not until I reached the top did a truck come by. There, reaching for miles, was a great, grey plateau. Strewn with giant boulders thrown by God, in the mist of low cloud and dusk of end of day, the plateau seemed remote, desolate, unknown. I hitched inland to a railway station where the two mountaineers lay in their sleeping bags on the floor of the darkened waiting room. I did the same. Next I knew, the room was brightly lit and full of people chattering and laughing with excited expectation and looking down at us with puzzled curiosity, being careful not to tread on us. It was half-past four in the morning. They were there to catch one of the rare trains.

I hitch-hiked south, through rolling hills, past peat-roofed log-built houses and cornfields and dark woods of fir, and blue and white-flowered hedgerows and villages with spired churches. I travelled in anything that moved, once with a toothless, hunched, smiling woodsman in his plodding pony and trap. There was a stillness and eternity about the land we passed through. As I came to read later, the slow books of Knut Hamsun capture that calm. In them, little is said and nothing happens but change occurs.

Years later, when I had a design office in Oslo, a man in it took me to the head of a fjord. "My family," he told me, "have been in that valley for a thousand years." He wanted me to understand his values, so remote from the urgent and perhaps ugly profit-and-loss, rapid delivery, ones I tried to press on him

I slept in my tent, in fields, in haylofts, in a police cell, on the floor of an electrician's shop, on the table of a butcher, long sausages hanging above me, and in welcome, warm clean beds, beneath strange and slipping duvets.

Norwegians were overwhelmingly open-hearted, insisting on putting me up however they could. Undeservedly, I basked in the glow they felt towards England, the country that gave them hope and help when they were invaded by the Germans. The tall tree they place in Trafalgar Square every Christmas and will 'in perpetuity', a gift to London from their capital, Oslo, is an annual reminder of their constancy.

From Oslo I went to Drammen, where friends of B's let me stay, play tennis, go to a party on board three destroyers given by the Royal Navy. Then south, across the border into Sweden, speeding now in comfortable, American cars down to Gothenburg, south to Malmo, then across to Copenhagen, dazzling city of spiralling spires, rococo churches, the palace, Tivoli. There, too, people were kind.

My best chance of getting a lift back from Copenhagen, I thought, would be to take the car ferry that crosses the narrow waters to Sweden. It worked. A Danish businessman and his wife were driving in their Rover to Oslo. They said they would take me. Surprisingly, the wife sat in the back of the car with me. Soon she was fondling my knee. When we stopped for lunch her foot pressed mine. In the evening we wound down to the coast to the home of a well-known Swedish landscape painter. I was given a timber guest-house to stay in. The wife came to my room first at night, when I shoo'd her away, then early in the morning, to walk along the shore. I was much too young for this. Guilt, too, crept into it. Her husband was being generous to me, paying for meals then, later, hotel rooms. Well short of Oslo, my destination as well as theirs, and after more assaults (which have never happened since, I have to say), I made an excuse and left the car.

From Oslo, I made my way around the south coast of Norway. In a remote area of low, scrub hills, a Norwegian Air Force ambulance, a Humber, gave me a lift. The driver was a doctor. We chatted as we sped along. Then the car slowed and stopped. We climbed out and saw the cause: the battery had fallen onto the road. The doctor looked at me and said, "It's a good job you are here. I know nothing about cars." Neither did I. He smiled gently and we sat on the running board of the ambulance, chatting, gazing at the hills. We were miles from anywhere. We could still be there. Yet, from nowhere, in a few moments a man on a bicycle weaved towards us. Where had he come from ? Where could he be going ? It didn't matter; miraculously, the stranger was an electrician. He fixed the battery. We drove to the doctor's airfield, Spitfires on the runway, then to his home. I couldn't leave at that time of day, he insisted; I had to have a meal and a bed. Nor could I leave next morning; he hadn't shown me his town. And the next day he wouldn't hear of it because there was a tennis match and, anyway, he had arranged a party that evening for me.

Who can wonder that Norway and Norwegian people have always held a lasting place in my heart. When, years later, I had the chance to open an office in Oslo I leapt at it.

In England, that was Compton's summer. In 1947 he scored 3816 runs and 18 centuries, even though cricketers played less often than they do now. His average that summer was over 90 runs in an innings, scored in under an hour. Freddie and I went to Lord's when we could to watch him, above all. Denis Compton the 'Brylcreem' boy (his face appeared on posters everywhere) was insatiable, uncontrollable. He would dance down the pitch, go to swing the ball to his leg side, then change his mind and hit a perfect off drive. Perhaps unfairly, changing his mind became a hallmark. When there is the chance of a run, one of the batsman calls 'yes', 'no' or 'wait'. You have to be quick and clear. With Compton, other players said, whether to run or not was always a subject for negotiation.

I found those three choices useful in business. People think that to be decisive, you must always say 'yes' or 'no'. Cricket tells you there is a third call. Indeed, it was said of President Kennedy that his first question, whenever he was asked to decide, was 'How long have I got ?'

I have seen many justly-famous cricketers playing in Test matches at Lord's. Absurdly few stay in the mind; when, in 1950, the West Indies won their first match there and the crowd jogged around the pitch making up a calypso which became 'Cricket, lovely cricket'; when, during the Centenary match, Kim Hughes hit the ball into the top stand of the pavilion (and, in 1990, Wasim Akram did the same). I've watched Botham and Boycott score centuries, and Tony Grieg, at fourth slip, flying horizontally through the air to hold an impossible catch yards from him. There was Cowdrey, one blustery day driving sweetly through the covers and, on another, batting with his arm in plaster to save a match.

Sitting with an Australian friend who claimed he had been capped for three countries — Ireland, Switzerland and France — I saw Clive Lloyd bat majestically in a world cup final between the West Indies and Australia, a deafening match the West Indies won in darkness at nearly nine at night. John Arlott likened the lazy grace of Clive Lloyd scoring a boundary to "a man knocking a thistle-top off with a walking stick". I was at Lord's in 1990 for 'Gooch's match' when, playing India, he first bowled someone out, then scored 333 runs in the first innings and another century in the next. To crown it all, with a quick throw he ran out the last Indian batsman, to give England the match. "He was unlucky," said Gooch. "I haven't hit the stumps since I was at school." That was the match when India, last man in, needed 24 runs to avoid a follow-on. Kapil Dev hit four sixes in succession.

Think of moustachioed Dennis Lillee pounding down the pitch, for all the world like a wicked pirate, or Imran Khan, haughty chieftain, or Richie Richardson, in his floppy maroon sun hat, cutting the ball so ferociously that it flashes to the boundary faster than the eye can follow and, with a 'thwack', ricochets off the fence yards back onto the pitch. I see again the cricketing knights, Bradman, Sobers, Hadlee, Hutton; each legendary.

Stories swirl around such men, heroes all of a brave game.

There was the Nawab of Pataudi. A surgeon friend of mine in Barbados discovered that while the Nawab captained India in the West Indies he suffered from double vision. Two balls hurtled at him when he batted. "Which do you hit ?" asked the doctor. "I aim between the two," the Nawab replied.

Yet, to those who watched cricket during and just after the war, the half-remembered insouciance and dash of Compton and Edrich, driving and hooking and glancing and cutting the ball beneath the sun, bring a special smile of joy. It was delightful when, in May 1991, Denis Compton named two new stands at Lord's, one in his name, the other in that of his 'old chum Bill'.

Ten

From Olympics to Italy

'Eight men with but a single thought — if that,' was Max Beerbohm's verdict on rowing. But he was unfair. 'Consider the advantages,' the advertisement in the university newspaper ran, 'of a sport in which you sit down, there are no hills to climb and you don't even have to look where you are going.'

1948 was a good year for Reading. The rowing crew won the Head of the River race and the tennis team became 'Varsity champions.

It was the year when the Olympic Games were held in London, the first in Britain for forty years. In the summer vacation I got a job, one of many students from several countries, at the glamourously entitled Olympic Village. It was actually the RAF station at Uxbridge, no distance from Iver. Uxbridge had been the headquarters of 11 Group of Fighter Command. It was in the operations room at Uxbridge on 15th September 1940, the day when the Battle of Britain reached its desperate climax, that Churchill, visiting, asked Air Vice Marshal Keith Park where his reserves were. "There are none," replied Park. But that day the battle was won. Within the week Hitler postponed the invasion 'indefinitely'. Between August and October over 2000 German aircraft were destroyed over Britain. That battle, those famous 'few', in the end saved all Europe for generations.

My first job, manning the gate, didn't last long. We put a brick on the pedal which controlled the turnstile, so anyone could walk through. That was unpopular. Rather than fire us, the commandant gave me the task of working out a roster for staff involved. It worked quite well. The camp had a hospitality lounge, a place to receive important visitors. My job was to man it overnight. After a free dinner I went on duty at 9.30 in the evening. I had to stay awake until midnight, then sleep in a bedroom off it, in case there were 'phone calls. At 8 am I was off for the day. Even though I spent most of the time asleep, I was on duty for ten-and-a-half hours. Such devotion entitled me to two-and-a-half hours' overtime each day, free breakfast, then free bus to Wembley, where I saw not only the grand opening ceremony, but most of the field and track events. After splendid days, I bussed back to Uxbridge for more free meals and undisturbed evenings.

When the US athletes arrived they took a quick lunch, then went training. The British team ate, then sprawled on the grass to sunbathe.

One man who didn't arrive was Herb McKenley, a Jamaican. Because he had just broken a world record, the press was onto his absence at once. At the time I had a temporary job in the press office. That office consisted of a press officer, his secretary, five telephones which never stopped ringing, a typewriter, and me. This was the Olympic Games. At just the wrong moment, the press officer went away for three days leaving me in charge. All day I'd pick up one 'phone after another, shout "He's not here" and slam it down. McKenley arrived after a while. The rumour was that he'd just spent a few days in New York with a girlfriend.

In the 400 metres hurdles he came second to Arthur Wint, a former bomber pilot, now medical student at Bart's. Wint, six feet four inches tall, with a lovely long, easy stride, equalled the Olympic record of 46.2 seconds. He had been to the same school in Kingston, Jamaica, as McKenley.

Journalists came to write about the athletes from their own countries. A man from *The Times* handed me his card and wondered if he "might just have a word with...(someone)".. A competitor, from the *Daily Mirror*, hustled in and said, "What's the story ? If you don't tell me I'll guess." We never saw the man from *Paris Match*. He shinned over a wall and went into the French team's dormitory without asking anyone.

There were stories at Uxbridge the press would have relished. In those early, post-war days, bread in England was not the best. The US team had white, fluffy, bread flown in every day. Tasteless as it was, it was different from the still wartime stuff we were used to. How much of that white bread — or other rations — reached the athletes is hard to say.

A team came from Korea. At night, some wandered to the local pub. An habitué mistook them for Japanese, whose cruelty in the war was widely hated and against whom he had probably fought. The local man provoked an argument. Unfortunately, the oriental athletes he picked on were the Korean karate team. English bodies flew through the pub door and littered the pavement outside. Quick police work prevented a scandal.

During the day student workers, as we were, wore khaki denim overalls.

One man from Oxford wouldn't conform. Invariably, you saw him in a blazer, with the added affectation of an upturned collar.

That was when my love for people in the Netherlands began. They can have a wonderful sense of fun, hidden as it may be beneath dour respectability. Fanny Blankers-Koen, a Dutch athlete, won four gold medals (100m, 200m, 400m and hurdles). To celebrate this, Dutch students working at Uxbridge held a dance for her. We all wore suits. What did the Dutch students wear ? Pyjama jackets, the nearest they could get to blazers, each with its collar turned up.

Fanny Blankers-Koen won all the Dutch gold medals. European nations, still under-nourished, had small chance against the United States (twelve) and neutral Sweden (five), although that was the year when Emil Zatopek, from Czechoslovakia, won the 10,000m and broke a record held by Nurmi since 1920.

A slim, beautiful girl in the art department at Reading captained the British Universities' athletics team. She married a man from the psychology department. They went to Canada to live. One day he disappeared. Months later, a clipping from a small Ohio newspaper was sent to her. It reported that her husband had been killed in a car crash. It turned out that the man had planted the story. He was alive and well somewhere else.

Another girl in the art department was Anne Windsor-Williams. She had been to school at Sherborne with Anne Dible who became the axis of my life. They were in St. George's Hall, a modern building up the hill, near the playing fields. 'Windsor' lived in Neath, in south Wales.

Her parents gave her a big party for her twenty-first birthday. All the boys invited to stay changed in one large bedroom. (Off it, the bathroom had a loo on a dais. It was called 'The Deluge Adamant', a memorable brand-name.) Changing was embarrassing; I had only my father's dinner jacket. I worried about the wrong thing. Everyone else wore his grandfather's.

The greater distress came next morning. We wandered down sloping lawns and across a field to the edge of the garden. There, before mining was nationalised, was a private coal-mine. Dirty, tired men were emerging from a hole in the hillside. With a horror I can't explain, I grasped the picture through their eyes, labouring men being gazed down on by pale, clean, untested youth.

On June 25th, 1948 Dibby (Anne Dible) and I went to an exhibition at the Courtauld Institute, then to Wimbledon, where the US favourite to win, Frank Parker, was knocked out by Lennart Bergelin from Sweden. In the evening we went to Wyndham's Theatre. We saw Shaw's *You Never Can Tell*. It was directed by Peter Ashmore, whose brother I was later to meet. Although half Russian (their father had been naval attaché in St Petersburg during the Revolution and married a Russian girl) he became First Sea Lord of the Royal Navy while the Cold War was still cold.

Musicals in London that June, a number of which Dibby and I saw, were *Bless the Bride* at the Adelphi, *Annie Get Your Gun* — with Dolores Gray and a cast of 56 people, and *Oklahoma* (starring Harold, now Howard, Keel). At the Palladium Duke Ellington was playing and Pearl Bailey sang.

Priestley's *The Linden Tree*, was playing, with Lewis Casson and his wife Sybil Thorndike. Coward's *Present Laughter* was on and, surprisingly, Arthur Miller's *All My Sons*.

There was a new play by Aldous Huxley called *The Gioconda Smile*. Ian Hay and Stephen King-Hall had a new naval comedy, *Off the Record*. A.E. Matthews was at the Vaudeville, in *The Chiltern Hundreds*. (When he filmed it, years later, by then a good age, he was asked how he managed to carry on working so late in life. "It's easy," he replied. "Each morning I look in the obituaries in *The Times*. If my name is not there I get up and go to work".)

Cyril Ritchard and Madge Elliott were at the Phoenix in *The Relapse, or Virtue in Danger*. "Lor', stap me vittals," Ritchard, the fop, cried throughout. In that glorious summer Binnie Hale and Bobby Howes were at the Duke of York's, Sophie Tucker was at the Casino, Hermione Baddeley was at the Savoy. At the Garrick Jack Buchanan presented *The Lady Asks for Help*. Alicia Markova and Anton Dolin were dancing at Covent Garden and D'Oyly Carte were producing Gilbert & Sullivan at Sadler's Wells.

Sadly, I never went to The Windmill Theatre, where girls stood naked — although they were not allowed to move — and numbers of British stars began their career in vaudeville. It was famous as the theatre that 'never closed'. All during the Blitz the Windmill stayed open. More than once shivering girls on stage stood still as statues, as the law required, while bombs banged nearby and dust from the rafters fell on them. That's brave.

In 1948, with a continuous show from noon to 10.35, the Windmill was still not closed. Under the proud headline 'We Never Closed' (by then a household phrase) it advertised the 213th edition in its seventeenth year.

That same summer, Dai Williams and I hitch-hiked to

Rome, sipping coffee outside a café in Milan while, a few yards away, rioters tore up paving stones to throw at helmeted police. In Florence we admired Brunelleschi's magnificent dome on the cathedral and, before it, Giotto's campanile, 'the model and mirror of perfect architecture' according to Ruskin. Charles V considered it the most perfect structure ever built. It should be kept under a glass dome, he thought. We admired the great doors of the Baptistery, said, by Michelangelo to be fit for the doors of Heaven itself. Dostoevsky thought the same. He wanted life-size photographs of them to hang in his study. We crossed and re-crossed the Ponte Vecchio, climbed the Bargello, visited the Pitti Palace and studied, quite seriously, paintings and frescoes and sculpture in Santa Croce, S. Maria Novella and other churches, as well as the overwhelming but dull Uffizi.

Heading through Siena and south, tramping in the heat along dusty roads in shorts, shirts, army boots and heavy socks, with rucksacks on our backs, we teamed up with two Germans. For the first time no one would help us, guide us or sell us food. Germans, we found, were not liked. So we left them.

Through that hilly country a friend of mine, in the Grenadier Guards, had fought only a year or two before. All week they lived in mud and horror. On Saturdays, when they were north of Florence, young officers were detailed off to clean up, put on their best uniforms, then go into Florence. A Principessa needed young men to make up elegant tea parties she had arranged for suitable young ladies. After an hour or so balancing fine china teacups and mingling politely, they went back in their truck to the mud, bursting shells, bullets and battle. In their dug-out one night my friend asked their Italian liaison officer if he knew "that blue-rinsed bitch ?" "You are speaking," replied the Italian stiffly, "about my aunt."

We arrived in Rome very late at night. With nowhere to stay and little money, we took a tram as far as it went, to the outskirts of the city. In the soot-black night, we walked until there were no more houses, climbed a hedge, then camped in what seemed to be a sloping field. By the first grey light of the new day we saw we were in an orchard and there, before us, was a Basilican church. I recognised it at once. It was S. Paolo fuori le Mura. I had drawn it a few weeks before in an exam at the university. I had chosen that church because although it had eighty great granite columns inside, there are few on the exterior. It was, therefore, quicker to draw than many other more usual examples of the period. Was one being lazy or efficient ? The bizarre coincidence of arriving there, of all the churches in Rome, struck me as a good omen for the exam.

Elsewhere, in a travel article, I have written about Venice, Serenissima, Bride of the Adriatic, where we went next. Sipping coffee outside Florian's, in St Mark's Square, which Napoleon called the finest drawing-room in Europe, is one of life's pleasantest and most voluptuous sensations. The curving, encrusted, basilica glitters before you. Towering to one side is the campanile, rebuilt in 1912, *'com' aera, dov' era'*, after the original collapsed. The sun warms your face. A string orchestra plays. Lazy pigeons, disturbed by the slow stream of passers-by, flutter and flap a few feet from the ground, then sink back to their ceaseless pecking. People who have never been to Venice are fortunate; they have something wonderful to look forward to. Venice captivated me at once, although I was, on that first occasion, caught in another way.

Behind the campanile a dark-eyed, anxious man came up to me. Looking about nervously, he took me to one side, into shadows, and showed me a ring he claimed to have found. It was a diamond, set in gold. For some reason, compelling at the time, he needed to sell it quickly. I bought it. Thinking it very valuable and no doubt being looked for by the police, I hurried to the youth hostel and hid it in the base of my torch. When, some days later, I crossed the border I was in a state of great nervousness. The customs people were sure to find it. But they didn't. Even so, I'd heard of Interpol. Of course, police throughout Europe would have been alerted. But no. Finally home, I unscrewed the torch to give the ring to my mother. It was tarnished. The gold was brass, the diamond, glass.

Dibby filled my life the next year, both during term and vacation. She lived in a sprawling house in Gerrards Cross, a few miles by bike from Iver. Her father, a professor at the School of Oriental Medicine in London, was stocky, with thinning grey-hair, polka-dot bow tie and hairy tweed jacket. He was always welcoming, her mother kind and gracious, both so unlike the chill that greeted intruders to Tudor Cottage. We dared invite almost no one. Dibby was one of the few girls Freddie and I were ever bold enough to take home. When any came we sat stiffly in the drawing-room eating cake and sipping tea from thin china cups, silently wishing mother would stop exaggerating. Even when we married, our mother froze wives in the same way.

Because Dibby was reading modern languages, we saw Moliére and sat through the most affected, histrionic performance of Racine in incomprehensible French.

We watched the Varsity soccer match, Trevor Bailey playing for Cambridge, and rugby at Twickenham,

England playing Australia. Two weeks later, in February 1948, Daddy took us to see his impossible dream come true: Fulham in an FA cup final. They played Blackpool. I feel now the mounting excitement as we joined the thickening, hurrying, swelling crowd, as it pressed towards the stadium. Grey skies, wet pavement, long raincoats, scarves, hats: trilbys and pork-pies and caps. Imagine Stanley Matthews in baggy, black shorts and black and white striped shirt, on the right wing, dribbling past one man, then another, then a third, to arch the ball precisely onto Mortenson's head. The ball flicks into the corner of the net, past the outstretched hands of the sprawling goal-keeper.

That was the year when Lester Piggott became the youngest boy in living memory to win a flat race — on The Chase at Haydock Park. He was twelve years old. That summer, too, Australia played cricket in England. At Lord's Freddie and I saw Bradman score 38. The teams, listed in my faded programme, make sentimental reading. For England: Hutton, Washbrook, Edrich, Compton, Dollery, Yardley, Evans, Coxon, Laker, Bedser, Wright. For Australia: Morris, Barnes, Bradman, Miller, Brown, Hassett, Johnson, Tallon, Lindwall, Johnston, Toshack.

In that last year at Reading I took to studying Chinese art. How and why I don't recall. What remains sounds a contradiction: an almost physical, tingling, sensation of purity and lightness, the absence of anything that is not essential. I can almost reach out and touch the rare refinement of it. Occasionally, fine food has the same quality, but not often. The analogy fits. After immersing myself in Chinese art I remember the shock I felt when, visiting the National Gallery, I looked again at Rembrandt. His paintings, just then, seemed coarse and vulgar as raw flesh.

At the same time, I was an enthusiast for modern painting. Towering above all, in my eyes, was Picasso. It was not a view shared by everyone. That year the president's speech at the Royal Academy dinner was broadcast live. I heard it. Sir Alfred Munnings, the president, had as his principal guest Mr Winston Churchill. Munnings introduced Churchill, then went on, "I remember him saying to me, 'Alfred, if you met Picasso coming down the street, would you join with me in kicking his.....something....something ?' (Laughter, a record of the time notes.) I said 'Yes sir, I would'." (Prolonged laughter.) To be fair, the record continues, 'The speech, which was broadcast by the BBC, was deeply resented by many members of the Academy and there were resignations.'

In that same year, 1949, I went to extra-mural Italian classes at Reading. A young, slim, dark-eyed Italian analysed the work of contemporary Italian writers. He was above my head, but there was a sequel. In the summer of 1949 I was offered a two-year scholarship to the University of Pavia, in Italy, to study Renaissance painting. That was to be the future.

Waiting, I sat in the garden at home writing, a sickness I seem always to have had. Drawing no parallel except this: P.G. Wodehouse, with rather more success, wrote from the age of five. "What did you do before that ?" he was asked. "Just loafed, I suppose," he replied.

On the fading garden swing I wrote half a book about Chinese painting, then another, a history of art. I had the idea it was studied too abstractly. My studies, such as they were, were of a self-contained evolution of painting. The great achievements of one man became the starting-point for another. There was little reference to what was going on in the world they lived in. That seemed to me absurd. Art must be influenced by the times, I thought, as well as influencing them. Indeed, you can hardly hope to appreciate a painting without understanding its background.

Look at Egyptian art and Greece, the patronage of the popes, the banking power of the Medicis. Think of the rise of rationalism and the discoveries of science or even the impact of the invention of photography. And what about the Great Reform Bill of 1832 that heralded the industrial revolution? Did it have no influence on Ruskin and William Morris and the Pre-Raphaelites ?

First I traced a rough social history and, no doubt, still cruder political line. Then I wove into it developments in painting. The theory worked pretty well. I don't read enough about art now to know whether it might stand up still, although I am aware that a great deal of education remains myopic and wilfully removed from life.

Dibby and I went to see Roland Petit's *Ballets de Paris* and Freddie and I were often at Lord's, to see the Gentlemen v Players, Middlesex playing Kent (when Compton scored 145) and Middlesex against the New Zealanders (when he scored 148 and Sir Richard Hadlee's father scored 50).

Then my call-up papers came. Britain still had National Service. What should I do ? I wrote to the British Council, who had awarded the scholarship on behalf of the Italian Government. It is all right, they said. Do your National Service first, then take up your scholarship later.

Eleven

STAND BY YOUR BEDS

That first night in the army was like a film director's idea of a prison camp. It was black dark. Glistening rain slanted through the glare of light from the cookhouse. Just changed into newly-issued, ill-fitting, scratching uniforms and hard, new boots, we stood in lines waiting to eat. Strangers to each other in an unknown world, we said little. Those first sounds were strange, too; clanking mess tins, low voices, rain, then the swish, swish of gas capes and crunch of gravel as trained soldiers, other beings, hurried by.

It was the 20th October 1949. From all quarters of the country boys, or men as we were now to be, arrived at the reception centre for the Royal Artillery in Oswestry, Shropshire. Our names were ticked off. We were assigned to a hut with, perhaps, twenty others, then lined up to draw kit: anklets pairs 2, badges 1, bags kit 1, blouses BD 2, boots ankle pairs 2, braces pair 1, caps comforter 1, discs identity with cord 1, drawers cellular short 2, drawers woollen 2, forks 1, gloves knitted pairs 1, greatcoat 1, holdall 1... and the rest. I have the original inventory now. It includes, to my surprise, anti-gas kit (6 eyeshields AG, 2 ointments AG, 1 respirator AG), of course a button stick and cleaning brushes and, endearingly, 'housewifes 1'. The 'hussif' as we called it, was a canvas roll containing needle and thread and spare buttons. Piling everything on to our newly-issued and folded greatcoat (1), we tried to find our way back through the rain to our hut, one among dozens.

Lights out was 10.30. Before then we had to stow our kit as best we knew how and make our beds on straw palliasses. Having been a cadet — and scout — helped. Yet it was all colder, stricter, harder, greyer than one was used to. The lack of colour shocked me most. For the next ten weeks there was not a splash of red, or pink or orange or anything to relieve the dourness of that camp. Just cement, dark brown huts, mud and khaki.

We were woken by bugle: da da, di, da — da da, di, da — "get out of bed, get out of bed" — then da da, di, da da— "you lazy buggers". A sergeant burst open the door and hammered his cane on the metal stove, then banged it against each metal bed, shouting as loud as he could. "Stand by your beds," he screamed. After shivering PT, then breakfast, queueing in a huge mess-hall, we were issued with more kit. A tailor came to adjust our uniforms, to make them bulge and droop less. For two weeks we did drill and PT, PT and drill. And had our injections. The jokes are true; men may faint at the sight of a needle. Some of the injections were block-busters, there's no doubt. One was so strong that all who received it were excused duties for thirty-six hours. They gave that to us on a Saturday morning, effectively killing Sunday.

After a fortnight we moved for gunnery training. A number of us went to another regiment in the same camp, the 64th. We learnt to know and use 25-pounders, the field gun used during the war and still, in 1949, the British army's main field gun.

We learnt all the positions of a gun crew, kneeling smartly, backs ramrod straight. As an aiming point we used the chimney on a local hospital, a place we came to know, full of nurses we came to know too.

It was a long way from lounging about in corduroys at the university, whispering in the library and talking about the quattrocento, but not unpleasant. You got to know people. In the hut was Maxwell-Hyslop, now an MP and even then questioning everything. There was a large-headed man from Radley who hid food from home in his box under his bed. After dark we would hear the rustle, rustle of silver paper as he took cake to eat, without sharing. Witty souls stole the lot, carefully replacing the wrapping. One night we lay in bed waiting for that rustle, rustle. It came, followed by most unladylike language. There was Bob Woods, a Rugburian and Tony Harris who seemed to know every line of Gilbert & Sullivan. Head tilted to one side, seemingly shy and nervous, Harris proved to be determined. Our tall right marker was John Glazier, whose uncle owned Herbert Johnson, the hatter then in Bond Street, supplier of hats to generations of officers. There were Brian Reading and Norman Gavin, particular friends.

Slowly, we turned into soldiers. Our drill became more orderly, we stood taller, marched more crisply, became used to the life, started to take pride not only in ourselves, but in the troop as a unit, a band you wouldn't let down.

'Spit and polish', taken to mean general smartness, is a precise description of what you do to new boots. When you get them the leather has a rough, almost mottled, surface. To make them shine you burn off the roughness. First, you lard the boots with Kiwi black boot polish (so much better, bombardiers advised us, than Cherry Blossom). Next you heat a spoon over the stove. Then you press the hot spoon into the polish. It hisses. You grind the spoon around and around, in small circles, spitting as you go at the part you are working on. It takes hours and hours and weeks and weeks before the boots shine as they should. In the army, of course, it is a crime to damage your boots, and burning them is seen that way. But that is what you do and are expected to do. With the same logic, it is an offence to scrape the floor of your hut with a razor blade. But that's what we did every Saturday morning when we had what they called 'Stables'. Then we scrubbed our huts clean and scraped the planked floors until they were unnaturally white, white as a Pierrot's mask.

In the beginning, cleaning your boots, washing and blancoing your webbing, and polishing your brass fills most evenings. We ironed our uniforms under a damp cloth and slept on our trousers, laid carefully each night under our bottom blanket. Some old soldiers lined the inside of the creases with soap. It would set when you ran an iron over it, and so make the creases sharper. But that, too, was damaging property. Worse, it was 'not done' in decent regiments.

For some weeks we weren't allowed out. When we did go we had to pass by the guardroom and recite some fact of regimental history. Since the Gunners' battle honour is *'Ubique'* (everywhere), there was plenty to ask us. We were inspected and had to look at ourselves in a full-length mirror, to see we were properly dressed: beret straight, one inch above the eyebrows, cap badge over the left eye, greatcoat pressed with cutting creases, anklets and belt blancoed, brass and boots gleaming.

I was lucky to be in the regimental, then brigade hockey team. Pitches we played on were sometimes grass, smooth as bowling greens, and often like hard tennis courts, red dust rolled flat.

They were marvellous. The ball flew as straight and sure as it was hit, which wasn't so on every pitch. While at the 64th, I was selected to play at centre half in a divisional side. Then I saw that the night before the game I was down for guard duty. "It's all right," said my troop commander, "I'll arrange it."

The pattern was this: twelve gunners went on parade. The smartest, called the 'stick man' was let off. The scruffiest, (the 'shit man') went on punishment duty. The remainder went on guard. Because it had been pre-arranged so that I would get a good night's sleep before the game, I confidently expected to be picked out as 'stick man'. Oh no. I was the other. All night, while the guards took two hour turns and at least had catnaps, a bombardier made me throw coal on the guardroom floor, smash it to dust with a shovel, sweep it up, scrub the floor, then throw coal on the same floor, smash it to dust with a shovel, sweep it up, scrub the floor, then throw coal on it... with no rest all night.

We went to dances at the hospital, sometimes legally, sometimes not. One night, after 'lights out' someone came into the hut to say there was a dance on. In the darkness, we pulled uniforms over our pyjamas as quickly as we could and slipped out. Jitterbugging, when you throw your partner around, skirts flying, was the latest craze. One thing that happens when you jitterbug is that your pyjamas slip and show below your uniform trousers in no time. But, standing in the crowd with the nurses, watching the frenzied dancing, were officers. Glimpsing them, we gunners vanished as we had come.

The hospital was an orthopedic one for children. An attractive nurse there, Johnny Parker, from Mildenhall in Suffolk, invited me in at Christmas to talk to the children.

Most were in bed, strapped in braces, unable to move. It was heart-rending, but I was glad to give them presents collected from the camp.

The Gunners do Christmas well. First order of the day, at 0700, is 'gunfire'. What, I wondered, did that mean ? It means the officers serve tea to the men in bed. Better, the tea is laced with whisky. At lunch-time, too, the officers wait on the men. One Christmas I spent in a barrack room being waited on, the next I did the waiting.

After a few weeks we could volunteer to go to a selection board, to be considered for officer training. It was called a 'Wosby', or properly, War Office Selection Board. There were three or four in the country at that time. I went to Chester for perhaps the most curious, frightening and surprising three days of my life. You were shown, with some politeness, to a billet with four beds. One of us in the room, rumour had it, was a 'mole' or 'grass', there to spy and report on us. It was probably untrue, but that was the mood. You felt you were watched all the time.

There were strange physical exercises, crawling as fast as you could through low, canvas, tunnels, and leadership tests you couldn't begin to do. Mine was to get two oil barrels and four men across a stream. All I was given were two planks of differing lengths and a short rope. I looked in dismay. Helplessly, I gathered the team together and explained the objective. "Anyone," I asked expecting no possible answer, "got any ideas ?" Someone had, so we did whatever he said.

There were written psychological tests and we all had to give a five minute talk. Hoping the officer judging us would find my ignorance hard to spot, for my subject I chose to talk about Picasso. The talk went on and on. My five minutes long since passed. Then the officer, behind me, said I could stop, but he would just like to ask a question about Picasso's blue period. Had I found, I wondered, the only expert in the entire British army who knew all about Picasso ?

The assault course needed faith. Having shinned over walls and run and climbed, the last obstacle started with a high rope net. By now sweating and covered in wet mud, you clawed your way up that net, over the beam that held it, then jumped to grab a rope hanging in front of you. We had been told to to use the rope to swing over a still higher wall, then let go. You had no idea what was on the other side. It was only a ditch, with more mud. Safely over somehow, I was told to report at once to a major.

He couldn't have been more charming. He 'oozed charm', even before Alan Jay Lerner wrote about Zoltan Caparthy in *My Fair Lady*, 'from every pore'. Wouldn't I sit down, he asked when I saluted him, as though, really, between us there was no need for such formality. He waved me to an upholstered, wing back chair. As I sat I became conscious of muddy water from my boots spreading in a puddle onto his carpet. When I moved my arm I saw a damp patch on his chair. The major, in stark contrast, had the cleanest, shiniest Sam Browne and brown shoes I had ever seen.

"It's exhausting, that assault course," he murmured, "you'd love a cigarette, I'm sure. Here..." He opened a silver cigarette box to offer me one. Fortunately, I'd been warned. "If you are offered a cigarette," my sister's husband, an RAF officer, had advised me, "don't accept it. You'll find there is no ashtray in the room." He was right, there wasn't. I declined. The major spoke charmingly, asking questions in the most diffident manner. "How many boys were in your school corps ?" he wondered. "Two hundred and thirty-seven, Sir," I replied without hesitation. The major smiled. That was another thing my brother-in-law had said. "If you're asked any numbers, say anything you like, but say it firmly, at once. They're not interested in the number, but how you answer the question."

The interview was as skilfully devious as one I had years later in a murder investigation. A Detective Inspector Diamond, from the Murder Squad as he announced himself, came to my office. He chatted for an hour and a half, apparently casually, about the murder of someone I knew. Only later did I spot four or five traps a guilty person might have fallen into. No doubt there were others.

Even the disadvantage of being filthy and out-of-breath was programmed, I am sure. Tension was stretched to the last minute. The time came when you were to hear whether you had passed or not. You were told to go to a corridor and sit. On no account were you to speak to anyone. In the corridor were two hard-backed seats, facing each other. In one was a soldier who had had his final interview. You sat in the other, gazing at his face for any clue that might help. Minutes passed in silence. Then you were told to go into a room. It was small. There was just a sergeant, sitting at a desk. He asked your name, then told you to turn right, take two paces, halt and salute. You did.

Suddenly, shockingly, you find you are no longer in a small room with a sergeant, but before a long polished table facing a battery of officers. Help. Which is the senior one ? Who should you salute ? Nobody warned us of this. Panic.

Keep calm. Eyes front, you try to scan the badges of rank on their shoulders. You salute and stand there, still as a statue. They ask a few questions, then you are told to march out.

You go back to the corridor, to sit opposite the next candidate, your mind racing. What did they ask ? How did you reply ? Then you are told to see another sergeant. Wordlessly, he hands you a slip of paper. The words are so telegraphic, so few, that you find it hard to seize their meaning. You have passed.

After a few more days at the 64th, three of us left for officer training. There were three schools at that time; Sandhurst for regular officers, Eaton Hall, the Victorian mansion belonging to the Duke of Westminster in Cheshire, for infantry officers, and Mons Officer Cadet School, at Aldershot, for the cavalry and gunners. We went to Mons.

Warnings were as dire as they were inadequate. "You better get yer 'air cut," warned one sergeant. "They're 'ot on 'air there." "Take a candle, you'll need a candle," said another. That, he explained, was because, from what he'd heard, we'd be up half the night cleaning our kit. "They're 'ot on cleaning at Mons," he added. So we bought candles — "going to Mons, then, are you ?" asked the store-keeper with a knowing smile. It was not comforting. Thoroughly alarmed and although it was short enough, army style, we had our hair cut to nothing the morning we left.

Kit bags over our shoulders, we arrived at Mons late afternoon on 20th January, 1950. The date is indelible. As far as we could see was a huge square with blocks of men hurtling back and forth to the shouts and screams of red-sashed drill sergeants. "'Ere, you. Come 'ere." Our eyes flickered from the square below us to a ramrod-backed, cheese-cutter'ed soldier thirty yards away. We saw a sergeant in the Irish Guards calling us. We marched over. "Git back," he screamed. "When you come an' see me you double." We did, three times. Heaving for breath, we stood before him. "You look like pansies," he snarled, "git yer 'air cut."

We did, for the second time that day. The barber took everything off with an electric razor, except a tuft on top. "Wot's under yer 'at," he confided, "is yer own." But first we drew new kit, from top to bottom, including white boards cadets wear on their collars (they are called gorgets, which the dictionary describes as 'a patch of colour on the throat of a bird') and white discs to go behind the cap badge. A different colour blanco was issued. That's what the candles were for. Long after lights out we were trying to sew on flashes, blanco webbing, clean weapons, polish brass, press uniforms and prepare for next morning. We blew out the candles, a letter home noted, at 2.15 am. Next day started, like a vicious whirlwind, at 5.30 am. Our platoon sergeant for the first few weeks was 'Sarn'

Wilde, Royal West Kents, as lean and tough a man as I ever met. He was the only non-Guardsman at Mons, a fact that seared his soul. "You will win the competitions," he announced when he introduced himself to us. "My platoon always does." So afraid of him were we that when the time came, we did. Only in the boxing did we come second. After our platoon won seven fights in a row, I lost mine. Sarn' Wilde was furious, not least by the bad example I, by then company commander, had set. In self mitigation I would say the man I fought was Ken Wilmshurst, a tall Scot who not only had arms eight feet long but later captained the British athletics team in the Olympic Games. For a week, Wilde took us, at first morning light, behind gun sheds for what were surely illegal punishment parades.

Those first few weeks were one high-pitched, fast-paced, screeching, accelerated ordeal. They called it 'chasing' us. When not on the square marching in quick time — as Wilde screamed "Lif' tarn, right tarn, ahboot tarn, lif' tarn, halt. Quick mar'. Lif tarn, right tarn" — for hour after hour, we doubled everywhere. Even in the middle of the night. His room was at the end of our hut. "Double," he squealed when he heard anyone creep carefully, touching his way in the dark, from metal bed to metal bed, towards the lavatory. We had hundreds of hours of drill, acquiring a snap and precision unknown to us before. "Hit the rifle," he'd bark, then, the only humour from him I heard, "if it breaks we'll get yer a new one." Slope arms, order arms, slope arms, present arms, slope arms, order arms, hour after hour after hour. Their idea, they were quite clear, was to 'break us, then re-shape us'.

Our sergeant major, who drilled us occasionally, was a

Grenadier. He insisted on being known by us as Company Sergeant Major Bennett, MM. He was proud of his MM, as he should have been. It was for gallantry. "What's my name ?" he bellowed, as we quivered to attention before him. "Company Sergeant Major Bennett," we shouted back. "MM," he roared. He took us for a church parade one day. One cadet called "Sergeant Major" and stepped a pace forward won, won tew. He asked to be excused because he was an atheist. "You can't be an atheist," reasoned Bennett, "that's not Christian. Fall in."

It became my job to get the whole company on parade ready for him. I can see today early morning stragglers running from the hut, clutching their rifles, trying to put on their berets, pulling up their trousers after what a major advised us was necessary, a "morning rear".

Three mornings a week the whole school was drilled by the Regimental Sergeant Major. His name was RSM Brittain, MBE, Coldstream Guards, a legendary figure, said to have the loudest voice in the British army. It was reckoned his voice carried from Chelsea Barracks to Victoria station above the roar of traffic and trains. From Mons to the Army School of Physical Training, a mere half mile, hardly counted. He drilled with a big bass drummer by his side, banging in time with a metronome. Tibby Brittain really did frighten us. "I don't believe in molly-coddling the soldier," he used to say. If we saw his back two hundred yards away we turned and fled behind the nearest building. But though he had a voice that screamed like a diving jet, he had humour too. As cadets, we were called 'sir'. As the RSM, so was he. He soon put us in our place. "You call me sir, sir," he explained one day, "and I call you sir, sir. The difference is"... He paused, then snapped, "YOU'LL MEAN IT."

There was a film on at the time about the Guards Armoured Division in Normandy, called *They Were Not Divided*. Brittain was in it. Taking drill, he screeched one day, "Look to your front. Don't look at me. If you want to see me," he paused, "go to the pictures." Another pause. "It'll cost you half-a-crown." Pause. "WELL WORTH IT."

His favourite thing in life was 'the book'. Well, there were two books. One was the charge sheet. "What's your name?" he would ring out to some erring staff sergeant. When he heard, he'd say, "It's in the book." Or, as often, "Sar' major, put that man in the book." That was one kind. The other was the drill manual, where, in infinite detail, how to execute every drill movement is described. He'd bark out orders for the correct movement, then add "It's in the book. I should know. I-I-I-I-I," pausing for effect, "WROTE IT."

Because Mons was large and our programme packed, we had bicycles. Dashing in from weapon training or drill, we would tear off our denims, throw on a uniform, then rush off, helter skelter as fast as we could ride, to the next lecture. Brittain didn't like that. He put cadets on a charge for 'being idle whilst riding a bicycle'. There was a way to do that too; sitting up, back straight, arms straight, eyes front. You could be 'idle whilst...' doing practically anything. They were, indeed, 'ot on that there. Sandhurst too. A friend heard a sergeant scream to Hussein of Jordan, when a cadet there, "You're a very idle king, sir."

There was a story attributed to RSM Brittain, perhaps falsely. After Dunkirk, when troops from all kinds of units were camped together, he mustered them for church parade. Some wore forage caps, others 'cheese-cutters' (hats with a peak). Still others wore glengarrys, the Scottish berets. Some troops still had their greatcoats and wore them. Others had gas-capes. Some were coatless. Faced with this motley, what was the sar' major to do ?

"All those with greatcoats," he shouted without hesitation, "you're Church of England. Fall in."

"All you with gas-capes, stand still. You're Roman Catholics." Everyone sorted into tidy squads, he had them marched off to each church as he had decided.

'Tibby' Brittain served 38 years in the army. When he died, in 1981, his picture was on the front page of the *Sunday Times*. Thousands of cadets who quaked before his awesome gaze and shook as he screamed, "Wake up there," or "I've never seen anything like it in all my L-I-I-I-F-E," will never forget him. The same might be said of RSM Copp, another Coldstreamer, at Eaton Hall. "No one," he told his cadets one day "is allowed to walk on this square, except me and the 'Oly Ghost, and 'e can only do it because I can't see 'im."

On Fridays, when Copp took his parades, he ended by giving a homily, a piece of advice. "This morning," he announced one day, "I am going to talk about saluting. Saluting. I was in Chester yesterday," he went on, "when I saw two gentlemen cadets, in uniform. A funeral went by. Very properly, they saluted. Very properly.... but, oh gentlemen, what salutes. If I'd been the bugger in the box," he expanded, "I'd have flipped the lid open and given them a couple of quick 'as you were's'."

Wonderful men. From them I first learnt the idea of excellence. Things wouldn't just do, they had to be right. Exact. 100 per cent. A pocket undone was 'half-naked', the gossamer whisper of unshaven hair was 'dirty flesh', a speck of blanco on the brasses of your belt was 'covered in mud', each to be 'sorted out' at sweating punishment parades. If that sounds inhuman, on infantry exercises I saw the other side. They'd drive you as far as you could go, then further, then a bit further still. But food came on time, whatever ditch you were in, and they always saw you were clean and fit, able to carry on. CSM Bennett, MM was always there, like a gruff hen clucking protectively over her chicks. Look after the horses first, was the rule, men second, officers last. It is a paramount lesson many executives in business, greedy and selfish, seem never to learn.

We became used to the hard chasing, adept at cleaning our kit, at home with our weapons. Our rifle, ancient now as the Brown Bess, was the .303 Lee Enfield. We knew every inch of it. It was made, I remember still, of 'Hoak, Hash or Helm'. We fired service revolvers, hitting the target only occasionally, and Sten guns, said to be dangerous because they jammed at the wrong time. (It's true about Stens. Months later I was standing behind a line of gunners firing Sten guns. One swung around to face me. "Sir," he cried, "this gun seems to have ja....". Phut, phut, phut, the bullets thudded into the soft earth a foot from me, splattering mud on my boots and raincoat.) We fired thousands of rounds on the Bren at all ranges. When, on television, I see wild Moslems and others waving automatic weapons in the air and spewing whole magazines of bullets into the sky, I shudder. Aim. Short burst. Aim. 'Johny-get-your-gun'. Aim, da-da-da-da-da, re-aim, da-da-da-da-da, re-aim... that's the disciplined way.

A year ago I told off a gardener for leaving his tools dirty. "Bright, clean and slightly oily is how they must be," I said, a phrase remembered from that weapons training years before. Although I later went on a course at the Special Small Arms School, becoming still faster and more fluent with weapons that seemed lighter every day, it was at Mons that I learnt to strip and re-assemble a Bren in the dark.

We were encouraged by a story told about David Niven. An infantryman, he had to teach the Bren first thing on a Monday morning. To be safe, he collected the Bren from the stores on Friday before going away for the weekend and locked it in his room. When he returned, on the milk train on Monday, the gun was missing. He conducted his lecture in mime. "First," he said, "you see the breech is empty. You do like that like this." He pulled back an imaginary cocking lever and peered at an imaginary breech. "Then you take off the magazine. There's a catch here you press. There. We'll put it— there." He laid the imaginary magazine carefully on the table. "Next," he went on "you twist the barrel locking nut. That is here." He twisted the imaginary nut. "There you go. We'll lay the barrel there." When he had stripped the gun entirely and laid all the imaginary bits on the table, he began to re-assemble it. "Now, where's the trigger guard ?" he asked the class. "There, sir," pointed a soldier at the empty table. So good was David Niven's mime, and so compelling his performance, that his class knew where every imaginary bit had been placed.

The climax of the infantry part of our course was a week of exercises. Instructions were handed out the evening before an early morning start. Each of us was given a role. Indeed, during the week we all did all the jobs of an infantry company. To my horror, I was the first company commander. I had to get us to the right place. In a panic I rushed around the huts. "Who can read a map ?" I asked. "Fine," I said to one — it was Brian Reading, who'd been a a friend at Oswestry — "Your job is to get us there." "Who's good at signals ?" To the cadet press-ganged into being signaller I said, "Your job is to get all the radios on net the minute we arrive." They were marvellous.

After our convoy of trucks and gun limbers had driven through the Surrey countryside for nearly two hours we arrived at a small path cut between high gorse that reached as far as you could see. That was the destination. Thanks entirely to Brian, who had map-read the whole way, we were two minutes early. I bundled everyone out of the trucks and, as we all knew, spread them out in defensive sections. Within another couple of minutes the cadet in charge of signals reported "all radios on net". It was copy-book stuff, as was the attack that followed. There was the first sign of a principle I followed in my firm for many years: I always surrounded myself with people who were cleverer than me.

For a week we attacked and defended, switching roles after each. We slept, if at all, in slit trenches we dug as soon as we stopped. We shaved, as dawn light streaked the sky, using warm tea left in our mugs. On and on we went. Finally, exhausted, we marched back to barracks. We fell on our beds, too tired to move. Our mud-stained kit scattered where we dropped it. In came a sergeant. He shouted at us to pick up a chair. We each had a folding wooden chair by our bed. With our rifles slung on one arm and grasping the chair under the other, wearing battle-kit and tin hats, we then went for a five-mile forced march. That is twice normal marching pace. Swearing, filled with anger, our legs searing with pain, we completed that. But there was more to come. Back once more in our huts, we were told to put on 'best BD', our best uniforms. We went on the square for forty minutes high-quality drill.

Finally, we had to shower and were allowed a 36-hour pass. Not having to do it now, I see the sense both of the forced march after that harrowing week and of the final drill. I imagine they wanted us to get used to being pushed further than we expected, and to be pulled back onto a tight rein of smartness.

I arrived home, in Iver, at four o'clock on Saturday afternoon. After a quick cup of tea with my mother and father, I went to bed. My father woke me at six on Sunday evening. "Time to go back," he said.

Although, as cadets we were in limbo, neither gunners nor officers, we moved with the snap of the guardsmen who taught us. Now, we went to new huts in another part of Mons and focused more on gunnery, with hours of lectures and gun drill and exercises, towing guns about the country. They tried to turn us into officers. This included becoming, on command, a bit less smart. We practised saluting casually and thwacking a stick against our trousers, as officers do. We were very unconvincing. Sergeant Ford, Grenadier Guards, a tall, strong, shot-putter, led us through these Jekyll and Hyde days, chasing us ferociously ("shoulders back, head up, chest out, tummy in, brace your legs back, dig your heels in, lif, ri' lif'") one hour, then coaxed us to march less stiffly another. We wore white riding coats off-duty and bought very particular tweed flat hats. The transformation was in train.

Officers at Mons were invariably extremely smartly turned out. One who attracted our envy may just have been visiting. I had turned the squad out for a special parade. Two cadets were numbered off to get us ready. After we were dressed, they folded our trousers neatly over our anklets, pulled our battle-dress blouses into perfect shape, brushed our uniforms and ran a duster over our shining boots. We formed up outside our hut. It was a fine spring day, sunny, with a light breeze. When the officer came to inspect us we crashed to attention; one sharp crunch. I saluted. The officer, a major, wore the DSO. It was said, we learned later, to have been earned behind the lines. He meandered slowly through our ranks. Hair curled up the sides of his worn service hat. The cuffs of his battle-dress were folded back. He was followed by a little Yorkshire Terrier.

When he had finished, he turned to me and said, "Tell me, can you tie a Windsor knot ? Do that." And he wandered off, dog busily sniffing behind him. The Windsor knot, named after the Duke of Windsor, is a way of tying your tie so that the knot is wider than usual. That was all, except for Sergeant Ford. He was less relaxed. "You're in shit, Mr. Pilditch, sir," he muttered as he passed behind me. He didn't mean a button was undone or my brass didn't dazzle, nothing like that would happen, but perhaps a speck of gravel, invisible to anyone but a guardsman, was on my boot. 'Like glass' was how boots were supposed to be.

But it wasn't all work. I played hockey for Mons, against both Sandhurst and the Parachute Regiment, and went on leave to Reading, for dances.

We went to a firing camp, on the west coast of Wales. It was bleak and barren, without trees, just the wind and rain whipping in off the sea. On Saturday evening our major, Singleton, asked, "Anyone want to go climbing ?" None did, but that was one way of giving an order. So, on Sunday we climbed Cader Idris, a peak in a range of Welsh hills. I took troops up there often after that, but the first time was harrowing. Feeling we needed to prove we had those elusive 'OLQ's', officer-like qualities, we scrambled and heaved our way up scree and rock face until, exhausted, we reached the top. We had done it. We felt marvellous until, that is, we saw a man there with a tea-trolley.

After those exertions, there was an even more humiliating sequel. In 1990 a Mrs Rachel Gibbs wrote to *The Times* that her family has a tradition that you have to climb Cader Idris (2927 feet) before you are six. Her second grand-daughter had just achieved it aged five years and three months. The family's rules, wrote Mrs Gibbs, are that 'you are not allowed to be carried and must not whinge, but you can have your hand held.'

As the train took us away from that camp I turned to Ken Wilmshurst, the Scot I had boxed, and sighed, "Thank God we'll never see that hell-hole again." Both he and I were back within three weeks, for eighteen months.

It was all over. The day came when those of us left marched, so proudly, digging our heels in, crisp, crisp, crisp, pulling arms back, heads high, bayonets gleaming, band playing, on to the gravelled parade ground. As the passing out troop, we marched to the front and centre of the entire school of cavalry and gunner cadets, halted and turned sharply (they liked the word SHARPLY) to face the front in Review Order. As guardsmen do when they troop the colour, after inspection we paraded around the square first in quick time, to 'The British Grenadiers', then in slow time, to the regimental slow march. As the SUO, senior under-officer, I had to shout the commands. Mustn't for-get; mustn't get one wrong. Tibby Brittain was behind us, silent, watching. The adjutant, a captain in the Coldstream Guards, mounted on a white horse, was in front. On either side of him pickets held lances. Stretching away in long lines of fluttering, flowered dresses and fancy hats, the men in dark suits, were parents invited for the occasion, my mother and father and small sister among them.

The cadet, in the cavalry, who was to have been awarded the sword of honour, or 'stick' as it was, was found drunk the night before, it was rumoured. So, as an afterthought, it was given to me. Although a mysterious honour at the time, it soon became unwelcome. In those days the British army was everywhere. We could volunteer for where we wanted to be posted. My three choices were: Far East, Middle East, Near East; as much travel at the Government's expense, in other words, as possible. 'King Georgie he payee' was the idea, a phrase heard in Ethiopia by a friend of mine who served in the Somali Scouts. From my passing out parade two men went to Kingston, Jamaica, one to the 1st RHA in Berlin, another to Cyprus, someone else to Hong Kong.

I was sent to Wales, to the camp we had left so exultantly a few weeks before. My major apologised. "I have a direct order," he said, "to send the 'best cadet'," as the one who won the stick was called, "to that training regiment in Wales."

Still, I was commissioned, in the service of King George VI. Although hundreds of thousands of men passed through officer cadet schools like that without, apparently, any lasting impact on their minds, to me it was a signal and lasting experience. I don't know why. Perhaps it was the hardness, the driving, the 'crispness' and being tested I liked. Or the companionship, the sharing. It may have been the sense of extreme fitness and smartness. Without doubt, the excellence I mentioned impressed me then, as the memory of it — and each year Trooping the Colour — does now. Certainly, clear thinking and unmistakable orders, sometimes expressed unforgettably, were better then than you generally find.

When the Brigade of Guards Troop the Colour over 600 musicians in the band perform what is called 'the spin wheel'. How to do it has never been written. Each man's drill is passed on by word of mouth. As the great block of the band wheels, bandsmen on the outside march smartly. Those at the centre, by contrast, mustn't. They are told to "loiter, with extreme intent".

So many lessons were ingrained. Decide the AIM and state it simply; that was one. Lead by example was another. Look after the men before yourself was a third. You had to see they were all right before thinking of yourself. This concern took a strange turn one day. A cadet complained that he had something stolen from his locker. Had he left it unlocked ? Yes. He was punished for putting temptation in someone's way. Punctuality, of course, was another lesson. Two cadets went skiing to Switzerland on leave. They were late back because the airport had been snowed in. Nonetheless, they were RTU'd (returned to unit), sacked, that is, from the school at once. See for yourself what is going on and keep everyone informed, are other rules I tried to follow in my business later.

Two up, one back, always hold a reserve, may have proved the most valuable lesson of all. In business people often over-stretch. They run risks. In my firm I always felt rather dull, cautious — cash in the bank, having sound reserves — until being reassured by an article about entrepreneurs in *Time* magazine. It found that successful entrepreneurs are seldom the swashbucklers of popular imagination, but more often conservative and careful.

Mons has gone. Aldershot, once filled with thousands of men in khaki living in red brick barracks redolent of Victorian England, has changed. The army has adapted to new times. But, wherever they are, I'd be sure — and experience shows — those splendid colour sergeants and sergeant majors are still as steadfast and dependable as ever. Gerald Kersh, who volunteered for the Coldstream Guards in 1941 and wrote a book about them called *They Die with their Boots Clean*, said it all. "They are," he wrote simply, "the backbone of things."

Twelve

More Welsh Rain

Oh, Mr Porter, Gracie Fields sang,
What shall I do ?
I want to go Birmingham
But this train goes to Crewe.
Take me back to London
As quickly as you can.
Oh, Mr Porter, what a silly girl I am.

Even after midnight Crewe station, a cavernous, dimly-lit hub was crowded with hundreds of laden troops criss-crossing in all directions, trying to find, then squeeze into, trains back to their camps. The one I took rattled slowly through the dark across Wales. However new, as an officer I travelled first-class. Often this meant having a carriage to oneself, to stretch full-length and sleep in. After a trip or two, imagine it today, the guard woke one up with a cup of tea; in time to see, by early light, the rushes and dunes of the coast, grey sea beyond. We passed around the sleeping town of Aberdovey, at the head of an estuary, sometimes dank and dour in rain, occasionally white and sparkling, cheerful and sunny as a Cornish fishing village.

Weather dominates Wales, the west, anyway. In summer we had healthy tans. In winter it could rain and blow without end. Often I used three coats a day until each was wet through; a white riding coat in the morning, a gas-cape in the afternoon, a long, pinch-waisted greatcoat with a deep collar and generous, folded cuffs, in the evening. In sun, the landscape is beautiful; green hills that change colour as clouds pass over and splashes of ochre and yellow, distant corn. In rain, the world is grey. The sky is grey, the low, heavy clouds are grey. The slate hills are grey. Even the grass seems grey, all colour soaked out of it. Sheep, roaming throughout the camp, were the same. And the wind. The wind rattled windows and made doors hard to open. You had to lean hard against them to push into the day. Often filled with stinging rain, the wind made us lean forward as we walked, bellow when we spoke. Fighting the wind, hour after hour whipping in off the sea, put your nerves on edge, made everyone tense.

The camp, at a place called Tonfanau, in Merioneth (now the site, fittingly, of a far-removed atomic power station), sloped back from a ridge of dunes and the sea. There was neither tree nor shrub nor flower of any kind. Wooden huts and characterless brick buildings, gun sheds along one side of the concrete square, and at the top, as you walked up the slope, the officers' mess; that was it. Two regiments dwelt there: mine, and a 'service' regiment. We were unalike. Constantly refreshed by new intakes of men, the training regiment was driven with urgent purpose. The service regiment was slower; nothing happened. You sensed that in the mess. One expensively-faced major drank pink gins with his breakfast. Others over their whisky mumbled their regret that, as gunners, they no longer rode horses. Although we shared the mess, squash courts and a cinema, known as 'the Gaff', the two regiments hardly mixed.

Exaggerating the contrast, perhaps, Ken Wilmshurst, in the training regiment and who later captained the British athletic team in the Olympics, liked to complete *The Times* crossword over breakfast. From Mons at the same time, he and I became troop commanders, joining other subalterns. Every ten weeks we would each receive one hundred and twenty young soldiers to train. After eight weeks they would pass out, being posted to service regiments. We had a fortnight to clear up and prepare for the next batch.

These training troops were grouped into three batteries. Anyone who saw the film *Tunes of Glory*, with John Mills and Alec Guinness, will recognise the majors of two of them. Mine was a gentleman, his hats made at Lock's, holder of the OBE, a slight, ginger-haired, fussy man. The other was 'Mad Jack', who had risen from the ranks, far from common then. On his chest he wore an MC with two bars, the Croix de Guerre and still more gallantry ribbons. A direct man, plain-spoken, he had no time for niceties. Although it is strictly not done, indeed most improper and illegal, to touch a soldier, I saw Jack pick up a man by the throat and pin him against the wall, his feet off the ground. He was almost as blunt with the colonel. One day, the colonel reprimanded one of Jack's NCO's. "You leave him to me." Jack bellowed to the colonel and everyone in earshot, "It's my fucking battery." Yet we all thought little of the gent and the world of Jack.

'Ged' Palmer, the colonel, whose father had been killed at Gallipoli, learnt his soldiering on the North-West Frontier. He had served in India, the Sudan and elsewhere and had been decorated for gallantry both in the Mohand and in the Abyssinian campaign, where General Wavell's forces, outnumbered ten to one, defeated an Italian army of 350,000 men. Both 'Ged' and our brigadier had been in the Long Range Desert Group, operating hundreds of miles behind German lines. *The Times* described Ged as 'indomitable'. To him nothing was impossible, everything could be done and had to be right.

'Ged' liked sailing. He had sailed in the Gunners' own yacht, the *St. Barbara,* and took part in a 440-mile race from Brixham to Santander. He helped found the sailing club at Aberdovey where the regiment moored a number of boats. On afternoons off it was the acceptable thing to go sailing, although there could be consequences. Next morning, a runner would come to see you. "Colonel's compliments, sir. Would you go to see him at once." What had you done, you wondered nervously as you walked up the hill. "Ah," the colonel would say, looking up from his desk, "yes, I know why I wanted to see you. The way you went about yesterday was horrible." His house overlooked the bay where we sailed; he had watched us through binoculars.

Manners, as well as sailing, had to be learnt. All the officers, except Mad Jack on occasion, treated the colonel distantly and with deference. After lunch one day, as we reached for our hats and clipped on our belts to go back on duty, I asked the colonel if he had enjoyed his leave. "Yes thank you." he answered gruffly. An older subaltern reprimanded me. "You must never ask," he told me. "It would be more courteous to express the hope that the colonel enjoyed his leave."

When you see how little industry trusts young people, it is salutary to remember the responsibilities given us then. Even my small experience, so slight beside that of millions of others, makes me argue that youth is capable of far more than it is allowed, a confidence I hope I proved later in my firm. There were absurdities — aged twenty I had to deal with marriage problems and more than once defend soldiers at Courts Martial — and surely one made mistakes but, on the whole, everything worked.

At Mons, 'ot at that', I had two sergeants, both distinguished wartime soldiers, and six bombardiers. One, 'Sarn' Crook, was the stiff-backed, hard-shouting, drill pig. He had been trained at the Guards depot at Caterham and somewhere acquired a taste for glasses of whisky laced with peppermint. At a sergeants' mess party one night I counted him drink thirty-nine, as upright and orderly when I left as he had been when I arrived. The secret lay in the system and making sure you had the best NCO's in the entire world. Of Caterham he told this story. An orderly sergeant, doing the rounds one night, saw one of the lavatories locked. He hammered his pace stick on the door. "Oo's inside ?" he demanded. "Jesus Christ," he heard. "On opening the door," he accounted to the officer taking misdemeanors next morning, "I found that this was not so." From behind his desk, the charge sheet in his hand, the officer looked up wistfully, touched the edge of his moustache, and said, "Sergeant, who am I, a sinful port wine drinker, to say that this man is not the Messiah ? Case dismissed."

The other sergeant, a more thoughtful man, led gunnery training. He came to me one day and said "Sir, Gunner has just cut off his thumb" (it happened when they shoved a shell in the breech and the breech block snapped shut). Ineptly, I asked, "How much of his thumb ?" "This much, sir," said the sergeant. He opened a matchbox and handed it to me. The thumb was in it.

The bombardiers were excellent too. One, old as the army, was a Liverpudlian, Bdr Pruden. Not unnaturally, he resented a youngster like me telling him what to do. He was always well turned out and did his job but, you felt, the least he could get away with. One day he came with a request for compassionate leave; his wife was ill. I got him a weekend pass at once. From then on, he was the most efficient, loyal NCO you could find. Whatever the 'man management' lesson, that was a successful conversion. They became an outstanding, sure, team.

When we weren't working out training programmes, and overseeing gun drill and other training, occasionally teaching, taking pay parades (where, as long as I was there, men I'd never seen before turned up from snug stores, and other 'cushy billets' where 'char' was always brewing up), dealing with discipline, sorting out the men's personal problems and a hundred other tasks, we played lots of sport.

The regiment was one of three in the brigade. All who joined the Royal Artillery, then larger than the Navy, came through one of them. Without them knowing it, if they were good at games their route was fixed. One regiment, the one I'd been in at Oswestry, specialised in athletics. Chris Chataway was one of their subalterns. To the second regiment good rugby players went. To mine came footballers.

When the troops completed their training, we had to fill in their papers, then hand them to the adjutant's office. I'd sent in my pile after one course. Most of the men were going to Hong Kong. The adjutant asked to see me. "What do you think you're doing ?" he asked. "You're sending Gunner Griffiths to the Far East." "Yes, sir." "Do you realise he plays football for the Arsenal ?" "Sir?" So he stayed, to become yet another runner. On our permanent staff we had twenty-three professional footballers, thirteen from the first division. Last I heard of Gunner Griffiths he was manager of Wrexham Football Club. I became first the regimental hockey officer, then was given basketball, a game I'd scarcely heard of. Both meant going on courses to Oswestry. In the evenings there you would see Chris Chataway running around the track. He would ask volunteers to pace him. We would pick him up as he approached, then run one lap of the twelve he ran. In that one lap of 440 yards he would beat us by 200 yards. Because we trained daily, played squash often and were not unfit, that shows how vastly superior good athletes are. On May 6th, 1954, on the Oxford University track at Iffley Road, Chataway paced Bannister to break that most famous of all records, the first four-minute mile. In the same year he broke the world record for 5000 metres. Both in 1952 in Helsinki, and 1956, in Melbourne, where Ken Wilmshurst was captain of the British team, he competed in the Olympics.

At Oswestry one day a bombardier saluted me smartly as he passed. Correctly, he looked in my eyes and I looked in his. I recognised him at once. It was the one who had made me smash coal on the floor of the guardroom, then clean it up all night, the year before. Did he recognise me and remember ? I half think he did.

In Wales we shot; for pheasant, in woods brown and golden in autumn, and for geese. Crouched in rushes at the edge of the dunes, the sky lightening with first streaks of day, we waited for that steady woosh, woosh, woosh of flapping wings as a formation of birds flew towards us, then over, bang, bang, bang, and out to sea.

One of the officers in our mess, Bill Petrie-Hay, a captain, flew. He had his own aeroplane. One afternoon he crashed into a hill, happily unhurt. In no time, Sergeant Jones, of the police, arrived on his bicycle. Like all the local people, he had no time for the English. "Got you this time," he said to Bill in his slow, lilting, voice. "Show me your papers." "I'm sorry," replied Bill, "I'm afraid I haven't got any." "Oooh," said Sergeant Jones slowly, weighing up the enormity of this admission, "you can't crash without papers."

We didn't get on with the neighbours. People in Merioneth were unwelcoming. We had a joke. A woman goes into a chemist's shop to buy something for her daughter, who is getting married. "Myfanwy getting married, is she ?" asks the shop-keeper. "And her not pregnant. There's swank for you."

The officers had continuous training, as the men did. (A lesson still largely unlearnt by British industry. Perhaps worse than most, one managing director was quoted by Roger Eglin in the *Sunday Times* in the 1980s. He was asked what he spent on training his managers. "Why should I do that ?" asked the managing director. "They're meant to be trained. That's why I hire them.")

Some days, in bright sun, wispy cloud drifting high in the blue sky, we were in the heart of Wales not with the sound of music, but gunfire. We were shooting at targets to our front, some miles away. In turn, each of us took the various duties, including hiding with a signaller on the forward slope of a hill, the guns behind us, out of sight. There, as an OP, the task was to identify the target, give its map reference, call the kind of shell and number of shots you wanted, then tell the guns to fire. Once I did all that and the signaller relayed it. Then he shouted into his radio — "STOP!" That is an emergency signal. He realised he had given the map reference of the spot we were in. Still alive, our second attempt was better. Then Bill Petrie-Hay had a go. Peering forward to see where his shots were landing, we noticed puffs of smoke far away to our right. Bill was ninety degrees out.

As well as his aircraft, Bill owned a long, green, open Bentley. With the battery captain, John Matthews, who had been airborne, and another subaltern, we drove, one weekend, to London. We were going to 'the shop', the RA depot at Woolwich, where the King was coming to a ball. It was a weekend of accidents. First, another car banged into the Bentley while it was parked outside The Blue Cockatoo, a restaurant on Cheyne Walk. I used the braces that held up my blue patrol trousers to tie the bumper in place. That made us so late that John Matthews's girl-friend, a nurse, wouldn't come. After the ball, John and I slept in barracks. When we woke his plain clothes suit was missing. "Fifty guineas, Savile Row," he exploded. When he called the military police he told them, "Don't look for the suit, look for a pawn ticket." They did, and found the culprit in minutes.

It happened again. As well as being experienced, John was

intuitive. In my troop one day a gunner lost his wallet. John told the military police to look in the lavatory cistern.A policeman stood on the seat and reached up. From the cistern above he pulled out the soaking wallet.

Poor John. Skiing, he met an attractive and very wealthy Australian girl. She wrote from Sydney to say she was coming to Beirut for a party and asked if John could join her, not meant as the joke it was on his pay. Later, she stayed in her father's flat in Half Moon Street in Mayfair. "If only I could fall in love with her." moaned John.

Another time I went to 'the shop' was to deliver 120 trained soldiers from the camp in Wales. With a bombardier to help, we arrived by train in Paddington station during the evening rush hour. Trucks we expected weren't there. So we plunged into the Underground. Platforms were jammed. The men, heaving their heavy kitbags, squeezed into the train where they could. When, after changing trains, we arrived at Woolwich it was dark and raining. We 'fell the men in' and marched to the depot. There, an officer met us. Happily, he didn't think of counting the men. The minute he signed a piece of paper to say they had arrived, I fled. How many completed the journey I dared not ask.

Years later, well into the 1980s, my wife and I were invited to dinner at 'the shop'. As I stood sipping a drink, a stranger said, "Do you come here often ?" "Oh no," I replied, "I haven't been here since the King came to dinner and that was a hundred years ago." "Do you mean then ?" he asked, pointing to a picture behind me which I hadn't seen. It depicted that same evening.

On other Saturday evenings a misnamed 'passion waggon'

drove officers into Aberystwyth. That is, unless the adjutant caught you. "Ah," he'd say as we were slipping out, "care to make up a four at bridge ?" "Why yes, sir, how kind," a disgruntled subaltern would say, and that would be his evening in ruins.

Not that the alternative held any delights. Aberystwyth offered little, although, at nearby Towyn there was once a concert with comedienne Maudie Edwards as top of the bill. She had been 'secured', the poster said beneath her name, 'at great expense'. Mostly, we sat in a dirty, half-empty pub, drinking warm beer until it was time to go back. There was a dance hall, though, and we got to know three girls. The names we gave them told all. They were known as 'Peg leg', 'Granite gob' and 'Deaf aid'.

Braver souls flirted with the scarlet-caped nursing sisters, from the Queen Alexandra's Royal Nursing Service, but, since they shared our mess most of us feared they were 'doorstep stuff'. Apart from them, there were no girls. Dibby wrote while I was there to say she was getting married, a sad blow. Mike Shepherd, a tall, languid, beautifully-dressed officer who became a particular friend, fell in love with a girl he had met on leave, Dorothy. I was best man at their wedding, after I'd left the army.

The wedding was in Peterborough. The night before, after dinner, Mike's father, a brigadier who had become head of transport police in Scotland, invited the men to his hotel room for a night-cap. He always carried a bottle of whisky with him. We hadn't enough glasses. "It's all right," he said, "follow me." We stepped quietly into the corridor. Mike's father took a pass key from his pocket. "It'll open anything," he whispered. Carefully, he put the key in the first bedroom we came to. He turned it, stepped silently into the darkened room, then came out, with a tooth-brush glass. He collected four that way.

Next day, wedding over, I managed to move the party to the railway station, in time for the Edinburgh-London express. The train roared in and hissed to a standstill. Mike and his wife climbed aboard. We all waved good-bye. Nothing happened. The train didn't move. We waved good-bye again. Still the express stood there. I turned away from the knot of guests, thinking what to do. Then I saw the station master go up to the brigadier. "Is it all right if I take the train away now, sir ?" he asked.

I made a discovery. There was a Palladian mansion in Shropshire where painting was taught over weekends. My major thought it commendable that a young officer should want to educate himself. He encouraged me to go. The army paid the fee, provided first-class travel and a living allowance. What the major didn't know was that the house-keeper there was an extremely attractive girl, Diana, who brought me breakfast in bed.

Perhaps because one was new, being orderly officer at the weekends was not unusual. Then, things could happen. One summer weekend I had to deal with a gun that, as the towing vehicle turned a corner too fast, snapped from its fastening and sped straight on — deep into Lake Bala. Another night the orderly sergeant, my own Sergeant Crook, came to me and said, "There's a fight in progress, sir, outside the gaff."

"Have you called out the guard?"

"Yes, sir."

"Have you told the MP's ?"

"Sir."

"We'd better have a look," I said.

Outside the 'gaff', the cinema, on a broad concrete area, Scottish 'Territorials', with us for summer camp, were fighting. Perhaps they were just finishing, heaving, moving slowly, their main passion spent.

"Stand still," I shouted, so loudly that they paused. Then "Orderly Sarn', fall them in." He did and they obeyed. Without pause, we marched them to the guardroom. Minutes later, Sergeant Crook and I realised how remarkable that was and how lucky and perhaps foolish we had been.

That experience worked a second time. In France, in 1969, I went to the business school at Fontainebleau, called INSEAD. One night, three of us were sitting outside an estaminet sipping pernod. A bunch of very untidy French soldiers came to the next table. They had finished their military service that day. Celebrating, they became drunk and rowdy. One of us, an executive from a British steel company, began goading them. "Leave them alone," we said. He wouldn't. Sooner or later it had to happen: one of the soldiers threw a glass of beer in my friend's face. He leapt to his feet and adopted the stiff boxing pose you see in nineteenth-century prints. In seconds, he was on his back, on the cobbles, being kicked by the soldiers. I had no idea how French commands go, but as we two remaining ran forward, I shouted *"Arrêtez-là"* and *"Cessez, cet instant"* as firmly as I could. Incredibly, they did. It can't have been the words, perhaps the tone of voice did it.

Thirteen

Ritual for Dinner

One rainy Saturday night I was leafing through a magazine in the mess, as orderly officer unable to leave camp, when the parents of a soldier asked to see me. The wife was distraught, the husband protective. They had come many miles because we were mistreating their son, they charged. I asked the orderly sergeant to bring him. When he came, he stood limply, his mouth open. With dead eyes he stared at the wall. He appeared not to recognise his parents. The mother burst into tears, her fears confirmed.

The following weekend the *Sunday Pictorial* (now *Sunday Mirror*) published a piece about him. They called ours a 'horror camp'. Then came the thing the army dislikes most, a 'ministerial enquiry'. Soon everyone was talking about him. Officers, NCOs and the men in his hut were interviewed. "He's just trying to work his ticket," they said. They were interviewed again. They were sure again. "He boasts at night about how he is having you on," said the men in his hut. But still he behaved as though he was mad. He peed against the wall of the colonel's office. On the parade ground he wouldn't obey orders. When the drill sergeant gave a command — "Quick march," for instance— the soldier ignored it. That took more courage than most had.

He was sent to the army's psychiatric hospital, in Chester. Doctors could find nothing wrong. What was to be done?

The colonel admitted it was awful if our training, admittedly demanding, had pushed this man too far. "The least the army can do," he decided, "is to try to restore the man to full health." He was sent to the psychiatric hospital for the remainder of his national service. So he got away from us, but not from the army.

Most stories were better. There was great satisfaction, indeed, in receiving pale, pigeon-chested boys from the cities, sometimes under-nourished, often short of sunshine and fresh air, then watching them fill out, both in body and mind. I wrote home at the time, "Physically, the effect of PT every day for the first time in their lives, is revolutionary. They put on stones of weight and seem to wake up from a daze." As they grew broader and stronger, able to throw heavy shells from one to the other and push and shove guns into action, as the drill on the square made them stand up straighter and respond quicker, so they became more self-confident, prouder. It gave me a pleasure in helping young people grow that remains.

"Half this life," the same letter says, "seems to consist of checking cleanliness of one sort and another. Although it is usually only kit, there is the odd bod we scream at for 'dirty flesh'." One man, I am ashamed to record, we doubled to the shower. Four men scrubbed him with brooms and he had cold showers twice a day for a week. Inspecting feet for 'trench foot' was one regular job.

After a few months the regiment formed what it called an 'extension' troop, or 'E' troop, for advanced training. I was put in charge of it. When they had finished their basic training, selected gunners were moved over to me for a further six weeks. That was good. The soldiers were fit, they drilled well, they could handle guns, they knew the ropes. I started badly, refusing all the NCOs allotted to me.

But the major supported me, and arranged for me to pick and choose from throughout the regiment. The 'E' came to stand for elite. I even managed to get a special flash for the soldiers' epaulettes, to distinguish them from the general run under ordinary training.

As well as more gunnery and still more foot drill, we took them for days in the Welsh hills, splashing through streams, rifles held high, clambering up slopes, digging in where we stopped. We pushed them, and the more we did, the tougher and prouder they became.

They welded into a tight, taut unit. If proof was needed, one mistake I made provided it. We had a report that men in one hut had been gambling. That was strictly illegal. I paraded them, and asked the guilty ones to own up. No one did. Foolishly, I said they would have punishment drill until the matter was cleared up. The men grew resentful, and more silent. They would never shop one of their mates. After two days I had to stop. That was another lesson in man management.

Occasionally, this troop took shining guns out for displays at public events. At least once I had two outriders, motor-cyclists in broad white gloves riding in front. We arrived at a camp. Seeing the outriders, the guard commander called out the guard. He ordered them to 'present arms', an honour reserved for senior officers. A captain, told of the outriders, bustled forward and saluted. When he found a second-lieutenant returning his salute his annoyance matched my embarrassment.

Before taking a convoy through any town I had to ask for a police escort. This, I was told, is not only practical, because the guns and limbers were large and clumsy, but is daily confirmation that the civil authority in Britain is greater than the military authority. Whenever I see the Household Cavalry trotting through Hyde Park to change the guard each morning, I always look for the policeman in front, and he is always there. That, in this age of terrorists, is not to protect the cavalry, others do that, but to re-state the important principle.

The same principle was exercised in another way by President Truman. The Korean war was on. Dressing one night, I heard on my cracked, Bakelite radio that Truman had sacked General MacArthur. Even in Britain we knew that MacArthur was a near-God, adored by the American people. Truman was asked later by Ed Murrow how he had he come to sack the general. "Well," replied the President, "I travel a lot about the country by train. When I do, I read history. And I remembered how the Roman senate had dealt with a general who got too uppity. They had to show their authority was greater than his. So they sacked him. I reckoned that was right," said Truman. "So I did the same."

In Wales, I volunteered for the Korean war. The opportunity was to become what is called an 'Air OP', someone who flies over enemy positions telling your guns where to aim. Waiting to be posted to Barton Stacey or Middle Wallop, wherever the army learns to fly, I tried to learn to play the mouth organ. It would entertain troops in the dug-outs, I imagined. But I couldn't master that any more than I would ever have mastered an Auster, the aircraft used then. Perhaps fortunately, I never had to do either.

As officers, we had a room each, and a batman to look after

both it and our kit. My batman was a cockney, called Dad. I read in the paper one day about youths in London fighting each other with razors. "Do you use a razor ?" I asked Dad. "Oh no, sir," said Dad. "Bicycle chain, me." When he was on leave and took his 'old mum' for a drink, he hid a bicycle chain under the collar of his jacket.

"Any trouble," Dad told me "and I'd give 'em one across the eyes."

One of my men, on leave, got into such a fight in Nottingham and injured somebody. With two guards, I had to escort him to a civilian police station, then watch his case in court. His mother came too. She was asked to give evidence. A gypsy, she wore a bandanna around her head and a full-length, flowing black skirt. As a barrister questioned her she paused, rummaged in her voluminous clothes and pulled out a pipe, a knife and a plug of tobacco. Carefully, she cut the tobacco and stuffed the pipe. The courtroom fell silent; everyone was transfixed. She struck a match on the sole of her boot before the judge leaned over and told her to stop.

That was a winter when there was coal rationing. In the camp we had none at all. It was freezing. We had no heat for weeks. In desperation, I asked Dad one day if he couldn't find some coal somewhere. Next thing I knew, the coal hole was overflowing, spilling onto the corridor outside our rooms. "Where did you get this ?" I asked. "Don't ask, sir," he said. I lit a fire in the stove in my room. In minutes, black smoke, worse than any warship could make, billowed out of my wet chimney, a beacon and signal for the sleepiest orderly officer. My pleasure was momentary.

As officers we had interesting TEWTs (technical exercises without troops), lectures and visitors. 'Manny' Shinwell, the Labour government's Minister for War, was one. For all Labour's 1945 election victory, troops marshalled to hear him just drifted away. A lecture about the Soviet army cast a new light on communism: soldiers, we were told, earned one-third of the pay ours do. Their officers earned four times as much as British officers.

There was a ritual for dinner in the mess. On some nights you wore service dress, on others, mess kit. At weekends, perhaps, you wore plain clothes, suits for some occasions, tweed jackets and flannels for others.

For the young officer it was all confusing. It went like this. You'd ask what to wear. Someone would say, "service dress." You'd change into it. Then, as you left your room, ready, there'd be a couple of officers chatting idly in the corridor, wearing tweed jackets. "What the hell are you wearing ?" they'd ask. "It's always sports coats on Wednesdays." You'd rush back, tear off your khaki , throw yourself into plain clothes. Ready once more, you would walk out. An officer would be walking along the corridor on his way to the mess. He'd be wearing blue patrols. "C'mon," he'd shout over his shoulder, "get dressed, you're going to be late." You'd turn back and while you were struggling into your tight patrols there'd be a knock at the door. An officer would walk in, wearing a dark suit. "Mind if I borrow a comb ?" he'd ask. Then, looking at you, he'd say, "But what ARE you wearing ? It's suits tonight...You'd better get a move on." You'd puff to the mess last and late, in a state. On a good day you could get a new officer to change maybe four times in ten or fifteen minutes.

On mess nights, when the table glittered with regimental silver, one charming custom was that the most junior officer was invited to toast the King. He would be placed at the end of a long table. After the meal, the port would go round. The colonel would stand up and say, "Mr Vice, the King." That was the signal to stand up and say "Gentlemen, the King." When it was my turn, officers either side of me grabbed my legs and held them, firmly, on their laps. I couldn't stand up. "Mr Vice," the colonel repeated, then, edgily, a third time. They let me stand up at the neatly judged moment, an instant before the colonel lost his temper.

Mess nights ended with whisky and snooker (I once played with an amiable man who was visiting his son, a quiet man whose fair hair was thinning and whose grey eyes twinkled behind glasses. He was Stephen Potter, the creator of 'gamesmanship', although he needed few wiles to beat me.) Occasionally there were exuberant rugby matches, using cushions or anything to hand. Sometimes there were singsongs.

Smokin' my pipe in the mountings,

the Kipling words went, to the tune of the Eton boating song,

Sniffin' the mornin' cool,
I walks in my old brown gaiters
Along o' of my old brown mule,
With seventy gunners be'ind me,
An' never a beggar forgets It's only the pick of the army
That handles the dear little pets.
For you all love the screw-guns
— the screw-guns they all love you !
So when we call round with a few guns,
O' course you will know what to do - hoo,hoo.
Jest send in your chief and surrender -
It's worse if you fights or you runs:
You can go where you please,
You can skid up the trees,
But you don't get away from the guns !

The screw-gun takes to bits. Wheels, barrel, other parts were carried by mules. They were used in mountain warfare. Today the words seem, at best, out of place. Glorifying guns, hankering for the distant duties of Empire, will be thought absurd, awful, ridiculous. Maybe so. I was never in a war, never learnt the truth. People who did may forgive me for honouring the army and its honour none the less.

Earlier I'd been invited to go to Sandhurst, to become a regular officer. Now I was invited to stay in, offered as a compliment. But, while enjoying the life and my job, I was conscious that this was an enclosed order. The world outside was bigger, richer. Slightly frightened, I decided to try my luck. There was the scholarship to Italy. I wrote to the British Council reminding them of it, and of their advice to go in the army and pick up the scholarship later. They replied that since I was no longer a student of a British university, I was no longer eligible.

How annoying.

Then my old battery commander at Mons, Major Singleton, wrote to say a friend of his who grew coffee in Uganda, needed a young man to help him. Kindly, Singleton had thought of me. Would I be interested ? A date was made for lunch one Saturday at the East India Club. Me as a planter in the sun; I quite liked the idea. More annoyance: that very weekend, as a last-minute substitute for someone else, I was made orderly officer. There was no escaping. The coffee grower returned to Africa on the Sunday, so we never met.

Entering the Colonial Office was another thought. The idea of such service was appealing. I wrote for the forms. Then it struck me, with some prescience considering how far-flung the British Empire then was, that soon there wouldn't be many colonies to serve.

As rain streaked down the windows of our cold barracks, the 'schoolie' (Education Officer) attached to the regiment used to tell us about America. He had been evacuated there as a schoolboy, and brought up in one of the Ivy League schools on the East Coast. The world he talked about was sunlit and open and generous. One vacation, he had hitch-hiked down to Florida. Tall, broad-shouldered, blonde-haired, with a charming manner, he was so handsome that he got a job lying by a pool. He didn't have to work, or even swim; just lie there. The boss thought his good looks would attract custom. (That was him, always lucky. From the army, he joined BAT, was sent to the Far East and, within three months, won a state lottery.) Back in the camp, he regretted that you couldn't get to America now. Visas were impossible. I remember saying, "There must be a way." I bet him five shillings I could find it.

Until then, though, I had to get a job. I wrote dozens of letters. Three people replied. Cliff Michelmore, at the BBC, was one. But most were less polite. (Experiencing that discouragement, I later made it a rule in my firm that any letter we received from anyone asking for a job was acknowledged the same day.) In the end I joined an oil company, Socony-Vacuum, now Mobil, as a management trainee.

The last training course came and went. My army days just petered out. All that fitness, all those experiences, drifted away to nothing, distant memory. One sunny October morning I took a train and left, forever, the dunes, shimmering sea, hills rising beyond the camp where, on summer evenings, we watched a shepherd gathering his flock. I left the men, by now marching in small squads to their tasks, the NCOs no doubt flicking the papers on their clip boards to see what the day held for them; all gone. As many more qualified than me must have felt over the years, I was suddenly empty, sad, alone, filled with apprehensive anticipation.

Fourteen

When Cows Had Names

There was the world outside. From the regular, restricted, khaki-filled and colourless life of an army camp, whole kaleidoscopes of interests beckoned. 1951 was the year of the Festival of Britain, with events everywhere.

After years of war, with rationing and shortages still and anything decent going for export, the Festival of Britain was planned to bring the tired British people new hope, even light-heartedness. Max Nicholson, in the Lord President's office, called it "jam on a large socialist pill". Although the Korean war was going on and it opened to a national dock strike, the Festival was timed well, just one hundred years after the Great Exhibition of 1851.

Austerity was to be forgotten, and perhaps was. Crowds came to see wonders of a new age and, at night, danced — even in the rain — to the music of Joe Loss. In the Dome of Discovery was more than one hint of the future, including a thing called cybernetics. A central feature of the whole

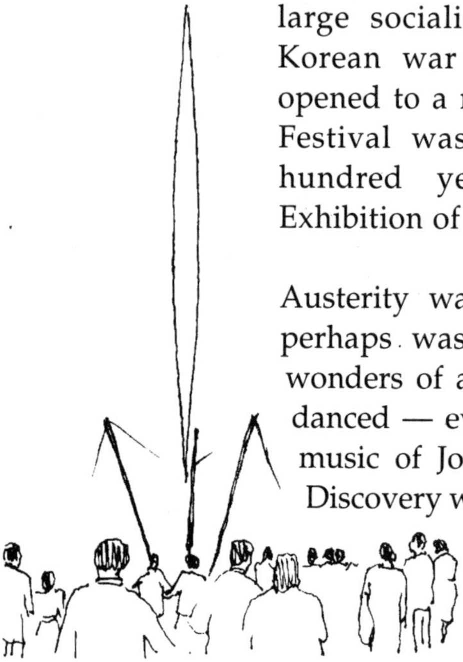

Battersea site, the pencil-slim Skylon, was meant, in the words of Sir Hugh Casson, the principal designer, to "hang up in the air and astonish". Cruelly, some critics likened it to the state of Britain herself "held up with no visible means of support".

The Festival generated an enormous amount of wonderful activity. I am looking at a *Radio Times* from one week in May, 1951. Bertrand Russell spoke optimistically about living in an atomic age: "Human skill," he said, "has reached a point where the human race can be happy if it chooses to be so. What we suffer, we suffer owing to our folly. But if we can open our hearts and minds to hope, the world can quickly become a world full of joy."

In that same week, on the radio, J.B. Priestley, a prolific author and playwright whose *Postscripts* on the BBC after Dunkirk gave huge comfort, talked about Britain during the Festival year. Known to everyone in the land then, perhaps he is forgotten now. Late in his life he lived in Albany, off Piccadilly. He crossed the road to Hatchards to buy books. I saw him ordering one. The young shop assistant asked his name. When he gave it, the assistant said, "How do you spell it ?" and then, "What initials ?"

Monsignor Ronald Knox preached the sermon at Westminster Cathedral, Alistair Cooke led a Transatlantic quiz one day and read his Letter from America on another. Jean-Jacques Servan-Schreiber, who later wrote a powerful book called *Le Défi Americain*, broadcast a Letter from Paris. Andre Gide's play *Oedipus* was performed (he had died a month or two before) as well as *Macbeth* and Shaw's *Pygmalion*. Angela Baddeley played Eliza, Terence de Marney was Higgins. Freddy, remarkably, was played byAndrew Faulds who left the stage to become a Labour

MP. Emlyn Williams — and Angela Baddeley again — were in *The Winslow Boy.*

At the Lyric Theatre, Hammersmith, Peter Pears led the cast of Benjamin Britten's music for *The Rape of Lucretia.* At the Albert Hall Yehudi Menuhin played Brahms's violin concerto. Over the river at the Festival Hall, Sir Malcolm Sargent (known as 'Flash') was conducting Brahms too.

Danny Kaye, who was appearing at the London Palladium, and Max Miller, Robb Wilton and Gracie Fields appeared in a Festival of Britain variety show. A young Petula Clark sang in a programme called *Calling All Forces* led by Ted Ray. Henry Hall's *Guest Night* was going strong, *Take It From Here* was on and the unmissable, weekly excitement of *Paul Temple, Special Agent* continued.

In that same week the King and Queen of Denmark came to London and the Prime Minister of Australia celebrated the fiftieth anniversary of his country's parliament. England played Argentina at football, the Walker cup was being fought at Birkdale, and the South African cricket team was in England.

For all that, for me, civilian life in London began in days of damp November drizzle. But first, people who did National Service had to become Territorials. I enrolled in the Royal Buckinghamshire Yeomanry, a gunner regiment, and went one evening a week to its drill hall.

Working in the oil company, in Victoria Street by Westminster Abbey was awful. Every morning I travelled from Iver in a dirty, crowded, train. Every morning the same people read the same papers. Day after day I swept the arm of my coat across the steamed-up window to see the same hoardings in the same place at the same moment. Paddington was cold and smelt of soot from the spires of smoke drifting upwards from the waiting engines. Each day I pushed through the criss-crossing commuters, then skipped down the steps into the underground, changed trains at Baker Street, then up to the daylight at Victoria; same turning, same walk, same 'good mornings'. It was all so repetitive.

After months in the open air, with wind on my face and responsibilities and command, however slight, to be at a desk in a Dickensian accounts department whose boss was a Mr Penny, was unendurable. Piles of orders from customers were dropped on my desk. Some were entitled to a twenty-five per cent discount, others to fifteen per cent. It was my complete job to work out the discount and pencil the price to bill. "How," the American song went after the First World War, "are you going to keep 'em down on the farm, after they've seen Paree ?" Not that the west coast of Wales is Paree, but the idea is the same.

Socony-Vacuum certainly had no answer. Nor did the

management training programme, conceived without imagination, hold promise. It took some weeks to discover that we were to spend two years doing menial jobs in one department after another. Then, if our work was satisfactory, we were to become petrol salesmen, driving from garage to garage. Three of us had been recruited. Within six months all had left.

The bet hadn't been forgotten. While still in the army I had joined the English-Speaking Union, then found that you could get to America to study. I applied for, and was accepted by, Dartmouth College in New Hampshire — then found I couldn't afford the fees. The American Embassy confirmed the schoolie's opinion; a visa was out of the question. There were just too many more deserving applicants. "Of course," said the consular officer, "people who are travelling through the United States and then on, to Canada, say, or Mexico, can get a visa for ten days." That was it, the chink of light in the black-out, the bet could be won.

The Canadian Embassy wasn't as welcoming as I expected. The man who interviewed me wanted to be sure I was serious. "We don't want any casual people who just stay a year or two." "Oh no," I agreed and lied. Persuaded, he marked me as an immigrant, an idea that hadn't entered my head. He recommended Ontario and a city called Toronto, neither of which, despite all that geography at school, had I ever heard of. I pretended to be enthusiastic. It was arranged. I was to go in February.

Back at Reading for a ball, in a whirl, I became engaged to Molly, who had been reading Geography and was now taking a year-long teaching course, paid. A major was once asked to write a book about India. "If I had been there a week I could have written a book," he replied. "If I had been there a month I could have written a chapter. But, you see, I have been there all my life. So it is impossible." Talking about Molly is the same for me. She was everything; gay, loving, loving life, generous, interested, with quick intelligence, able, supportive, a friend. She was attractive, with her dark hair shorter than shoulder length, arching eyebrows, smiling full lips. She played tennis for the university, was well built with a good figure and stood confidently and squarely, unnervous.

'Put another nickel in/ In the nickel odeon/All I want is loving you and music, music, music.' That Teresa Brewer record blared out at party after party we went to then. 'Baby, it's cold outside' was another.

At one party, I asked a girl who'd been in the art department at Reading what she was doing. She had joined something called The Council of Industrial Design in the Haymarket, London. "It's like the civil service, it's a rut," she said, "but I like it. Ruts are so comfortable." That was in 1951. Years later I came to know its successor, the Design Council, intimately, serving on several committees and its Council. Not so much has changed.

Molly's family lived in an ancient, untouched village in Somerset, called Hinton St. George. By a Saxon cross, their house is long and low, thatched and bending, medieval. It is called The Priory. (One icy bedroom beneath the rafters, used only when the house is full, was known as 'The Chapel'. When, years later, new owners tore out the Victorian interior, there, indeed, was a chapel. If there are such things as ghosts, I felt one in that room, a chilling but strangely unafraid sensation that recurs as I write.)

I'd been to Molly's home before, wedged next to a woman holding a lamb in the back of a green bus that swayed and rattled through the high hedgerows. Now I had to go again, to ask her father's permission to marry. Molly's father, Arthur Jeffery, was a farmer; broad arms like oaks, a fine, large, head, full hair now white, dark bushy eyebrows, strong nose, slow, burred West Country speech. After dinner Molly and her mother left the room. There was an awkward silence. Her father looked into the fire. He fumbled in his pocket for his tobacco pouch and filled his pipe. He looked out of the window, then at the curtains. He harrumphed and turned back to concentrate on some particular of his pipe he had never seen before. "Well ?" he asked, his eyes turning slowly to mine. I stuttered my request. Neither of us knew what to say. He remembered he was supposed to ask me about my prospects. Slight, would have been a truthful answer. After a few moments he let it be known that that was enough of that. He was a dear, strong, man. I came to love him and the whole family more and more as years passed.

In 1951 the still villages of Somerset had scarcely changed since Thomas Hardy's day. They were complete, self-contained, isolated. Seasons came and went. Cows gave birth, crops were harvested, there was Christmas and Easter; life passed as it had for centuries. For a week we talked about a fox that burst into the chicken run and killed some birds. "Right beneath my bedroom window," complained Molly's outraged mother.

On the farm cows had names, Daisy and Maisy and Betsy. They were milked, and crops were sown and cut by men whose families had worked there for generations.

In the fields on a hot summer day, making a poor fist of

being a suitable son-in-law, I slithered, in slippery, 'typically townie' shoes, on top of a hay cart wielding a long pitchfork to catch stooks of hay thrown up at me. Each turn of the meadow, we stopped for cider. Hay-making done, all the workers went to the cider barn where, surrounded by huge wooden barrels, we drank cider again, now from a two-handled mug we passed around.

Each summer evening a green bus veered into the village. Looking through the window, waiting for it, became our entertainment. Always there was one woman standing at the bus stop. The bus approached her, then accelerated, to roar past, screeching to a stop fifty yards up the road. The woman waddled and puffed up to it. Other evenings, the bus would see the lonely woman and stop short. The game never ceased.

Later, we cut slices from a great wedge of cheddar cheese, dipped a fork into a jar for pickle and drank local cider. Meal over, we played cards or dominoes, which Arthur, pipe in his mouth, face creased with delight, always won.

His cider mug had a verse, worn but legible, on it:

Let the wealthy and great
Roll in splendour and state
I envy them not, I declare it.
I eat my own lamb,
My own chickens and ham,
I shear my own fleece and I wear it.

I have lawns, I have bowers,
I have fruits, I have flowers,
The lark is my morning alarmer.
So jolly boys now,

Here's God speed the plough,
Long life and success to the farmer.

Under the verse was a solemn verity:

NOTHING WITHOUT WORK.

Molly's father was one of twelve children. Nine had emigrated at the turn of the century, five of them to Canada where they created what is now the Alberta town of Jeffery. He went to Australia, shearing sheep. At the start of the First World War he enlisted. Though he never spoke of it and the only evidence was an old Australian slouch hat that hung by his desk, its brim turned up on one side, he fought, as an infantryman, in Gallipoli, in the desert and in France. When the war ended he reckoned he had travelled enough. From then on, while he made occasional outings to nearby village fairs and, some years, went with a brother to the Dorset coast, even, in 1926, during the General Strike, took a load of vegetables to Covent Garden, he seldom budged. But that simple life, the one I saw, deceived.

One weekend, Molly and I were talking about a play we had seen in London. It was *Ross*, with Alec Guinness as Lawrence of Arabia. I described to this Somerset farmer who Lawrence was, his courageous journey across the desert to Akaba, how he raised a fighting force among the nomadic arabs. I spoke of his achievements, then disillusion. All the while Mr Jeffery gazed into the fire, sucking his pipe, saying nothing, hardly listening. Then, without turning from the fire, he muttered, as though to himself, "Rum chap, that."

"You mean, you mean," I stuttered, "that you know about him ?""Oooh," he replied, "many's the time I've sat 'round a camp fire with that fellow." And that was all.

When cows wouldn't calve, or the fire wouldn't burn, or an engine wouldn't start, he'd call it "a proper Turk", perhaps another memento of Gallipoli which has drifted into the language of Somerset. It was an expression we all used. Molly is one of five daughters, each of whom I'm fond of. I think I have heard them all say, "Tis a proper Turk."

And when, years later, I bought a house in Somerset our gardener, an old farm hand more at ease laying hedges than cutting grass, called a broken mower "a proper Turk".

Certain scenes, Thomas Gray remarked, would awe an atheist into belief. Like so many in England, that Somerset village is one of them. More than six hundred and fifty years ago the present church was built, its tracery carved from local stone in the new Decorated style, in place of one which had already stood there for three hundred years. One earl in the great house had fought with Henry VII, another had locked Cardinal Wolsey, when he was a curate in the neighbouring village of Lopen, in stocks for being drunk at the fair, a third had served the King against Cromwell. Such continuity is something to cherish.

Yet the long, slow life of rural England has changed, swept away in a jarring tangle of television masts and Toyotas, computer-fed cows and mean rules from Brussels. Centuries of gentle, good and simple wonder, along with much that was poor, have gone. Not even the inherited confidence of the local earl, thirteenth in a line now ended, could be countenanced today. As the vicar mumbled through his tedious sermon one Sunday, Molly heard Earl Poulett, from his chapel pew to one side of the aisle, bellow,

"Get on with it, you clerk in holy orders."

My mind swells with vivid pictures. Here is Arthur Jeffery in his checked shirt, leaning forward carefully, his broad, strong body slowed by age, to pour cider from a large barrel into his mug. Molly's mother, Dorothy, slim, slight, the mildest of women, has just banged the oven door shut and stands in the kitchen wiping flour from her hands on to her apron. Her pale complexion is flushed, her grey hair, tied in a loose roll, is awry. There go Molly's sisters, laughing and pushing through the old door, running to the dining room, their shoes clattering on the worn stone floor, in some giggling race of their own.

All, for me, summon 'thoughts' as Wordsworth wrote, 'that do often lie too deep for tears.'

The great house, as I write, is owned by a Texan. Outbuildings of the Priory have been converted to new houses. The old barn is one, the stables another, the carpenter's workshop a third. No longer do cows meander at dusk down the High Street. The churchyard, where Molly's forebears lie, is grassy, overgrown. Tombstones, shaded by ancient trees, leaves rustling in the wind, are worn, patterned and stained with moss.

Fifteen

Times Square and Toronto the Good

During the blitz, while sirens wailed and bombs fell and black-clouded fires burnt and, as Sir John Colville, Churchill's secretary, remembered, to walk across Trafalgar Square on the morning after a raid was to crunch glass underfoot, the King and Queen had stayed in London. Perhaps it is hard today to judge how much that meant. Asked whether the Princesses shouldn't be sent to safety, perhaps to Canada, the Queen Mum said, "It's not possible. The King won't leave London, I won't leave the King and the children won't leave me." So that was that. Then Buckingham Palace was bombed. "It means," the Queen added, perhaps with some pride, "that I can look Londoners in the face." When, on the 6th February 1952, the brave, shy, King died and we saw photographs of the Queen, shrouded and still, scarcely a soul was unmoved. They were emotional days.

A week later, the Wolseley jammed with mother, Patience, Freddie and me, our father drove me to Euston. Near to tears, we said good-bye. I wedged into the train to Liverpool and the Cunard ship, RMS *Samaria*. Destination: New York. I had £25.

On the evening tide, after a final, long hoot, the ship cast off. Slipping her moorings, she moved slowly away from the dock. The umbilical cord was being cut. For me, I confess, it was a terrible, eternal moment, so like the sad couple in Ford Madox Brown's 'The Last of England'. I watched the Liver Building slip away, smaller and smaller, until it was gone. Choked with emotion, every sentimental thought pushed into my mind: 'England, home and beauty,' 'There'll always be an England,' 'Keep the home fires burning (while our hearts are yearning'). I was leaving not only family and fiancée and friends and everything I knew, but a land of lasting values; muddled, grey, but steadfast.

In our wearier, perhaps more cynical or truthful world, these clichés embarrass me now. I simply record them, dated as they are. The whole voyage was a cliché. From stem to stern, main deck to holds, the *Samaria* was crowded with every caricature of emigration. Red-faced Irishmen, picked up from a cutter off the Irish coast, sang mournful songs around the piano in the saloon. Raggedy-dressed families, doubtless from displacement camps in Europe, clustered in corners. Bearded men with patient eyes, mothers clutching babies, truly the 'huddled masses', all shorn from their war-ripped roots, to struggle again in unknown cities.

Day after day the ship sliced through the great, grey ocean. Rolling gently and heaving, its course was steady, always away and further away from the Europe, or England we had known.

Beyond Ireland the ship heaved and slowed and stood up and crashed down through two storms. Crockery slid off tables, chairs slithered back and forth across the dance floor, books fell, stewards slammed hatches shut. Thrown from side to side, grasping for railings, I made my way on deck. In the lee of a lifeboat I found shelter from the strongest, whipping winds. I clung to a steel hawser and was elated by the wild sea, waves crashing, threatening and going away.

Then, seas calm, marbling away to stern, we were no longer going away, but churning towards. And there, one magical morning, its towers piercing through early mist, was Manhattan. The scene is familiar. Yet to approach it quietly from the sea, all rage gone, engines throbbing gently, lighters steering you to your berth, is an unforgettable experience. Arriving by air, as we do today, when we are thrown without pause into the mad maelstrom of New York, is as aggressive as that early moment was tranquil.

The voyage was over, the ship we had got to know no longer ours. The new womb was ripped open. We shuffled down the gang-plank into a large Customs shed. Then, black porters, a line of yellow taxis, bright sunshine, New York. Absurdly, I remember feeling jubilant to have won the bet. It was absurd because that is why I had come, absurd because I almost never bet, absurd because I have not seen that schoolie again.

I had a small plan. First, I took a taxi to Grand Central station, where I left my luggage. Next, I went to the New York headquarters of the English-Speaking Union.

A woman in a blue dress, her greying hair tight and neat, looked coolly at me over her spectacles.

"You must be English," she said.
"You haven't any money."

She thought for a bit, then added: "Come back at two o'clock."

Did you have a good journey? How was the weather ? Do you know anyone here? How long are you staying? Did she utter any innocent pleasantries? No.

At two o'clock, no more forthcoming, she thrust a card at me.

"Go here" she said.

'Here' was an apartment on the west side of the park, in the eighties. It was the town house of a Mrs Thomas Lamont, said to be among the richest women in America. She generously put up itinerant strays from England. I was the lucky one now.

Mrs Lamont was as enchanting, as amiable, as courteous as she was generous and businesslike. At breakfast each morning, she had two white cards by her plate. On one was typed her agenda for the day. On the other was a synopsis of the news and reviews of new plays and films. She was armed. Meeting anyone, she could say something about whatever was going on. "They say the second act is marvellous," she could coo, as she moved away.

Mrs Lamont gave me tickets for some of those plays. Alone, in the fourth row of the stalls, I saw the Oliviers in *Julius Caesar*, for example.

Returning one evening, I intruded on the end of a dinner party. Mrs Lamont spoke, with concern, about the Royal Family. "How are they ?" she asked me. How was one to reply ? "Very sad," I said. Later I learnt that the Lamonts knew the King and Queen well, staying with them in summer.

On one of those trips, when he was in London, Thomas Lamont went to the British Museum to check the legend that Karl Marx had spent many days there. Lamont found the oldest librarian he could and asked if he had met Marx.

He described him carefully and guessed which shelves were most likely to occupy him. "Ah yes," replied the old man. "I remember the gentleman. I often wondered what became of him."

During the day I toured New York, visiting museums, galleries, the Rockefeller Centre, Empire State building, Broadway. The sky was bright blue, the air sharp, high windows sparkled in the sunlight, taxis bumped by. Somewhere, perhaps after lunch at the Stork Club, Walter Winchell was tapping out his one-line stories, to be syndicated across the country. It was New York, New York. That was before drugs and the current sleaziness. There was, at least to me, a lingering note of Damon Runyon about Broadway. Smoke puffed from the Camel ad. News flickered round from a million bulbs on the motorama, Budweiser horses tossed their heads. New Yorkers strolled along Broadway, enjoying their city. There was none of the hunted hostility you so often sense now.

Everyone was wonderful to me. I have been to New York perhaps sixty or seventy times since and found many friends. At that time, though, being so close to the shared war may have added to their natural kindness. From the war, intimate links between the United States and Britain seem to me as right and natural — and sensible — as breathing. I now know that, from 1942 on, there were half a million American airmen with bombers and fighters spread over 100 airfields in Britain. At least 30,000 airmen were killed. To me, with the countless doughboys, they are to be honoured forever.

During that first visit to New York I remember thinking, 'If this is how kind Americans are, won't Canadians be still more marvellous ?' At that time, after all, most came from

British roots. In the so recent war Canadians, like Australians and New Zealanders and others in the Commonwealth were, perhaps, as brothers.

It was time to find out, time to leave New York. One night I took a Greyhound bus, up the Hudson, across the dark, windswept Adirondacks, north, into the dull, flat, snow-covered lands of Southern Ontario.

Although Canada flew the Union Jack then and had the Queen's head on its stamps, I was soon to learn that my expectation was the most ignorant — and they'd say arrogant — anyone ever had. Canadian money, too, bore the Queen's head, a reassurance. Except that, if you looked carefully, you could see her hair had been engraved wickedly with the devil's face. The story of the time was that the mint, where money was produced, was in Quebec, and that seditious engraving was the work of a French Canadian.

From the bus terminus in Toronto, I went to stay in the YMCA. I dropped my bag in a cream-painted room and stepped into the primitive street of a Wild West town. Where, I asked, is the main street ? This, I was told, is it. An icy wind lashing my face, I walked in mounting dismay. Sidewalks were wooden planking. The road was dug open. A tangle of electric cables looped from pole to pole above the traffic. Shops were small, single-storey, with cheap green roofing. This was Yonge Street, spinal cord of Toronto. 'Though I didn't know it, the subway was being built.

Before I'd left Iver my sister, Julie, made me promise to stay two years. "You'll be homesick" she warned, "you must give time to live through that. Give the place a chance." If I hadn't promised, I'd have taken the next bus away.

Friends of friends in England, a retired man and his daughter, let me live with them, a kindness I overstayed. I had to get a job. One dentist paid me to open packing cases newly-arrived from England. I hacked at them with a chisel. When the crates finally fell open, the contents, white-enamelled dental chairs, were pock-marked where my chisel had been. That was that job. A kind man employed me to build a bookcase. (Shades of carpentry at school, when the instructor, exasperated by my inability to cut dove-tail joints for a tray, told me to keep cutting them, and make a match-box). With a will, I sawed and planed and sand-papered all day. I cut joints and glued them. Assembled, the book-case looked fine. I was inordinately proud. The man, too, seemed pleased. With a gesture of satisfaction, he tapped the bookcase. It collapsed to the floor, noisily. I went for a job as swimming instructor in a boys' prep school. Mercifully, the headmaster hired someone else.

In *Performing Flea,* a letter from P.G. Wodehouse describes a Finnish girl he heard of in New York. She was interviewed for a job by a wealthy hostess. "Can you cook ?" she asked. "No," replied the girl, "my mother does that." "Can you make beds ?" "No, my mother does that, too." The hostess persevered. "Can you look after children?" Again the girl said no. "Then what can you do?" asked the exasperated lady. "I can milk reindeer," replied the Finnish girl. Not that it would have helped, but I couldn't even do that. Still, there was a living to earn.

Each morning of that cold winter, I caught the streetcar going downtown. At least it was warm. The rear section had a hot metal stove with its chimney sticking through the roof, not unlike those I'd known in barracks. I scoured the papers looking for vacancies. More than one advertisement, most days, said 'Englishmen need not apply'. I trudged through the icy snow, bent against the freezing wind, from interview to interview.

One evening, the daughter of the house I was in, Dorothy, anxious, no doubt, for me to leave, said, "You'll never get a job. You English are too modest or truthful. Whatever they ask," she advised, "say you can do it. They'll cut whatever you say in half anyway."

Next day I did as she said. I had three offers. Home again, in the warmth, we talked them over. One was with an oil company. I didn't want that; I'd just got away from one. The second was an insurance company; safe, I thought, but dull. The third was the opposite. It was to be the production manager of a new movie magazine. "But," I said, "I have no idea how to do it." "Oh, never mind," Dorothy replied, "you'll soon pick it up. Anyway, people there will help you."

So that was the job I took. At Reading I had learnt how to measure type. I knew the difference between an 'em' and an 'en', and what a 'pica' was. I could see the difference between Bodoni and Perpetua, so the work wasn't wholly foreign, only ninety per cent. The editor, Vic Kelly, who wore what I thought then were cheap, tanned double-breasted suits, and who had a small, dark moustache, but also had several children and a peaceful earth-mother wife, and Bill Lytle, a freelance designer who did the layout, helped me through, as Dorothy said they would.

Not only did I mark up text and rush it to the printers, but within a few weeks I was choosing pictures, writing captions and even a fashion page. I published the first picture, certainly in Canada, of Marilyn Monroe wearing only a sack. She was little known then. My caption said she would look good in anything.

Most of the material poured in from the Hollywood studios. We subbed what were no more than publicity puffs, trying to make them look sharp and original. The words of one actress have stayed forever: "Never," she was quoted as saying, "believe your own publicity." That is good advice. I have known numbers of people in the design world who go to great lengths to have nice things written about themselves and their firms, then believe every word that is published.

Movie News was the title of the magazine. Pocket-sized, it was published every other Monday. As well as articles about stars and reviews of new films, there was a theatre page. In May, 1952, I see that Honor Blackman had her first role on the stage in Canada in Jean Paul Sartre's *Crime of Passion.* The actor who became famous as the father in the TV series *Bonanza,* Lorne Greene, was in the same play. That must have been his break. When I first arrived in Canada, he read the news for a local radio station.

We covered the Academy Awards. Humphrey Bogart was best actor in 1951 for his part in *The African Queen*. Vivien Leigh was best actress (*A Streetcar Named Desire*). Best picture, with a clutch of awards, was *An American in Paris*.

It was all fun. But the magazine had a fatal flaw. Each issue carried a competition with a $1000 prize. There were pictures of twelve stars. You had to write their order of popularity. One issue in April 1952 pictured Doris Day, Alec Guinness, Rhonda Fleming, Montgomery Clift, Paulette Goddard, Robert Young, Jane Russell ('Mean, moody and magnificent' was how she was described in a film called *The Outlaw*), James Cagney, Joan Fontaine, Stewart Granger, June Allyson and Alan Ladd who, it was said, was so short that he had to stand on a box when he was filmed with an actress. Or she stood in a trench; it amounted to the same thing.

On Saturday evenings we drove in Vic's station waggon through the Canadian winter to one popcorn-smelling cinema after another, sometimes hours away. Half way through the programme, the house lights would go up. Vic, nervously at first, would go on the stage, shake hands with the manager, then announce the winner. He would say something and hand over the cheque. The trouble was, the magazine couldn't afford it. One Thursday the proprietor came in and sacked us all. No notice, of course, nothing like redundancy pay. I don't think he even paid that week's wages.

Pressing against the icy wind of more streets, climbing more stairs for interviews, I got a job with a book publisher, Longmans, Green. Book publishing: what could be more interesting? Well worth leaving that dull job in the accounting room of an oil company in London... except I was to be in another accounts office. The job, I now see, was almost the same; working out discounts on orders.

The company had two lists, one for the book trade, the other for schools. Although it had some famous authors on its list (Pearl S. Buck was one I processed a thousand times), steady money came from school books. Whoever wrote *Geometry Part 11*, say, received royalties year after year.

Sitting next to me at a long table was a tall, fair-haired, slump-shouldered Englishman from Oxford University

Press. There, he told me, he had been sent to Manchester to give lunch to the author of successful travel books about Africa. "It must be wonderful, Africa," began my friend, "do tell me about it." The author looked at his plate. Awkwardly he confessed he had never been there.

My neighbour hated Canada. "They call Oxford the city of dreaming spires," he muttered. "They should call Toronto the city of screaming tyres." His unhappiness made him heavy and sour, his lugubrious speech shafted increasingly with giggles of near hysteria.

Behind a glass door sat an editor. Occasionally he stepped from his room to speak to the air in front of him, addressing a remark to no one in particular. Mr Burton, perhaps that was his name, was short, plump, with a round pink face and full white moustache. In summer he wore a linen suit and panama hat, as though he had just stepped in on his way to Lord's. "If you are going to write a book," he said to the far window, "you'd better do it before you're thirty." Research he was doing suggested that most famous authors had published by then. I made that a goal and just met it.

Being short-staffed, no doubt, they asked me to read new manuscripts that came, several a week, without warning. It was a foolish error. One book I read was by the aged widow of a Baptist minister. She described her girlhood in Ontario sixty years before. Coming home one day from playing tennis, she met, on the verandah of her parents house, a young man. She was so struck by him that not only did they marry, but from that day, she never called him or referred to him as anything but Mr.... as he had been introduced. Her husband became a missionary among Indians in far parts of Northern Ontario, Manitoba and Alberta. That was the life she described. I tossed aside the manuscript and turned to the next. My notes to the editor dismissed it. Months later another publisher took the book and had a bestseller on his hands. Still, I am told that, like fishermen, every publisher has his 'one that got away' story.

By then I had a front room on the first floor of a house in a leafy road north of a cross-street called St Clair. Molly wrote. Her year's teaching course was coming to an end. Could I suggest schools in Toronto she might apply to ? I sent eight names. Molly, by post, was offered five jobs.

Waiting several hours at the dock to meet Molly when she arrived in the high humidity of a hot Montreal summer, I was a disappointment. My pressed suit was crumpled, new, white Dacron drip-dry shirt soaked, tie torn off, hair short; what had she come to ?

She came to a very good, preppy, girls' school called Bishop Strachan, to teach geography. The school, founded in 1867, the year of Canada's confederation, was solid, built of granite in what they called the 'collegiate gothic' style, ivy-covered, with acres of well-kept grounds. It was Church of England and strict. The headmistress, Grace McNaughton, was a Scot. Girls wore 'middy' tops, like sailors, short, pleated blue skirts, and black stockings. When I went to collect Molly in the evening, they called from windows, "Hi, lover boy."

Molly spent several happy years at the school. And we were in love. Crunching along snow-packed pavements on black nights to eat with friends or go to the cinema or eat apple pie à la mode on the yellow-topped tables of the drugstore in what was called Forest Hill village, a strip of shops nearby, our life was full of fun, dreams, promise.

We married in December 1952 in a Catholic church. Our reception was held in the large house of a fellow teacher. Because he was of Ulster Protestant stock, our friend's father wouldn't join us. He stayed upstairs. That was Toronto. Yet his bigotry became ironic and tragic. Within a year or two his daughter ran away to the Far East with a Catholic where she died from a rare disease.

Molly and I flew to New York for our honeymoon. We danced to Guy Lombardo and his Royal Canadians at the Roosevelt Hotel, shiveringly window-shopped along Fifth Avenue, laughed at a Yorkshire terrier wearing a mink coat in Saks, bought leather picture frames and a writing set in Mark Cross, were given a free meal while we watched ice skaters at the Rockefeller Plaza. We went to the Radio City Music Hall to see the Rockettes, a line of long-legged chorus girls who danced with perfect precision. We visited the Frick and other galleries.

Appropriately, we saw Frank Loesser's *Guys and Dolls*, the original production with Vivian Blaine and Stubby Kaye.

When you meet a gent
paying all kinds of rent
for a flat that could flatten
the Taj Mahal ,
Call it sad, call it funny,
It's better than even money
The guy's only doing it for some doll.

Imagine being able to coin images like 'a flat that could flatten the Taj Mahal', or control words as well. There is more. Miss Adelaide, the heroine suffers permanent sniffles. She is reading a medical book at her dressing table at the Hot Box. She sings: (Sneeze)

It says here in this book
'The average unmarried female
Basically insecure,
Due to some long frustration
May react
With psychosomatic symptoms difficult to endure
Affecting the upper respiratory tract.'

In other words (here he goes),
Just from waiting around
for that plain little band of gold
A person
Can develop a cold.

I look at the craft of turning long words into those we use every day. The plain way to say things. George Orwell said of Arthur Ransome that he wrote prose "like a window panel". He meant it was effortless to read and understand. Especially when I give talks that is my aim, scarce-achieved. I write and cut, time and again. The snag, I have found, is that if you say things simply listeners think you are saying simple things.

Sixteen

Sorry, Mozart

Our flat in Toronto wouldn't have flattened the Taj Mahal, although we enjoyed it. It was the first floor of one of the settled, comfortable houses in Forest Hill, 305 Russell Hill Road, a few yards from the school. In the front was a large, parquet-floored bedroom. Across a bare hall we had a small, panelled, sitting room with an open fireplace. Behind was our kitchen. A former conservatory, glazed all around, it had no running water. We got that from the bathroom around the corner.

Forest Hill is an area north of a main cross street in Toronto, St. Clair, and west of the city's spine, Yonge Street. Houses there are large, solid, satisfied; set back behind lawns that run forward to tree-shaded pavements. It is a prosperous place. The local greystone church, Grace Church on the Hill, is no less well-to-do. It stands almost mid-way between two exclusive schools, Bishop Strachan for girls and Upper Canada College for boys. On Sundays, lines of shining Cadillacs and Buicks parked along the verges, under the great maples. Their owners, mink-wrapped, came regularly and gave generously. Both were the social things to do. The church responded handsomely. Any want of humility was more than compensated for by the comforting credo that it was godly to be rich. Hadn't God shown, by the favours they enjoyed, what He thought of Grace Church's parishioners ?

By now I was a writer on an employee newspaper, searching, so slowly, for letters on an ancient, noisy, typewriter, then pecking them one... at... a... time. With three or four colleagues around, I now had my own desk in a warm, brightly-lit, open plan office.

The company was Canadian General Electric, subsidiary of mighty GE. It had six plants in Canada. Each week, a writer in each factory produced four pages of local plant news. A department in the head office, where I worked, wrote the outside pages and sometimes a centre spread that was common to all. The whole endeavour was exemplary. If you see employee newspapers, even today, so often they show the boss doing this and the boss doing that. People in the firm hardly count. GE's way was better. The stories were only about the people, or written through them. Directors rarely appeared. As impressive, there was little blarney. Our editor, a busy Englishman with a large head and short, pumping legs as he rushed everywhere, whose whole life this was, believed and had us believe, that he was running a newspaper, not a puff-paper.

Morale, however, was central to our aim. One plant was building generators. Those for one big order were being painted white. Why was that? They were part of a huge hydro-electric scheme in the north of Canada. We wrote about that, showing how people in CGE were helping to build Canada, a popular theme. It was the old idea: "What are you doing ?" a man working in the road is asked. "I'm digging a trench," he answers grumpily. A second man is asked. "I'm digging a trench to take a pipe," he says. A third worker is asked. "I'm building a cathedral," he replies with pride. "In this trench, you see, goes a pipe that will be part of a new cathedral."

I did my first interviews. One lady I met was a shy, fair-haired Estonian in the statistical department. She could use an abacus faster than an adding machine. That gave us the chance to talk about her and how her work fitted in to the overall picture.

Market research, just being explored, was a revelation. A young, bespectacled man called Jack Roberts was the pioneer trying to convince executives of its value. I interviewed him. He explained: each year people in every department have to write their budgets and plans for the coming year. How do they do it ? They see what has happened in the current year, then add a bit, maybe ten per cent, for growth. But suppose the market isn't like that, said Jack. They'd never know. Think about light switches, he went on. Take Quebec. Say we sold 100,000 there this year. Add ten per cent, that's 110,000. But then look at the new 'housing starts'. If you see those figures you will have a much better idea how many switches you need to make. Our market could be several times our estimate. Indeed, he found it to be nearly three times as large as the company thought. I accepted the argument then and have ever since. Thanks to Jack, though decades later, I bought several market research companies. Even now, six firms in ten in Britain do no market research. The main reason they give is that they "know enough about their customers already." Jack would have doubted that, and so do I.

Never any use at office politics, there was one trick I acquired then. Whatever we wrote had to be approved by a director. As soon as you laid the papers on his desk, I noticed, he picked up a pen. He wouldn't have done his job diligently, was the impression, unless he corrected something. I soon put mistakes in for him to find. Then he was happy and so was I. My eternal prose was untouched.

At that time there was talk of atomic war; the trigger I don't recall. But it was serious enough for a newly-married American friend to keep a station waggon, full of food and blankets and with a gun, at the city limits, and for me to join the Militia. A tubby advertising man, a major in the reserve, offered me the rank of officer-cadet. Even in this field, I remember thinking, they bargain. Because I insisted, they admitted me as a lieutenant in a mounted regiment of the Royal Canadian Artillery (Reserve). To do so I had to give up my British commission, receiving a new, Canadian one from the Governor General.

It was all a waste. We met on Monday evenings in a drill hall, standing around uselessly. There was nothing to be said for it, except that once in a while one went away for a week-end course. On one I took a party of men to Camp Borden where we learnt to drive tanks, roaring and ploughing and plunging through deep snow, line abreast.

Canada was smaller and meaner-minded than it is now. The population was little over twelve million. In Toronto, a large, sky-scrapered modern city today, there were fewer than one million people, the majority with British roots. Many had a chip on their shoulder. But they faced a dilemma, a dichotomy. On one hand they were still trying to get away from Britain and resented her. On the other hand, they struggled to resist the inexorable and inevitable impact of American commercial power. To signal the Canadian wish to be on its own there was a competition for a new flag, to get rid of the Union Jack. It was won by the maple leaf design we see now.

'Canada for the Canadians' was the cry, one which led to absurdities. The Governor General, Vincent Massey, the actor's brother, put his name to a decree which said that henceforth half the music taught in all Canadian schools was to be Canadian. Sorry, Mozart, beg your pardon, Brahms.

In *The Night Manager,* John Le Carré twice referred to the province we lived in as "stodgy Ontario". Toronto, its main city, was known, variously, as 'hog-town' (Canada Packers and the big meat yards were there) and 'Toronto the Good'. It was a Scottish Presbyterian and Ulster Protestant town. The main department store, T. Eaton, with branches across the country, pulled blinds down its windows on Sundays and was said never to have employed a Catholic. Englishmen complained that, even in a bar, you couldn't have a drink standing up. You had to sit. Nor could you drink out of doors. Officious neighbours could call the police if they saw you having a drink in your own garden.

The tallest building in the city was the best hotel, the Royal York , now dwarfed and hard to find. A friend, like the rest of us young and broke, expansively took a girl to dinner there and was both surprised and alarmed to be treated as a prince, shown to the best table and offered the best of everything. Later he learnt why. In Toronto lived a millionaire with the same name. The head waiter confused them.

There was a castle in Toronto.

Called Casa Loma, it was turreted, conical-spired, seemingly medieval Transylvanian, where bats or even vampires might flutter from the high windows. The dreamer who built it, a wealthy man who had raised his own regiment to serve in France in the First World War, was unlucky. As soon as it was completed, the city passed an ordinance to impose exorbitant taxes on 'all castles within the city limits'. So he never lived in it, never used the gold-plated taps in his bathroom, nor did his wife use the silver-plated taps in hers. We could visit the castle, though. "The doors you are passing through," a guide intoned, "came from France. They cost $280,000. The mural on your left is Italian. It cost $173,000. This master bedroom is from a Venetian palazzo. It cost $434,000...."

Perhaps changed since, Toronto then was all about making a buck. Cultural life, now flowering, was limited. Ed Mirvish who, in 1982 bought London's Old Vic, sight unseen, and spent £2 million on its facelift, was still building his wealth with 'Honest Ed's' a discount shop in a poor part of town. However, a Victorian theatre, the Royal Alexander, was restored. We saw *The Boy Friend* there, with its English cast. The hero pushed his way through the curtains before the show started to speak from the edge of the stage. "The English," he apologised, "aren't very good at dates. There was 1066, of course and the Armada was in 1588. Then", he continued, "there was 1776." He looked down at his hands. "That was an off year for us." Then came the twenties. "England didn't have the 'Roaring Twenties'," he pointed out, because "in England ....nothing ever roars. Ours were more like the 'twittering twenties'."

In the ice-hockey stadium, Maple Leaf Gardens, we saw Margot Fonteyn in *The Firebird* and two English people started a new theatre, The Crest. But mostly it was the cinema we went to.

Toronto's first coffee bar opened, the Concerto on Bloor Street. Lance Percival, later to be seen weekly on British television in *That Was The Week That Was* (TW 3), wandered between the tables strumming a guitar and singing calypsos. The Concerto was owned by a Brigadier Claude Dewhurst, something of a pretender who made his name at the end of the war, racing around Berlin in a white Jaguar. He became foreign and military correspondent on Canadian radio. After Suez, as a member of the Imperial Officers Association of Canada, I was among a dinner audience who heard him explain the invasion. One of the guests present was the British Royal Marine general who had been in charge of the landings. His face grew purple as the ignorant travesty went on.

Through the company and Molly's school, our social life opened. One journalist from my firm found it hard to believe Molly taught geography. "Where," he would ask, "is (say) Port au Prince?" "I really have no idea," Molly would reply. "What," he wanted to know, "is the population of Rio de Janeiro." "Not the faintest," Molly would say. "When I need to know anything like that I look it up." That didn't satisfy his scepticism a bit. He looked up military details to trick me about that too. "On which side," he asked me carefully, "is the plume on a Grenadier guardsman's bearskin ?"

One parent Molly met at school wrote novels under her married name, Vicky Metcalf. Her husband, working for Garfield Weston, ran Loblaws, a supermarket chain. According to his wife, in all their married life he had never taken her out. Then one day, a bank holiday, he invited her for a drive. She was so astonished and delighted she 'phoned her friends. When they reached the highway, the husband said, "Now, you count all the poster sites on your side of the road, and I'll count all the poster sites on mine." When he found what he wanted to know they returned home.

In summer we had tennis parties, using the deserted courts of the school as our own. In winter Molly skated and I played squash at the university. There, too, I went on an accountancy course. It availed little. I remember the instructor explaining patiently that a debit is a credit and a credit is a debit. Although I have since chaired a public company and been treasurer of more than one body, I'm still not quite clear what that means, or why it matters.

Winter followed winter. I became used to digging out my car, buried beneath overnight snow, then slithering and sliding to work on icy roads, windscreen wipers thumping, thumping, thumping, as soft snow fell. In summer, top down, elbow resting on the hot car door, we drove through now familiar streets, past drugstores and supermarkets and cinemas, jewellery and clothes and fur stores and car lots and the church on the corner, braking without thought as the rattling streetcars hissed to a halt to let their passengers climb down.

Many young English people started careers and, often,

married life, in Toronto. They moved into newly-built apartments which smelt of fresh plaster, then filled them, bit by bit, with furniture, 'aloominum' pots and pans, and prints of the Impressionists. Yet most never quite felt they were there to stay, or belonged. We were looked on, and felt, foreign.

The United States was scarcely two hours away, and New York the glistening mountain-top of city sophistication. We watched Jack Paar on late night television and took *The New Yorker*. We swapped the wit of the legendary round table at the Algonquin, where Robert Benchley, S.J. Perelman, Dorothy Parker and Alexander Woolcott, whose offices were across the road, were said to lunch. Two examples I remember, one I often associate with Margaret Thatcher. Perelman wrote an article about the then rising ranks of women who traded what might be called 'the gentle comforts of the marital bed for the hurly-burly of the chaise longue' when they shed domesticity to join the tailor-suited fight to the executive boardroom. He headed it 'The hand that cradles the rock'.

Dorothy Parker (Men don't make passes/At girls who wear glasses) was asked, over lunch, to turn the word 'horticulture' into a well-known phrase or saying. After a brief pause she replied, "You can lead a whore to culture but you cannot make her think." Hearing that Calvin Coolidge, a dry and ascetic president of the United States, was dead, Dorothy Parker asked, "How could they tell ?"

With her first paycheck, Molly bought me a Smith Corona portable typewriter. I began freelance writing, tapping in the evenings and weekends not only non-fiction articles, but also dreadful short stories.

They, as Benny Green said of certain songs, were "not worth the paper they were rotten on". You must expect to paper your walls with rejection slips, I'd read, before you start to sell articles. That is a sound warning. But gradually the balance swung. We went to Washington at Easter. I wrote about that. Again, as happily and appropriately as seeing *Guys and Dolls* in New York, we saw *Call Me Madam,* where Ethel Merman played the part of Perle Mesta, said to be the inspiration for 'the hostess with the mostest'. The film opens with an apparent newsreel clip of a great banquet, tables glittering with silver, stretching into the distance. There, facing into the camera, Merman made the remark that made Mesta famous: "I'll take the check."

The English *Geographic Magazine* published a piece I wrote about the Canadian oil industry. On pages following was an article by a James Callaghan MP, future prime minister, about oil pollution of the sea. For a photographic magazine I wrote a monthly series. And there were others.

Off Toronto is an island. Today it is chic, built-up and busy. Then it was neglected, overgrown, seedy. You reached Centre Island on an old steam ferry. Just a few minutes across the lake from down-town, it seemed to me a wonderful place to live, close yet a world away. Although I meant to write about the people who lived among the scrub in the collapsing timber houses on the island, a marine artist I met changed my mind. He had a passion: to restore a 2196-ton ship, built in 1907, that had been 'the Queen of the Lakes'. She was called the *Cayuga*. For nearly fifty years she carried passengers between Toronto, Niagara and Queenstown, one of ten or twelve ships that sailed daily. In the 1950s no ships did so. People who lived in Toronto, on the edge of a great lake, were shore-bound.

Alan Howard, the artist, wanted to put that right. Bay Street financiers were uninterested, the mayor thought the *Cayuga* should be sunk off-shore to make a sea wall. But Howard persisted and I believe the *Cayuga*, spruced up, did sail again.

Then one day I had an idea: what about a travel programme on the radio ? The local stations were parochial and dull, one ad squeezing out another. What I'd do, I thought, was write about cities. The radio station would sell the programme to TCA, the airline (now Air Canada), and others in the travel business. I put the idea to CKFH, one of the better radio stations. Remarkably, they invited me in and, with no fuss, put me in a studio in front of a microphone. Tight with fear, I read a ten minute talk I had prepared about Paris. Without me knowing, they had put suitable French music behind my voice. We listened to a play-back. The music made all the difference; it sounded quite good. Next day, I had a letter inviting me to write thirty-nine programmes, three a week for thirteen weeks. The task was too daunting to tackle.

Seventeen

Let the Water out of the Pool

Tom Patterson was a remarkable man. Of many articles I struggled to write at night and over weekends, the one I like most was about him. He grew up in Stratford, Ontario (population, when I wrote, of 19,000). Lying on the banks of the Avon, he wondered why his Stratford shouldn't perform Shakespeare as well as its namesake in England. Why not have a Shakespeare festival ? He approached the City Fathers. They agreed he should explore the idea and gave him a bountiful $100 for research. With the money, he went to New York to ask for the advice and support of Laurence Olivier, then playing there. Olivier wouldn't see him. With the few dollars remaining, Patterson 'phoned Tyrone Guthrie, in Ireland. Guthrie listened, then said, "If you want to make money I'll tell you how to do it. Get a line of dancing girls from New York. Put a band and some lighting behind them... though, of course, I won't be with you. But if," he continued, "you want to produce the finest Shakespeare in the world, I'll be with you all the way."

In the summer of 1953 the first Shakespearian festival was held in Stratford, Ontario, in a blue and terracotta tent holding 1500 people, said to have been the second largest ever built. Alec Guinness turned down a Hollywood contract to come. Irene Worth from the Old Vic, known in Canada for her performance in New York in *The Cocktail Party,* led the cast with him. They played *Richard lll* and *All's Well.* Tanya Moisewitsch designed the costumes,

Tyrone Guthrie, tall, patrician, popular, produced with a freshness and dash seldom seen before. One Canadian actor in the cast was asked when he started acting. "June 2nd, 1953," he replied, "when I started to work under Mr Guthrie."

The stage was an 'apron', jutting into the middle of the tent. No one in the audience was more than fifty feet from the action. It swirled on the stage. Actors ran down aisles beside you, the play was all around you, an exhilarating experience.

Taking notes for my article, I looked at the cars parked in lines across a field. There were number plates from every state in the United States. Patterson's dream came true.

Summer comes to Toronto on May 24th. That was Queen Victoria's birthday. Whatever the temperature (often hot for weeks before) that is the day you put away your winter clothes, wrestle the heavy snow tyres off your car, unscrew the storm windows and clip mosquito screens in their place, and open your summer cottage. It was a Canadian version of 'ne'er cast a clout 'till May is out'.

The cottage we went to was on an old Indian island in Georgian Bay, part of an area of Lake Ontario known as Thousand Islands. To reach it you drove north of Toronto for maybe an hour and a half, then took a boat with a screeching outboard tearing the silence as you roared and buffeted your way across a still lake for another forty minutes. You slowed, and bumped against an old wooden jetty.

From there the only land you could see was some miles away. It had belonged to Orville Wright, the first flyer, and was said to be deserted since his death.

Climbing up a narrow path, twisting around granite rocks, you came to the house. Built at the end of the last century, it was timber, with a high pitched roof, one big room with kitchen and bedrooms sliced from it, a screen-covered porch where we sat in the evenings and a privy outside at the back.

It belonged to Mary Kirby, the secretary at school and close friend of ours. She had been given it by an admirer. That is all that was said and all we knew. Mary, then perhaps in her fifties, was short, gay, with sparkling light blue eyes, always happy and effortlessly able. She could spend the morning with you on the beach, slip away, then ten minutes later serve lunch for a dozen people. We made rostas for washing up and dusting and other household chores, it is true, but everything was light-hearted fun. To me, Mary was a mother to yearn for.

Her husband, Fred, was tall, lean, severe, a modest banker with silver hair and bright blue eyes in a tanned face; tanned because he spent his days stripped to the waist on the roof, always finding holes to repair and probably something to grumble about as well. Then, in the evenings as we sat on the porch sipping a drink, he spoke, in his deep, slow voice, of his dream. Never realised, it was to buy a small hotel in Jamaica.

They had a son, Bruce, who became a mathematics lecturer at Queen's College in Kingston, Ontario. (The syllabus there suited him. Three days a week his lectures were at eight and nine in the morning, so he was finished by ten. The other two days, his lectures were at nine and ten, so his work was done by eleven). On the island, together, we composed stories in the style of *Time* Magazine. So he was

Bruce J (John) Kirby (26). He didn't step out of his car or climb out of it, but 'hopped from his Loewy-designed tan-coloured Studebaker'. Canasta was popular then. We played that each day as well as timeless Scrabble. One of us would lay down a word, then leave, to swim, lie on the beach, row the boat, read. Hours later the other would complete his word. This timeless test led to huge scores.

The island was rocky, covered in dense woodland, dangerous with poison ivy. (A brother-in-law of Mary's a scientist who worked in the Toronto museum, ate some poison ivy one day to see its effect. It made him very ill indeed.) The island, too, was inhabited by raccoons the size of foxes which, with long, delicate paws, ruffled through the garbage after dark. Twice a week a chugging boat deposited groceries on the jetty. Apart from that arrival we saw no one, we were alone.

North Ontario was empty then. Once in a while we chugged across the lake to a headland. There, long since overgrown, rose the remains of a wooden hotel. It had been built by a worker in a timber yard in Yorkshire, who

had eloped with the owner's daughter. They had come to this remote spot. When he died it was winter, the ground too frozen to dig. His wife had nowhere to put his body. She propped him outside her back door until spring came. These brave pioneers had two sons. One, Wilf France, brought the groceries. The other lived alone on the upper floor of his ramshackle house, the stairs to reach him broken. The downstairs rooms were filled with his miserly passion, his collection: a towering mound of dead dry-cell batteries and empty Carnation milk cans.

Fred Kirby, far from wealthy, bought an expensive picture. Well beyond his means, it was as he put it, for 'his old age', an extra pension. The painting, of a sunlit bay, was displayed proudly over the mantelpiece in Fred's small sitting-room in Toronto. Its story was poignant. Although the artist, an Italian, was enjoying considerable acclaim in Canada, he had never been there. Sadly, he was bed-ridden in Capri.

I was alarmed. It was quite clear to me that the picture was worthless. What should one do ? By now Paddy Gunn, who had been in the art department at Reading, had become assistant curator of the art gallery in London, Ontario. I 'phoned her. "That's curious," she told me. "People keep calling to ask about this painter, and we can't find a thing about him. None of our books has a word..."

That was that. Months later, Paddy called. "You remember that painter you asked about ? Well, I've tracked him down." Paddy had been to an art gallery in a small Ontario town. The shop was empty, a curtain drawn across the back of it. Paddy, unable to resist the smell of fresh oil-paint, peeked behind the curtain. There were several pictures, still wet, destined to be by the Italian master. They were being painted and smuggled into the reputable art market by a group of Ukrainian immigrants.

There was a final step: should I tell my friend, who was so proud of his picture ? I didn't dare. I told his son, hoping he would find a way to persuade his father to part with it.

Through Mary we met two mean men who lived together. They were known as 'the millionaires', as they may have been. One evening they asked us to their house, not to eat but to see slides they had taken of a recent trip to Venice. To save money, they had gone off season, in winter. Their slides showed one grey, rain-drenched view after another. But in between their own they inserted slides they had bought. These radiated the glorious light and warmth of Venice. "That," they repeated to underline the point and seeing no irony,"is what it looks like in summer."

I suspect Canada had a more innocent air than it has now. It was fewer than ninety years, and those marked mainly by two world wars, from the days when the nation was founded. Quebec wasn't as divisive as it has become. Provinces distant and unalike were linked by rail, around the great lakes, across the great bread basket, over the Rockies, up to the Yukon. There were Eskimaux trapping seals, Indians on reserves, farmers and factory workers and doctors and lawyers and shopkeepers spread across a harsh continent. Back from the war, they shared a sense of building, not only their own lives but still forging a nation. In the far north the DEW line (distant early warning) was being built. Young men went to amass money. In the cities there was growth, growth, growth. Miles of new suburban housing sprawled across a treeless landscape. And always there were new car lots with shiny Chevrolets, fluttering pennants, special deals.

There were timber and oil and minerals galore. The stock market was ablaze with penny stocks that made millions. When someone found a deposit — oil or mineral — he would raise money on the exchange to fund drilling. Most found nothing, but some succeeded. Then shares that had cost a few cents, within the reach of most people, multiplied a hundredfold. There was a craze to look for uranium. You could buy a geiger-counter in the department store.

One weekend two boys went off with their geiger-counters. They returned home bubbling with excitement. They had found uranium. As they ate the supper their mother cooked for them they planned to go down to the claims office next morning to stake their claim. When they did, they were crestfallen to hear that the land had already been claimed; someone had been in a few minutes before. Their mother had overheard their conversation and beaten them to it.

We had an English friend who was employed by International Nickel to find new deposits. With his young wife, he had come from Peshawar. With two or three assistants and a cook, they set up camp in the icy wilderness of Northern Canada. One night his wife, Bridget, woke to see a bear coming into their tent. "What did you do ?" I asked. "I shot it," she said simply, as though she was explaining to the vicar how she made plum jam. Bridget was in the same tradition as those stalwart Victorian ladies who, bonnet firmly planted on their head, rode across the scorching Australian desert or painted watercolours among tribesmen in Africa, women of character.

Hugh and Bridget liked isolation. As he was successful

and their work came to an end, more people were flown into the camp. Bridget complained, "There must have been thirty people there. It was awful." From one site they were a week late leaving. That was enough for the thick ice to thaw. As they crunched across a wide lake in a snowmobile, the ice below them creaked and cracked. At any moment they could sink. They sped for all they were worth, hatches open, holding their breath.

We knew another man who prospected for minerals. More than once he left home without telling a soul where he was going. Secrecy was important. After a few weeks his wife put ads in big newspapers around the world asking him to come home. Reading an old book about Ireland, he saw mention of copper coins. Where, he wondered, had the copper come from ? Without a word he went to Eire. After weeks of searching, he arranged to see the Prime Minister. He threw a large map across the Prime Minister's desk. "You've got copper here," he announced. "Tons of it. What I want is your permission to drain this lake," He pointed to the map. It was Lake Killarney.

To our joy, Freddie came to stay. Being Freddie, within a couple of weeks he won five silver dollars on a radio show. He volunteered for the Royal Canadian Air Force, still determined to fly. But he was tragically unlucky. Our father became ill. Freddie went home, so soon, to run Daddy's business.

I flew over at Christmas, in a BOAC Stratocruiser, landing at Prestwick, in the gentle moist winds of Scotland, then continued down to London. Heathrow's terminal then was a collection of asbestos-roofed, cream-painted brick huts along the northern perimeter. Inside, seats were wicker. Irises in tall 1930s vases stood on glass-topped tables.

The family was there to meet me. We drove the few miles to Iver where Daddy, released from hospital for the holiday, was at home. No one would say what was wrong with him. The doctor, (I think the only person we knew who was Jewish, another reflection on our boyhood) who had been Hergowitz and was now called Harding, thought it best not to tell them.

We had to know. "It is better you don't know," he told me when I visited him. Perhaps with some North American aggressiveness now flowing through me, I insisted. It was cancer, he said, though he enjoined me not to tell Daddy. That advice, typical of the time, was mad and cruel. Just when we should have been closest we were farthest apart, pretending to each other. Sitting on a piano stool, already shrunken in his collar and suit, he looked forward to going to *Osiris*, a boat he moored at St Mawes, even wondering whether he should buy another boat. Whether he knew that would never happen but was determined to keep our spirits up I do not know, but it was awful.

Later I flew over again to see him for the last time. Molly went to help look after him in Iver for the whole of her summer vacation, a horrid, brave and generous thing to do. We wrote every day, letters I keep.

As he grew worse, my mother's faith in doctors faltered. Determined to keep Daddy alive, she fed him strange, dusty herbs, what would now be called 'alternative medicine'. For a while there seemed progress. But no. He died in pain. Faith in the church fell away too. God had let mother down. She turned to spiritualism. At her first seance she was comforted. "There is someone here," the medium called, "with a broken third finger on his left hand." That, my mother recognised, was her father who had been trodden on by a horse. Next time, her brother claimed attention. "Freddie is all right," he told the medium.

The same medium, in Belgrave Square, said she was present when Lord Dowding, who led Fighter Command during the Battle of Britain, "witnessed" the death of two American airmen high over the Pacific.

From writing about employee relations for Canadian General Electric, I joined a marketing magazine as a news reporter. Although less brazen, it had the same format and role as *Campaign*, the British advertising weekly. "Every day," I wrote at that time, "I meet interesting people." And, I was surprised to read recently, began to get good stories. Letters say, more than once, "Maggie (Maggie Brown owned the magazine) says this one should go on the front page." One was about the introduction of the Vickers Viscount, first turbo-prop aircraft, into Canada. Trans-Canada Airways, now multi-lingually named Air Canada, had bought it and were mounting a big advertising campaign. For hours I wrestled at my desk to say that in a headline. Then the editor of the *Financial Post* came over to me. I told him my worry. He looked at the copy, picked up a pencil and at once scrawled across the top 'New whiz plane gets TCA push'.

We loved headlines. The famous one came from *Variety*, the American showbiz paper. It ran: 'HIX STIX NIX PIX'. When we gave up trying to work it out, someone explained. Fewer country people were going to the cinema, it meant. Respecting the Duke of Edinburgh though I do, my favourite modern headline was written when the Duke made an infelicitous remark in China. The headline in the

Daily Mirror summed it up by adding just one letter to a phrase known to every reader. THE GREAT WALLY OF CHINA it splashed across the front page. When the Queen had a good horse in the Derby, the *Sun's* headline was ONE'S WON.

My career in design may trace from that job. Whenever a design story came up it was assumed that I was the one to write it. Because I had studied fine art, I was the one-eyed man in the land of the blind. What I found was that design and art are different disciplines. In time I also discovered yet another flaw in myself. While others could write about subjects until they were experts, I couldn't. I needed to get engaged, to do it myself. Within three years I had joined a local design firm and within six had started my own design company.

Back from the island one hot Sunday evening I found a message to call an Australian who worked beside me. "Don't go to the office," he told me. "The firm has been sold. Go to 481 University Avenue." Next morning I did. That was Maclean-Hunter, the largest magazine publisher in Canada. *Macleans* magazine was its flagship, edited by Pierre Burton, a well-known commentator and author in Canada. The *Financial Post*, a weekly business newspaper, was another of its publications. *Marketing*, the magazine I was on, joined a stable of a dozen or more trade publications.

Most of the editors, by chance, were English. The editor of *Bus & Truck* was Arthur Hailey, who went on to write *Airport* and a list of bestsellers. Sandy Barrie, who had been a pilot in the RAF and then an architect from the AA who later, back in England, wrote a series of successful boys' books and a seriously-researched, revealing, book about men who dug tunnels under enemy trenches in the First World War, edited *Design Engineering*. A magazine for the electrical trade was edited by Cedric Jennings, whose father had been editor of the *Straits Times* in Singapore. Cedric, short, with heavy horn-rimmed glasses and a loud, vital voice, was a campaigning journalist. In Canada at that time there were many fires. Houses built of wood were the victims. The reason, Cedric's research showed, was that people were buying more and more appliances and overloading their electrical systems. What was needed was what he termed 'Adequate wiring'. His campaign became national, never far from the news. Then Cedric gave up editing to start a company. It was called Adequate Wiring Ltd.

One of the salesmen, a Scot, made history. He was the first non-graduate to be admitted to the Harvard Business School. Three vacations in a row he went to Cambridge (Massachusetts) to see the Dean and professors. Each time he was told that this was a post-graduate school; they simply could not accept him. He argued that businessmen with less education needed Harvard more than most. He persuaded them to take him as an experiment. If he was not up to the course they would all soon see. Happily, he passed out in the top ten. His point was made and remains Harvard policy.

I was promoted to assistant editor, then managing editor of a magazine called *Canadian Packaging*, the start of several happy, busy, fulfilled years among close friends. The publisher was Jack Daley, a warm-hearted, deeply religious Catholic with a large family. Always positive, encouraging, optimistic, he was a wonderful salesman, who drove the magazine to more and more success. His boss used to come around when each new issue was published. There were we, so proud of the stories we had written; the pictures, layout, every caption carefully-crafted. As we waited, hoping for his approval, the boss, without a smile, picked up the new issue to weigh it in his hand. If it felt heavy, which meant there was lots of advertising, he'd say, "That's a good issue." Still unsmiling, he walked off. On my shelves is a book by Stanley Unwin called *The Truth About Publishing*. The truth about magazine publishing is that boss weighing the ads.

Pressure on people like Jack, concerned with revenue, was inexorable. His boss had a bad habit that helped him up the ladder. He wrote critical and false memos to his colleagues, drawing attention to a failing of theirs. He sent a copy to his managing director yet, somehow, inadvertently, forgot to send the original to the man accused. More than once the managing director, saddened by the sorry collection of memos in front of him, called the victim to his office. The colleague, taken by surprise, defenceless, had little to say. Invented though they were,

these memos cast doubt on the man's future with the firm. One salesman on *Canadian Packaging* unaffected by this was Ken Scott, a bright-blue-eyed, blonde-haired, smiling, optimist from the north of England. He had been a purser of Cunard's luxury liner, the *Caronia.*

At home in England at that time, he was having a drink with a friend on the terrace of his family's dark, granite Victorian house. It was set on a hill, overlooking a soot-stained northern town, smoke pouring from a hundred factory chimneys. Ken was talking about places he'd been; Valparaiso, Rio, Jo'burg. His friend's father, hands dug into his waistcoat, butted in. "Aye," he said, "that travel's all very well. But what I says is," he paused to look lovingly over the black town below him "yer can't beat the place where yer makes yer brass."

My editor was John D. Harbron, as he insisted, tall, bespectacled, cautious. Behind high old typewriters on battered desks, we faced each other every day in a small room so hot in summer that sweat from our arms spoiled the papers we were working on. Thorough as I was slapdash, as interested in printing and packaging machines as I was in design and marketing, we probably made a good team.

John was a commander in the Canadian Naval Reserve. In his spare time he wrote a book about the Russian navy. His publisher in New York sent his manuscript to a naval expert for an opinion. The expert replied, "It must be false. We don't know that much about the Russian navy ." John was visited by the counter-intelligence branch of the Mounties. Where, they wanted to know, had he found this information ? John pulled open the drawers of his filing cabinet. There, meticulously referenced, was every fact in the book. Among other sources, he had found a Polish news-paper that published stories about the Soviet Navy. John had taught himself Polish to read them.

That book, I think, was not published, although in 1988, the tercentenary of the Spanish Armada, he produced an authoritative work on the subject from the Spanish point of view. For years a Spanish scholar, he holds a decoration from the Spanish court.

Editors were pressed by salesmen to write friendly stories about companies which might advertise. We resisted this, among mounting anger. In a showdown with the managing director we demanded that advertising and editorial must be kept separate and distinct. Handily, there was a recent precedent. The *New York Times* had provoked a stir by publishing, before it was announced, a photograph of a new General Motors car. Furious, GM cancelled their advertising, then $7 million a year. Then they relented. People buy the *New York Times*, they admitted, because it brings news. GM not only restored their budget, but increased it. Our boss conceded the same point. From then on, no interference.

Maybe his understanding was one reason why Maclean-Hunter enjoyed a golden patch. He brought in experts to teach us. One, from New York, had designed *Look* Magazine, then the best picture magazine in America, and US *News and World Report*. He taught us how to construct a magazine, what goes where, the basic architecture. He taught us layout; how to lay out a page, a spread. Then pictures; how to choose a picture, the need to link them in picture stories and how to do it. He taught us about headlines and captions, making them all marry. One of his remarks: "People like people best." He meant write about people and put them in pictures.

I have since laid out several publications for others. Doing so, I have analysed half-a-dozen highly successful publications; *Paris Match, Vogue,* the *Economist* among them. Although they look quite different, all follow exactly the same rules. At the same time, I looked at other, less successful, publications. They do not follow the rules. Even the one about people.

Another American who lectured to us had written a book called *The Technique of Clear Writing*. His enemy was the ponderous, lugubrious and often unintelligible prose you so often read, not least in reports.

Among many examples, he gave one pinned by the side of a store in a factory. It was three paragraphs long. He asked us what it meant. After a long time we deciphered the point: 'If you want thumb-tacks, ask for them.' See that in practice, once more in Frank Loesser's translations of a medical book, read by Adelaide, in *Guys and Dolls.*

This lecturer had developed what he called a 'readability index'. You counted the number of syllables in a sentence then multiplied it by a factor, maybe 0.7. His research, he told us, showed him that pulp magazines in the US, like *Confidential,* had an index of five or six. Big-selling publications, like *Time,* had an index of seven or eight. Higher-brow large volume publications, like *Atlantic Monthly,* had an index of ten to twelve. Most ordinary writing in daily use, most company outpourings and most limited circulation magazines, would have a 'readability index' in the 20s. What made this pseudo-scientific mumbo-jumbo compelling was an assertion he went on to make. Literature acknowledged universally to be good and read by generations, he claimed, is invariably in the six to ten bracket; Shakespeare, the Bible, Dickens.

We struggled to put his ideas into practice: use short words, skip the Latin when there is an Anglo-Saxon choice, chop participles from the end of verbs, the 'ings', to keep them active. Write short sentences. "A period (full-stop) uses less ink than a comma," he pointed out. "Write," he advised ungrammatically but well, "like you talk." A great deal easier to say than do.

Although Maclean-Hunter had its own art department, I managed to bring in a freelance designer, Chris Yaneff. He redesigned our magazine with a new typeface, more white space and, above all, excellent covers. With the more informed layouts and better , or at least more active, writing, results were immediate. In less than a year, circulation, readers' enquiries (a sign of readership) and advertising lineage all more than doubled.

As we got bigger we became more ambitious. We commissioned research studies, for instance, and published facts and statistics and trends until then unavailable. These, too, built readership and advertising revenue. I have now a long article I wrote in 1956, after study in the US and UK, about automation, then a new, feared word. It was optimistic, although not because it quoted a happy taxpayer in the United States who received a windfall of $5 million from an IRS (Inland Revenue) computer that went wrong. "Opponents of automation," a Federal cabinet minister in Ottawa remarked, "are barnacles on the backside of progress."

Tracking stories took me about and let me meet remarkable

people. Victor Papanek was one. He used his design imagination to create articles for people in the Third World who are poorer than we can grasp. One of many was a workable radio made with wire and a biscuit tin. He was thirty years ahead of our awareness. In Toronto I was taken to lunch by the manager of the Packaging Association of Canada. He took me to the restaurant of a large hotel. Known to be a big spender, waiters hovered over him as the lengthy meal wore on. At one moment, he took off his heavy, horn-rimmed glasses to make a point, and laid them on the table. From a far wall, a waiter hurtled towards us. He picked up the spectacles, breathed on them, wiped them with a napkin, laid them where they had been and slipped away.

Graphic design, and some advertising, enjoyed a style you don't often see in America now. Bill Bernbach had just created those 'think small' ads for Volkswagen. David Ogilvy, an Englishman who took New York by storm, had a bearded naval commander selling Schweppes and a man with a black eye patch to promote Hathaway shirts, and wonderfully written advertisements for British tourism and Rolls-Royce. 'Tread softly,' read one advertisement showing Westminster Abbey, 'past the long, long sleep of kings.' Ogilvy, or his agency, wrote that the 'loudest noise' in a Rolls-Royce 'is the ticking of the clock'.

There was Fedder's air conditioner, advertised in the *New Yorker*. The page was split in half. On the left was a full-length photograph of a skinny man. Below the photo it read: 'BEFORE: I was a 125 lb weakling.' On the right was the same man. Under, it read: 'AFTER: I am still a 125lb weakling, but boy, is my room cool.' Using the finest graphic artists, Albert Kner who ran the advertising for the Container Corporation, a board and packaging company in Chicago, ran a long series devoted to 'great ideas of Western man', each worth collecting.

In New York I interviewed many leading designers of the time. Raymond Loewy, whom I met again in Paris was the doyen. With Bill Snaith, a keen ocean-going yachtsman, Loewy had the largest design office in the world. A year or two before he had been on the front cover of *Time* Magazine. "Designing the Studebaker gets you on the cover of *Time*," a colleague told me, "but designing packaging makes the money." That, absurdly, is still true. Walter Margulies (who became captain of the US croquet team), a quiet-spoken Swiss, courteous and hard, was rising fast as a corporate identity designer of high calibre and even higher fees. In Canada we were impressed at a fee of $3 million he was said to have earned for designing five beer labels for Molson's, a Montreal brewer.

His salesman came to see me. He wanted us to write about that job. He claimed to be a Spanish duke, son of an ambassador. He was smooth, beautifully dressed, gracious, amusing. He claimed to have been in the OSS, wartime forerunner of the CIA. With his lightning brain it could have been true. He claimed to have Renoirs and Dufys at home, and that could have been true too. He claimed to have a Cadillac and driver, rich for a salesman. We were sceptical as, indeed, were people in a New York design firm he later bought into. They hired private detectives to check his stories. None stood up, yet he always had a way of talking himself out of trouble.

But the Cadillac was true. He invited Molly and me to New York for the weekend. At the airport there was the driver and the car. He lived with his beautiful, dark-haired wife, a television star, in an elegant 'brownstone' house in upper Manhattan. There, indeed, were small masterpieces, perhaps Renoirs and others he had mentioned. Behind a sofa was a small glass-boxed table where medals he almost certainly hadn't earned were on display. After dinner with her father, one of Bermuda's 'forty thieves', his wife took Molly to a charity ball at the Waldorf, sliding open a cupboard door to find a suitable mink to wear, from among a long line of them. The man and I settled down. He pressed a button by his sofa. One of the paintings slid back to reveal a black and white television set showing a wrestling match.

(The contrast reminds me of the after-dinner visit of homage an American friend made to Picasso. Excited as a schoolboy, he was admitted to the house by Jacqueline, Picasso's wife. After a moment, the apogee of his whole life arrived. He was shown in to meet *'le maître'*. Picasso, wearing shorts and a tee-shirt, was sprawled in an armchair with his feet on a table. In one hand was a can of beer. He was watching a Doris Day movie.)

The salesman took us to see Pearl Bailey in *House of Flowers*. She was a madam. One song kept her on stage forty minutes or more. The audience stood and shouted for one encore after another. Of the words, all I remember is 'a hammock's vain but a canoe's insane'.

Another side of his character showed when Molly and I tried to repay his hospitality. I asked them to dinner. He suggested Sardi's. My heart froze; that was far too grand for our pockets. But we went. The room was filled with famous faces, Noel Coward among them. It grew worse. Far from hiding unobtrusively in a dark corner, as Molly and I hoped, we were led to a large, round table in the centre of the restaurant. Half way through the meal, friends of our guests joined us. "Won't you have something to eat ?" I stuttered falsely. "No, no... well, perhaps a little lobster..." Each bite of my food tasted more ashen than the one before. "I'm never going to be able to pay for this," was all I could think. To my astonished relief, when the bill came I found I just could. Days later I realised my guest had quietly met the lion's share of the bill.

This man, still selling design, invited me again. Collected at the airport by the same driver, I was driven to Bucks County, to a turreted château standing above a lake set in rolling fields and woodland. The house had been moved, it was said, stone by stone, from France by the Ford family. Over the fireplace was a Reynolds, he acknowledged. Or was it ?

In London later my friend's name was in the papers. A young millionaire had died in a 'plane crash. Penny Brahms, his beautiful, socialite widow, was shocked to find she had been left just one shilling and two photographs of herself in the nude. My smooth friend, by now described as a Mexican banker, was one of two men convicted at the Old Bailey for forging the will.

I went to Chicago, once to see the packaging show held in exhibition halls at the stock yards, once about a job. Today Chicago is an open, pulsing city with some of the most magnificent architecture in America. Then the shades of Al Capone were not far. Buildings had hardly changed since his day. The city was grey, dirty, unwelcoming. An icy wind blew off the lake making people scurry indoors. The

'Windy City' was right.

The bar of the hotel I stayed in was on the top floor. Lonely salesmen nursed their drinks around a white grand piano. It was on a revolving dais so that, as you sat there, the lights of Chicago at night seemed to glide by. A playing card appeared by my glass, then another and a third. I looked up. A man, sitting on the other side of the piano was flicking them from his top pocket. I went over to him. "Why are you doing that ?" I asked. "To meet you," he replied. We went out to eat then, hurrying through the cold streets, into a night-club. My friend came from New Mexico. "What do you do to amuse yourselves in New Mexico," I wondered. "We play 'let the water out of the pool'." He explained. They have a barbecue, then someone suggests they have a swim. But no one has brought a swim suit. "Never mind," they say "let's go anyway." When everyone jumps in the water that's when they do it. "Do what ?" I asked. "Why, that's when we let the water out of the pool."

Louis Cheskin ran a place called The Color Research Institute. He spoke and wrote authoritatively about the effect of colour and how to use it, far better than anything I have heard or read since. Then it was a new field to me, one, I thought, with lots of potential. Cheskin claimed his remarkable findings were based on research. That impressed me too. I was keen to see how it was done. He offered me a job. I was quite interested. To my mounting surprise, the taxi drove me further and further from the city, into suburbs. This famous guru's office, if there was one, was in his bungalow, one of thousands. There wasn't much research there. It struck me that, like Ernest Dichter, famous at the same time as a pioneer motivational researcher, much of his excellent opinion was intuitive.

None the worse for that, but who, in America or anywhere, would buy intuition ? They needed to cloak their ideas in alleged research to be heeded.

Writing took me to Chicago, Detroit, Buffalo, Montreal, New York and plenty of places in between.

Sitting next to me on one of those trips was George Ball, the Secretary to the US Treasury. We were caught in an electrical storm. The turbo-propped aircraft dropped hundreds of feet, then swung and turned and climbed and skewed to one side, then fell again. On and on. As the sky calmed, we talked. The coming globalization of business was in his mind. National frontiers would collapse, he forecast. Try as they would to slow things down, governments would be powerless to arrest the trend. "Business," he added, "is always twenty-five years ahead of government."

When the World's Fair was held in Osaka in 1970, the French pavilion showed, on a giant map, where French is spoken. It included all of Canada. That is nonsense. In Toronto nothing could have been further from anybody's mind or competence. Even in Montreal, where I went for Maclean-Hunter, I never heard a word, although it is true that, living there later I found you had to say at least one word in French before anyone would put petrol in your car. Even so, today's terrible conflict, so close to tearing Canada in two, was barely nascent then. Indeed, a book by Lady Tweedsmuir, wife of a former governor-general (John Buchan, who wrote *The Thirty-Nine Steps*) expressed pride that, in their wisdom, the British founders of Canada had preserved both the French and English language.

Molly and I bought a car before we could drive. A Hillman,

it went wrong so often I wrote an article, 'What's wrong with British cars'. Then we acquired a beautiful, silver, raking convertible, a Sunbeam Alpine, with deep leather, orange-coloured seats, style and power. We drove to friends in Ottawa and to another whose father was a tobacco farmer in Rodney, Ontario where, for breakfast, farm hands devoured plates full of corn-on-the-cob. In the fields we chewed tobacco leaf and Molly astonished the farmer by shooting cans as mercilessly as Annie Oakley.

Eighteen

Sidling down Bonders

Books with new-found hope and confidence poured from Canadian presses. Their titles show the mood: *The Unknown Country* (a bestseller), *Canada's Tomorrow, Canada: The Golden Hinge.* (That was the term used by Monty — the Field Marshal— when he opened the Canadian National Exhibition in Toronto. He saw Canada as a hinge between Britain and the United States. He was wrong about that. "You don't want to worry about those Americans," he said, advocating closer links with, 'the old country.' Popular as he was, his talk was badly received.)

Two Canadian authors who stood apart from the rest were Robertson Davies, a fine novelist who at that time was a college lecturer, and Marshall McLuhan, later to dazzle us with a flood of penetrating ideas: 'The medium is the message', the 'global village', 'population implosion', 'hot' and 'cold' media. I found him hard to read. Only by taking a sentence from a page, then writing it down and gazing at it, could I understand his meaning.

Each success shifted my perception of our age. And how true it has all become. As I write, forty or more years later, we are more distressed and anxious to do something about people in Bangladesh, Soweto, Ethiopia and the Kurdish mountains than we are about our neighbours, all effects of the 'population implosion' and 'global village' he foresaw. In London *The Times* said McLuhan was 'at the frontier'.

The *New Yorker* put him with T.S Eliot, D.H. Lawrence and Oswald Spengler.

Books from the United States were no less challenging, although I always thought well-written novels never sounded true. I wanted to write one that had people saying "sod it" and swearing and scratching themselves and being natural. Then came J.D. Salinger. His *Catcher in the Rye* dazzled me. As far as I recall it is about little; the weekend of a sixteen-year-old boy, thrown out of a preppy school. But his language, fresh and irreverent then, made a huge impact. Perhaps Salinger gave adolescence a voice. If so, he had more power than he could have conceived or wanted. The man who murdered John Lennon in 1980, Mark Chapman, had a copy of *The Catcher in the Rye* in his pocket. At his trial, instead of giving evidence he urged the jury to read the book. Other assassins were as affected by it: the man who tried to kill President Reagan among them.

The Organisation Man, which coined the idea of 'the man in the grey flannel suit', was particularly damning. Its author, William H. Whyte, argued that US industry demanded too much conformity, which was true. Every job applicant had to sit through psychological aptitude tests, measured against norms of behaviour. But, wrote Whyte, original, clever, imaginative people would fail. They didn't respond in the same way as everyone else. Yet America needed clever people. "If you have exceptional ability," he advised, "you have a duty to cheat when you do those tests." If they don't, he meant, America would be deprived of their talent.

You could see what he meant at Maclean-Hunter. Not only were short hair, white shirt and black shoes *de rigueur* — salesmen wore plain suits, journalists wore tweed jackets— but even in the car park conformity was clear. You had to drive the car that placed you correctly in the pecking order. Although they bought their own, salesmen and executives drove precisely graded cars from General Motors or Ford. Nothing was said. It was just the way. In the same unspoken code, journalists and editors, not thought management material, were allowed foreign cars.

Whyte quoted David Reisman who, with a Harvard colleague, wrote *The Lonely Crowd.* They believed that advanced society, above all in modern America, was throwing up a new kind of man. They spoke of people being 'Tradition-directed', 'inner-directed' and 'other-directed'. Their theory went like this: for centuries the world was static. Little changed. A father could tell his son what work to do, whom he should marry, not to go beyond the village where wild animals were.

That changed in the Middle Ages, the time of exploration and imperial expansion. Sons and daughters went to parts of the globe about which their parents knew nothing. They couldn't advise them. What they could do, a point I touched on earlier as a possible basis for English public schools, was to give children a set of values to live by, a sort of inner gyroscope. With these principles, the son or daughter would survive.

Now, Reisman argued, even that didn't work. Ideas and opportunities had so exploded that the parent had no idea what to say. Their offspring, too, didn't know what to do. Was it better to be a doctor or an airline pilot, Christian or Buddhist ? Should a young man marry the girl next door or not marry at all ? To find answers, Reisman suggested, youngsters turn to their peer groups, or people like themselves who have 'made it'. He imagined them having radar-receiving dishes on their heads, tuned in, searching for what is going on. That explained the rise of mass media to the young. James Dean was perhaps the first of their models. Then they saw themselves in the Beatles and Rolling Stones. Until that explosion our heroes were always older: Gary Cooper, Cary Grant, Clark Gable.

Alec Guinness met James Dean in a Californian restaurant after flying the Atlantic. Dean wanted to show him a new sports car, perhaps a Ferrari, he had just bought. When he saw Dean with the car, Guinness had a terrible and clear presentiment that Dean would be killed by it. He was, next day.

I read books about creativity. In *Applied Imagination* Alex Osborn described how policemen in one American town reduced traffic offences. They stopped women drivers and gave them a rose, congratulating them on their good driving. Their idea was to reward success, in other words, rather than, as usual, punish failure.

Today there are thousands of books about design, whole departments, even whole bookshops, devoted to them. In the 1950s there were few. Perhaps the best was by Henry Dreyfuss with whom I was later to be interviewed. He was a wonderful, honest, industrial designer. In 1955 he published *Designing for People*. As if to encourage anyone starting a business in hard times, he had opened his office in Chicago in 1929, two weeks before the Wall Street crash. His first client was Bell Telephone. They ran a competition to find new designs for a sort of tea cosy that was put over telephones, to hide their ugliness. Dreyfuss astonished the Bell people by saying they were wrong. They should design better telephones. Bell remained his client all his life, a life ended tragically when, in 1972, he and his wife committed suicide.

Earlier, in 1950, Raymond Loewy, perhaps the most famous of all industrial designers, surely the only one to have his face on the cover of *Time* Magazine and whose designs for the Apollo space mission were auctioned at Sotheby's, had written *Never Leave Well Enough Alone*. More self-aggrandising, it was still worthwhile. Later, wanting to form a link for my company in France, I met him in Paris, in his office filled with photographs of Loewy with President Kennedy, Loewy with President De Gaulle, Loewy with Lollabrigida, Loewy with... Before rushing off for lunch with Brigitte Bardot, he offered to buy my company. Flattered and excited, we none the less said no.

I remember reading Colette and, of course we devoured English books. W.H. Smith had a bookshop in Toronto at that time. Diana Cooper's trilogy was published, elegantly written about a golden, departed world. Her father was among the first in England to install electricity in his house, Belvoir Castle. It would never catch on, he thought, because the generator in the basement was too noisy.

Diana Cooper was in the British Embassy in Paris at the end of the war and after when Duff Cooper, her husband, was ambassador. Her aim was to restore to Paris and the Embassy the glamour both had enjoyed before the war. She revived soirées and balls before people had the clothes for them. She insisted they were to be superb. All Paris came, including Jean Cocteau and his literary set. One day, Diana Cooper walked along the Seine. Under a bridge she found a tramp in rags. "How would you like a meal with the British Ambassador and his wife ?" she asked the startled man. She struck a deal with him. All he had to do was to come to the Embassy on a particular night and say nothing. She would do the rest.

Candelabra ablaze, jewels sparkling at white throats, long dresses, officers in scarlet tunics, an orchestra playing, the scene was set. The tramp arrived, smelly and dirty as before. He gazed about him in wonder as he shuffled up the steps to meet the ambassadress. Diana Cooper smiled and turned to her neighbour. "Madame la duchesse," she said, "have you met M. Dubois (or whatever his name was)? He's the most marvellous poet...you must have read the review in *Le Soir...*" So it went on. In no time, guests were claiming not only to have read the reviews but to admire his poems. The evening was a triumph. A week or two later Diana Cooper admitted in a poetry journal her deception. Cocteau was not amused.

At an investiture Duff Cooper presented honours to French people who had helped the Allied cause. One was to go to a rag-picker from Marseilles who smuggled airmen across the frontier into neutral Spain. Duff Cooper, with others, was embarrassed. In their view, the award she was to be given was too little; she would be insulted. To compensate, Duff Cooper sat the lady in Queen Victoria's chair, pride of the Embassy. He left her until last, then, with no citation or word, he crossed the room, kissed her on both cheeks and squeezed the medal into the shopping bag at her feet, baguette protruding.

One night in Paris Sir Peter Tennant, who was also in the Embassy and told me these stories, had dinner with Field Marshal Montgomery. Monty, in full uniform, turned to him and asked if he was interested in medals. Peter stalled. "You should be," said the Field Marshal, "they're very important." He then described each of the many ribbons on his chest. That done, he reached into his pocket and pulled out more which he threw on the table and described in the same detail.

"What about strategy ?" asked Monty. Yes, Peter could say he was interested. The Field Marshal called for maps. He spread them on the floor, kneeling before them. "To keep sea lanes open, and maintain world peace," he explained, "we're going to need bases. But people won't let us be in their countries any more. Those days are gone. They'll kick us out. What we've got to do is to find islands or atolls, or build them, to create our own bases."

"Here's one." he pointed to the map. "And here's another." He was convinced it was the way ahead. He intended to tell heads of government. That dinner, occurring shortly after the war, showed his grasp and foresight.

Although Molly and I had been in Canada a number of years, were fond of friends, enjoyed our work and much of life there, like many Englishmen we never quite left England. Indeed, one of the virtues of Canada, people said, was that you earned so much you could afford to go to England every year. That seemed dotty to me. Why not earn less and live in England all the time ? It would mean another leap in the dark. But the words of a wise old space salesman on the magazine helped us.

"If yer wanna go ter Philadelphia," he had advised, "the first thing you gotta do is git on the train."

Admittedly, as Canadians never stopped telling themselves, the future belonged to Canada. Each forecast was more ecstatic than the last. For all that, to us something was lacking. Everyone was on the go, on the make. What you saw was what you got. It was a simple world, its lines as sharply cut as the hard edges of buildings in sun beneath that bright blue sky. In winter it was cold, with thick snow. In summer, when temperatures soared into the nineties and higher, the city was hot and humid. For a few magnificent weeks in Fall maple leaves were deep red and golden. There wasn't much weather in between. The softness and subtlety of England is seldom seen.

No question, those are values we preferred. It was time to leave Canada; time to come home.

Many people feel submersion in North America once in a while is good for you. It makes you more direct, less elliptical or devious as Europeans, ever courteous, may be seen to be. Agreeing, and not without sadness, we set about coming home. For a year I wondered how much cars cost, should we bring ours home ? Where would we live ? And what would I do ? For a while, letters to Molly's father asked about potatoes. Perhaps what I could do was to sell clean, pre-packed potatoes, then unknown in Britain. Supermarkets were new. What about opening a self-service shop in a nice English market town?

Our friends were the same. We dreamed and talked about returning to England. One spoke of 'sidling down Bonders' in the Aston Martin he would have, being 'admired by the dollies'. Grown tired of the affectations you can find in people exiled from home, who drop names of 'dear friends' in England, to magnify or lengthen their roots, this man invented his own family, the Park Pruetts. When, at parties, ladies twittered about lord this and lady that, he would say, "You must know the Park Pruetts... charming people...they're in Hampshire...farming, ye know." As often as not, after a brief frown the lady would beam, "Of course, such dear friends...". They had no idea Park Pruett was the name of a mental asylum.

Sighing for home, another friend remembered the joy of driving up Box Hill in an old open Bentley. As he double-declutched to gain power, wind blowing through his hair, rolling Surrey farmland before him, " I wouldn't," he said "call the King my uncle." A third, newly-returned, sighed that, "There is something about the way of life, you know."

A fourth friend, who had been a bomber pilot and read five hundred books in a German prison camp and scarcely one since, at first wanted a chicken farm in the country, then a Queen Anne town-house, then a Victorian house he could convert.

In the event, what he did was clever. Back in London, he and his wife set their heart on the Vale of Health, a pretty road in Hampstead. But everyone else in England, it seemed, had the same ambition. "What can I do," he asked, "that others can't?" By then he was in a market-research firm. So he employed two girls to go from house to house, with clipboards, to ask questions. Among them were questions about moving house. "Well," said the woman at one house, "this is remarkable. My husband and I only decided at breakfast this morning to sell our house." My friend bought it and may live there still.

Gradually my ideas set. Having written about design at length, attended conferences and visited numbers of design offices, I decided to start my own design company in England. But first, I needed a job in one, both to learn the business and to understand the market. The question was: how to go about it? Where to aim? Where to start?

The answers add up to an encouraging example of job creation; not applying with dozens of others for a vacancy, but creating your own job.

I persuaded my boss that our magazine should publish a 'World Design' issue. It would encourage manufacturers in Canada to design their packages better, my argument ran, if they saw what was happening elsewhere. Once agreed, I wrote to as many design offices in the world as I could find. Hundreds of photographs flooded in. Spread over the carpet at home, they took days to sort out. I paid especial attention to those from Britain. Which firm, I asked myself, would I like to work for ? I pinpointed three, took pains to thank them for their submissions, published their work, then wrote again to thank them. It all went well. The only dissent came from the late and loved Willy de Majo, by then already well-known as a designer. Willy complained that pictures of his work had appeared on the same page as pictures of German designs. A Jugoslav who was decorated for his service in RAF Intelligence, Willy had strong feelings about the Germans.

Willy, who founded ICOGRADA (the International Council of Graphic Design Associations) later became a good friend. In his house in London he had gold swastika'd plates from Hitler's dining table. He explained he was one of the first into Berchtesgaden. He liberated some plates. Some he put in his battledress. Others he hid under his hat. Willy says that as he left the fortress an American sentry saluted him. Willy saluted back. In his nervousness, he knocked his hat off, and the plates crashed to the ground.

As a journalist I had sat through many conferences. Listening to one dull speaker after another, I remember asking myself what was the difference between the speaker and me. The difference was that he was up there and I was down here. It was a threshold to cross. That is why, while planning our return to England I arranged, through the Institute of Packaging in London, to give a talk. My very first, it was set for the Connaught Rooms. Terrified, my lips were dry and my heart beat faster for at least a week before. I wrote to the heads of the firms that interested me, said I was giving this talk, and hoped we might meet there. There were three of them. All three came and although the talk must have been dreadful, frightened and high-pitched, two offered me a job.

Another design firm I was invited to see was large and owned at the time by Richard Lonsdale Hands. His office was in to the

Commonwealth House, what Americans call a 'flat-iron' building, wedge-shaped. Lonsdale Hands' office was on the top floor, with a semi-circular window looking towards High Holborn. We had lunch by the window at a shiny black round table, the centre of which was electrically powered. He asked if I wanted salad dressing. I did. It glided towards me. After lunch he showed me a film about his company. It ended with him stepping into a Rolls-Royce, pausing to sign a letter brought to him by an elegant secretary. It was all a bit high-flown for me. Ashley Havindon, a distinguished graphic designer at Crawford's, an elegant advertising agency doing good work, offered me a job too, as an account executive. I thought that too general; it was better to specialise.

We had sailed on Cunard's *Ascania*. Ken Scott, the old Cunard purser we knew, looked after us. At the foot of the gang-plank an officer was waiting. He took us to our cabin, the cheapest. After one glance, he led us to a grand one. We sat at the Purser's table and were invited incessantly to parties. As the ship sailed in sunshine across a glistening sea, we recovered on deck not only from the parties but from weeks of overwork, tucking rugs around our knees and sipping morning Bovril.

From Southampton, we took a dirty train to London. Through the steamed windows, England looked grey in the morning light and small, small, everything small. After the broad sweep of Canada, its high, wide skies and simple optimism, the land we saw was so like the description by William Morris a century before:

> *Not much space for swelling into hugeness, no*
> *great wastes overwhelming in their dreariness,*
> *no great solitudes of forests, no terrible,*

> *untrodden mountain walls; all is measured,*
> *mingled, varied, gliding easily one thing into*
> *another, little rivers, little plains, little*
> *mountains, neither prison nor palace, but a decent home.*

Grey and small and dirty it may have been, but the moist air was caressing, English air, the voices and sounds ours. Sentimental no doubt, a line from *The King and I* captures for me the gentle strength of this decent, aggravating country. Thinking of home and the husband she has lost, the governess sings, "When the soft mist of England lies sleeping on a hill." Wherever you go in the world that remains an evocative phrase.

Nineteen

Design in Dover Street

Dressed in a bowler hat, stiff white collar, dark grey suit with a gold watch chain stretched across my waistcoat, my father's half-Hunter in my pocket, carrying a tightly furled umbrella, I walked the few hundred yards to work each day, past Gunter's, where the fashionable met for tea, past a shop with a girl in the window and, above her head, a neon sign advertising 'French lessons'. Soon the girls along the railings of Curzon Street saw I was a resident. As I walked home their pouting invitations changed to amiable "Hallo luv's".

Molly and I had moved into a one-room flat with a small wrought-iron balcony in a plain Georgian house in Derby Street. Off Curzon Street, it is behind where the Hilton hotel now stands. Across the road was Leconfield House, then home of MI5. Next door to us was another headquarters, of a brothel, said to be that of the Medina brothers, pimps of the time.

We didn't stay in London long. Within six months we bought a house in Buckinghamshire, in Burnham Beeches. A bungalow set in nearly two acres of sloping ground, opposite the entrance to a golf course, we called it Springfield. Unusually, it was centrally-heated, fired by a large boiler that devoured coal and old newspapers left by the previous owner. Of course the house was empty, the floors bare. My mother, by then, had Persian carpets three deep in Tudor Cottage. When she came to see us she brought a house-warming gift; a broken teapot. Gradually, though, we furnished the house with modern Danish furniture, lain on by a Persian cat called Hi-Fi. We bought a second-hand Lea Francis, a long black car with great chrome headlamps, raking mudguards and large doors that swung backwards. Daily, I drove to Burnham station to take the train to London, often in heavy, Thames Valley mist, trees dripping. I was commuting again.

THM Partners, the firm I joined, was a very chic, indeed snobbish, design office in Mayfair, at 40 Dover Street, a building since demolished. It was run by John Tandy, Lucy Halford and Derek Mills.

There were few design offices in London then. THM was exceptional, for its exclusiveness, quality and breadth of work. It designed packaging for numbers of household name companies, designed interiors of buildings and exhibitions and some excellent products

There is a story about Charles Saatchi who, with his brother Maurice, built the world's largest advertising agency. He was so shy, it was said, that when he saw a party of businessmen disgorge from a lift and walk along the corridor he was in, he pulled his handkerchief from his pocket and bent to polish a doorknob until they had passed. Derek Mills would have done the same. Rarely seen, he designed packaging with John Beadle, later to become my partner, and one or two others.

Lucy Halford, strident and autocratic, looked after the interior design. Among her staff was an eloquent and loquacious architect who wore a well-cut cavalry twill suit, suede boots and knitted tie. There, too, was a tall, languorous long-bearded man with a black eye-patch called Ronald Smith. 'Smithy' taught me something that has lasted. Speaking about exhibitions he remarked, "If you are aware of the design of the stand it is a poor design." You should be conscious only of the goods being shown, he meant.

Good design, in other words, is modest. I think of that to this day, when I argue with modern architects. At presentations in 1989 and 1990 of the design for Stansted airport the architect spoke at length about the roof. Repeatedly he asserted, "It will make a statement." This made me so cross that I replied, "Imagine you are a mother with two small children. You have just flown in from the Middle East. You can't speak English. It is first thing in the morning. You are tired and haven't enough hands to manage the children and all your bundles of luggage. What kind of statement would you want ? Would it be about the roof ?"

With the backing of my experience in North America, I talked to John Tandy and Lucy Halford about commercial television, about to start in Britain. Lord Reith, the director-general and to many the founder of the BBC, likened introducing commercial television to the Black Death. We had "sunk a maggot into the body politic" he complained. I thought that blind. "We'd better take it seriously," I said. "Oh, television," replied Lucy. "I never watch it. That's what the ordinary people do."

Poor snobby Lucy. A month or two later she was struck down with a slipped disc. She went to the London Clinic. I visited her there. At the foot of her bed was the largest TV set I had ever seen. It had been lent by one of her clients, the Arthur Murray School of Dancing, then in Leicester Square. I couldn't help myself: "Television, eh, Lucy," I

smiled rudely. "Yes," she replied with aplomb, "it is rather amusing. One sees so many of one's friends."

John Tandy, a kindly man, was no less superior. His father, he told me, a general known as 'Napper', bought everything by the dozen, "as a gentleman should". Nor, it seemed, did gentlemen carry briefcases. John carried his papers to and fro in a large brown envelope. (There was a story at the time of an ensign in the Brigade of Guards who bought his fiancée a diamond ring. Carrying the minute package down Bond Street, he was seen by a brother officer. Next day he was called to the adjutant. "If you insist on carting your luggage about London," he was told icily, "please take a taxi.")

Always beautifully dressed in identical soft white cotton shirts, plain blue wool tie, and loose-woven double-breasted blue suits, Tandy sat, silver- haired, eyes rather close set, finger-tips touching, behind a paperless table. He was a refined perfectionist. One day he had me knock on the door to his room, wait to hear him call, then enter. He stood, walked around his desk holding his hand out tome, and smiled, saying how good it was of me to come. No, he wasn't happy with that. I had to go out and try again. I knocked, waited, entered. This time John stood and moved around the other side of his desk towards me, arm outstretched. How good of me, once again, to come. We went through that perhaps six times until he had it as he wanted. Everything was rehearsed in this way.

Again remarkable for those relatively early days of design, John dealt only with the heads of huge corporations and he charged high fees, in guineas. One day he was not himself, he had suffered a sleepless night. What was wrong ? He had three large proposals outstanding, and worried about what he would do when they were accepted. "We'll have to take on more people," he told me. "That means we'll have to move offices. Where will we go?" His anxiety persisted for several days. In the end, none of the jobs came in. It taught me, when my turn came, to worry when it happened.

One client we had was Craig Wood, a famous marketing man from Proctor & Gamble who had become chief executive of Hotpoint. Everyone was fascinated to see whether a soap company marketer could help a so-called 'white goods' manufacturer to prosper. To my disappointment, I am not sure he succeeded. But he did get us, perhaps the first consultant designers to do so in England, to design a washing machine for them. Ronald Cuddon, the architect, did it brilliantly. His design called for two materials and three manufacturing processes the firm had never heard of. Yet they were in use elsewhere, in other industries. The washing machine became market leader. That showed both how myopic designers in a company may be, solving the same problems all the time, and the value of bringing in outside experience.

In Hotpoint then was John Kerridge, who became a colleague and close friend, and, for a decade, chairman of Fisons. He taught me another lasting lesson. Walking around the research and development department one day he asked a scientist what he was doing. When he heard, John wondered how that helped the consumer. "Well, not at all," said the scientist. "Then I suggest you stop doing it," replied John. Greatly concerned with helping companies develop new products since then, I have often kept that simple perspective in mind.

As part of learning, Tandy took me to visit clients in the textile industry in and around Manchester. Root of the industrial revolution, Manchester held romance for me. Buildings were blackened by a century's soot, gaunt, solemn, serious. Women who, according to my mother, scrubbed their doorsteps daily in an energetic struggle against the grime, wore wooden clogs the first time I went there. Year after year since, I wanted to paint those black mills. Now they are bright, full of boutiques. It is too late.

Helping John Tandy to reach the top people in industry was Douglas Sutherland. A big man with a mane of long, wild hair, his face turned to avoid smoke curling from a cigarette he dragged from the corner of his mouth, Douglas was one kind of archetypal gentleman journalist or public relations man of his time. (The other kind was beautifully dressed, shooting cuffs over tables in expensive restaurants.) Douglas and I shared an office. Since, he has written a series of witty but telling books about being a gentleman or lady. Then, he was an independent public relations man.

When not preoccupied trying to raise money to send a new Mayflower across the Atlantic (which succeeded), he arranged lunches to bring John into contact with others. One he organised was held in the French Embassy. Among his clients was the French Tourist Board. Another was Mrs Gerald Legge, later Lady Dartmouth, later Countess Spencer, step-mother to Princess Diana and now, at the time of writing, the Baroness de Chambrun, know to us as 'Acid Raine'. She was there to raise money for a charity. Jules Thorn, the industrialist, was at the lunch and next to him, John Tandy. They drank 'wine from the wood', supplied by another of Sutherland's clients. I assume he took a fee from most of them so it was all very efficient.

Perhaps as a result, John and I went to see Jules Thorn. John talked about good design. Thorn waved to an ugly, curved and veneered television set perched on a stand in a corner of his office. What, he wanted to know, did we think of that ? Aghast at its vulgarity, John didn't know how to reply. Before he spoke, Thorn interrupted. "That's the best-selling television set in England. When you know how to improve its sales, let me know." More concerned with fine form than revenue as we were, that should have been a salutary and lasting lesson for us.

Through John Tandy I met numbers of interesting people and was well introduced to the design world in Britain of the time. Henrion, a poster artist who went on to design the identity of large companies, was one. When he died, in 1990, Dick Negus, another distinguished designer, wrote: 'It is impossible to do less than lionise his career. He was a lion — powerful, courageous, gentle, with enormous presence.' Henri was born in Nuremberg in 1914. He designed posters in Paris before the war and maybe that is how his French name came. It was helpful, no doubt, when he came to England on the eve of the war. After being interned, he designed posters in the British cause, along with George Him, Hans Schleger and Abraham Games. He was one of the designers of the Festival of Britain. I first met him at a show of his work in Mayfair and he remained a friend ever after. Hugh Casson (now Sir Hugh) gave a talk. He spoke of a Lady someone who "had a tidy mind". She believed in a place for everything and everything in its place. She kept everything in boxes, each plainly labelled. One Casson saw was for "pieces of string too short to be any use".

Jack Beddington was another remarkable man in London. He was known for having discovered and helped a whole generation of British painters; Graham Sutherland, Raymond Piper, perhaps Paul Nash. Beddington was the advertising manager of Shell. For years he ran a series of posters filled solely with a contemporary British painting. Below, like the tobacco warning you see today, the poster had a subdued strap line which read 'You can be sure of Shell'. At Shell, too, he employed Sir John Betjeman, both as writer and commentator on film.

I sat at Beddington's feet one evening, enthralled. He told me how he first discovered one famous painter. "I was rushing back to the office after lunch," he said. "It was raining. I passed a gallery that had a small glass display at the edge of the pavement. Behind the glass I spotted a black and white crucifixion. I hurried in to the gallery and gave someone my card. 'Tell that artist to come and see me,' I said." The artist, then young, may have been Sutherland. It was someone of his stature.

Beddington had the eye. "Only ever buy pictures you

like," he advised me. When he died, there was a memorial service for him at St Martin's in the Fields. An obituary in *The Times* noted that in his house were over three hundred paintings, including, if I remember, eighty-five in his bedroom. He boasted to me that "I never paid more than a fiver for a picture in my life."

We met Bernard Levin and James Cameron. James was a war correspondent, a lean, haggard, chain-smoking, hard-drinking, hard writer (meaning good, spare, no waste) and fascinating weaver of tales. Bernard, then, was younger but already known. He wrote for *Truth*, became a political correspondent for the *Spectator*, a post once held by Dickens, then became an acerbic theatre critic. One play of the time he described as 'Chinese junk'. Of another he wrote, "This play hasn't been performed since 1752 and I quite see why."

One day I met Bernard in Kensington High Street. We stepped into a coffee bar. He told me he had just left the paper he was on (the *Mail* or the *Express*). Enough of that, he said. From now on he was going to write plays. But, I wondered, can a critic write plays ? There are plenty of precedents, he reminded me: Shaw, Pirandello among them. I was sad to read, a week or two later, that he had joined the other paper (the *Express* or the *Mail*) as its theatre correspondent.

For a while he had a calypso about the day's news on the wireless every morning. He wrote it on the bus going to work. During the heady days of *That Was The Week That Was* (TW 3 for short), to which he kindly invited Molly and me, he had a weekly slot. TW 3, a Saturday night television programme which tore into the week's events with sharp and unforgiving wit, could sometimes be savage. While he was saying his piece during one programme, a man bounded from the audience to knock him off his stool. Another evening, police waited at the back of the theatre to arrest a man who had appeared in an interview. Today, of course, Bernard Levin writes twice a week for *The Times* about anything he likes, with no strings attached, and is regarded by many as the greatest essayist of his age.

It was said of another journalist friend, Bill, possibly apocryphally, that his first job was cleaning windows. One cold day he decided it was warmer the other side of the glass. A man of considerable enterprise, he soon got a job in the office whose windows he was cleaning. It was the *Financial Times*. He went on to become one of London's most distinguished city editors, a television presenter, prolific author and publisher of a string of six magazines. A fascinating raconteur, clutching a glass of wine at parties in our flat, he would talk non-stop to a blonde girl who wrote a weekly love story in a women's magazine. Within days and surely without his knowledge, his adventures appeared in her romances.

We met an American doctor, just returned to London after being medical adviser to the Imam of Oman. Among his duties, he told us, he had to watch prisoners having their hands cut off for stealing. He was not allowed to administer any anaesthetic or pain-killer — beforehand I was going to say. As a concession to him, he won permission to treat the men afterwards.

After he had been there three months he had not been paid. He plucked up courage to mention it. "I'm dreadfully sorry," said the Imam, "I'll deal with it at once." The doctor returned to his quarters. Within a few moments there was a knock at his door. In came four tall, black, bare-chested men heaving a trolley. It was loaded with sacks they strained to lift. Each sack was full of gold coins.

London, to us, was a wonderland of people with fascinating tales.

Colonel Wintle was in the papers at that time for debagging a solicitor at gunpoint and pushing him into Brighton's high street, then 'phoning the newspapers. He wanted to draw attention to what he believed to be a miscarriage of justice. The solicitor had robbed his sister of a promised inheritance. Eventually, he took the case to the House of Lords and won. Facing five law lords, the monocled Colonel was supported only by a soldier. That made legal history. " Why didn't you have professional counsel?" he was asked. "Because," replied the colonel, "if I tell Trooper Mays to turn to page 185 he will do so. He won't say wouldn't page 203 be better?"

Wintle had met the trooper in hospital where he was visiting another man recovering from a broken collar bone. He had fallen off his horse, "not," he made clear, "as a dentist might, but as a cavalry officer would." A sister came to say that in the next ward a soldier was dying. Wintle went to see him. The following exchange took place.

> "What's your name?"
> "Trooper Mays, sir"
> "What's the matter with you?"
> "I'm dying, sir."
> "Of course you're not. Troopers don't die in bed. Get well at once. Furthermore, get your hair cut, you look awful"

Trooper Mays said later he did both.

The forebear of my first secretary ought to be in the *Guinness Book of Records*. As Home Secretary, he opened one of the early railway lines in Victorian England. The engine ran him down. He was the first man, ever, to be run over by a train. A man we know is in that book for winning $2 million from a $26 bet at a horse race. Talking over his shoulder, a taxi driver told me how he and a friend were driven by their wives to Heathrow, to play golf in Scotland. They flew, instead, to Colombo where they met two girls and, anxious to avoid a tell-tale tan, spent the week indoors. Another cabby, we read, became the 'The Brain of Britain'. A man I met then and know now, keen on shooting, gave his wife a ferret for her birthday. You don't find any of that in Canada, I tell you.

We went to stay with friends in their perfect, four-square Georgian house in Kent, all boarded floors, bare bedrooms and claret decantered in a butler's pantry. The husband, a stocky, pipe-smoking retired Para major, took the long train journey to London each morning. Under his arm each day was his copy of *The Times*. What was special was that his wife had warmed it for him in the Aga. Whether she pressed it, too, I don't recall.

The Aga, essential token of taste and discernment in every elegant kitchen of the time, had something to answer for. One golden summer evening we were at dinner in Regent's Park with a psychiatrist and his wife. As we sipped sherry, she slipped away, to return with glossy eight by ten black and white photographs of herself in the nude. They had been taken by a Harrison Marks, a photographer off Piccadilly Circus. She handed them around for us to admire. As we wondered what to say, another woman there, to the surprise of her distinguished and rather pompous wine master husband, confessed that she, too, had been to Harrison Marks. "Where did she hide the pictures?" he wanted to know. "Under the Aga in a brown envelope," she replied.

Not rare or admirable examples, perhaps, except for the Brain of Britain, but more instances of the variety, even eccentricity, of people you meet in London. Appearances, we soon learnt, are simply nothing to go by.

Not a day went by without meeting someone with a story to tell. At least, I thought that until, at a drinks party I stood opposite a heavy, silent, seemingly dull man in a brown suit. He was editor of a railway magazine. Then after a monosyllabic few moments his eyes lit and cheeks flushed with enthusiasm. He was talking about steam engines and meeting Ava Gardner on the set of *Bohwani Junction*, a film of the time set in India. Its adviser on trains, he was a world authority.

London, we were finding, really is a city of infinite interest. Every day was different and marvellous. But there is more. "Paris," I came to write later, "may be more glamorous, Rome grander, New York more exciting, but no city I know has the comfortable majesty of London. The very word has a steadiness about it, steady as the chimes of Big Ben."

Steady is a good word. London has a solid base. Yet that is not all its strength. Later I was to have Italian friends to dinner. For many years they have lived here. I asked them why. They came to England, the husband confessed, because as a student in Milan he read the books of P.G. Wodehouse. That world, he decided, was the one he wanted to live in.

If Bertie Wooster and Biffy and Bingo and Tuffy and Glossop

and Aunts Agatha and Dahlia and Lord Emsworth never existed and the great golf match didn't take place and England isn't like that, they half did and it half is. Wit and whimsy are strong strands in the English character. In the First World War, A.E. MacDonald was a Scot posted to an English regiment in France. So amazed was he to see officers go 'over the top' with nothing more than a walking stick, that he resolved, if he lived, to tour England to find out about these people. He concluded that the English were a nation of 'warrior poets'.

Twenty-two years later, early in the Second World War, remnants of the broken British army crowded the beaches of Dunkirk. More lines of tired men stood in the sea, waiting for rescue. By day and night they were shelled and machine-gunned and bombed. One of the soldiers there was a young officer in the Grenadier Guards who was to become Lt Col. Sir Eric Penn, an 'extra equerry to the Queen'. Up to his chest in water, he turned to his neighbour and said, "One can hardly believe the battle is going strictly according to plan." "No," replied his friend, just as hungry and cold and wet. "And if nanny could see me now she'd be horrified."

Not a bad place to be, wherever men with such gentle wit, not to say coolness, came from.

And here we were, home; shaped, perhaps forever, by the years you have read about. Before us, we scarcely saw, lay a new life; rich in people, adventures, joy - joy, we found later, to be tempered by unimagined tears.